JALAPENO CHILES, MEXICAN AMERICANS AND OTHER HOT STUFF

JALAPENO CHILES, MEXICAN AMERICANS AND OTHER HOT STUFF

◆

A Peoples' Cultural Identity

Raoul Lowery Contreras

iUniverse, Inc.
New York Lincoln Shanghai

JALAPENO CHILES, MEXICAN AMERICANS AND OTHER HOT STUFF
A Peoples' Cultural Identity

iUniverse, Inc.

For information address:
iUniverse, Inc.
2021 Pine Lake Road, Suite 100
Lincoln, NE 68512
www.iuniverse.com

ISBN: 0-595-29256-9

Printed in the United States of America

Contents

Part II   *GROWING BY MILLIONS, PEOPLE AND CULTURE*

Part III EDUCATION AND MEXICAN AMERICANS

Part IV   *MEXICAN AMERICAN NEGATIVES, POSITIVES*

INTRODUCTION

The fastest growing segment of the American population is Mexican American, or, people of Mexican origin, or immigrants from Mexico and a mix of these people who might be 100% Indian, 100% White, or a combination labeled, mestizo Some can even be descended from African slaves brought in to replace Indian labor in the sugar cane fields.

They can be Spanish-speakers only, English-speakers only, or speak only in some Indian dialect from Southern Mexico. Or they can speak two or three of the languages of Mexico, of which there are dozens. They can be short or tall, thin or fat, blonde or brunette. They can have blue eyes, brown eyes, green eyes.

They can have doctorates, or be school drop-outs. They can be poets or murderers. They can be priests and ministers, or nuns and nurses. They can be doctors of medicine, or what we call witch doctors, shamans. They can be pious or atheists. Some might even still worship the gods of their Indian ancestors (and, use cactus hallucinogens, peyote).

The old reputation of "lazy Mexican" has been laid to rest despite Hollywood's efforts. In today's America, the reputation of Mexicans as hard workers is almost universally held by people in the know. The people in the know, however, are generally uninformed about these new Americans. They even express surprise when it is pointed out that some of these people were here before Americans, or before even British colonists who eventually became Americans.

For years, Americans of Mexican origin were called the "Invisible Minority." They are invisible no more.

Here is their story as observed by this writer, a Mexican born American. These essays were written for and distributed by Creators Syndicate or the New York Times Syndicate and they were published in newspapers all over the United States during the Nineties, a decade in which the Mexican American population exploded by millions while maintaining their status as the vast majority of all American Hispanics. Almost seven of ten American Hispanics are of Mexican origin. In fact, within sight of Los Angeles City Hall, there are more Mexican origin people than all other American Hispanics combined.

Lastly, the food of Mexico has preceded the Mexican people as no other ethnic food has preceded any other ethnic group. The Italians, for example, offer up pizza and spaghetti, but without tomato sauce from tomatoes that Hernando Cortez introduced to Europe after he conquered Mexico, where would Italian food be? The Germans offer up German Chocolate cake, the Swiss milk chocolate and the Americans, Hershey Bars, but where would they all be if Cortez had not introduced chocolate to Europe after he brought it from Mexico in 1521. The entire world eats corn in a million different dishes and breads, but where would all of humanity be, food wise, if Cortez had not introduced corn to Europe after he first ate it in the Valley of Mexico, where Indian agronomists had created corn out of grasses native to the Valley of Mexico thousands of years before Europeans had rid themselves of pesky cavemen?

Culturally, where would America be without the cowboy culture, a culture introduced to America by Mexican cowboys, the vaqueros. To short circuit any argument that Spaniards were the first cowboys, one must ask how many "cowboys" existed in Spain before Cortez came to Mexico?

PART I

Chapter introduction—For anyone who has noticed that there are now over 38-million people who can be called Hispanics or Latinos, a careful examination of who these people are is mandatory if one wishes to live harmoniously with this rapidly expanding population.

First, the country must know who these people are, where they came from and where they might be going. Will the country improve in this 21st century with this growing community spreading throughout the fifty states, or will the United States morph into a Third World nation?

There are a number of questions the general American population has that are answered here.

Do Hispanics, especially those of Mexican origin, have dual loyalties or loyalty to Mexico only? Are they now or will they ever be loyal Americans? Are they new to the fight for freedom and liberty? Are there different views and misunderstandings about Hispanics and how they feel about the United States?

1

AMERICAN WARRIORS, PAR EXCELLANCE

When the March, 2003, war with Iraq broke out, the Black political mass in America despised the war, despised the President of the United States and was highly critical of the entire effort. The Black Congressional Caucus voted unanimously against giving the President the authority to attack Iraq. It opposes everything the President has put forth as policy or programs.

Joining the Black Caucus is the all-Democrat Congressional Hispanic Caucus in attacking the President and the quick and successful war. Nonetheless, unlike the Black Caucus, the Hispanic Caucus seems to not be in touch with the Hispanic political mass, especially with Mexican Americans.

Here is how Black activist writer Earl Ofari Hutchinson saw it on April 7, in the war's last days:

"That so many Latinos vigorously back the war is no fluke. A Pew Research Center poll in February found that far more blacks than whites oppose the Iraq war. The press has played up the differing black and white attitudes up as yet another example of the racial divide. But it makes almost no mention that in the same poll nearly seventy percent of Latinos support the war. A poll taken in March by Republican pollsters, Fabrizio, McLaughlin & Associates also found strong pro-war support among Latinos. At first glance, the strong pro-war sentiment among Latinos seems to defy political reality and public perception. Latino civil rights groups and the Congressional Hispanic Conference have pounded Bush for his assault on civil liberties protections, affirmative action programs, his tax cut giveaways to the rich, support of school vouchers, and further cuts of spending on social programs. The Caucus was near unanimous in opposing the Congressional resolution last October that gave Bush total power to wage war against Iraq. Latino activists have staged large anti-war marches in Los Angeles. And the majority of Latinos are Democrats. But things are changing. In Texas and Florida nearly one-third of Latinos voted for Bush in 2000. Congressional Latinos are politically divided. In March, four Latino Congresspersons publicly broke with the Congressional Hispanic Caucus. They called it too liberal, and activist, and formed the Congressional Hispanic Conference."

Hutchison can't figure out why Hispanics have declared their independence from the "plantation," the very plantation he and his fellow government party activists dream about. As the saying goes, he just doesn't get it. Of course, to begin with he uses Latino and Hispanic in the same sentence and doesn't define them further. What he saw in Los Angeles were not Salvadorans, Guatemalans, Puerto Ricans or Dominicans, he watched Mexican Americans, even if those words didn't cross his lips. Perhaps, like among so many other Black and White Americans, he doesn't know who or what they are.

***This article was published in the JEWISH WORLD REVIEW, Tuesday, April 8, 2003, Day 20 of the United States of America's war against the Saddam Hussein dictatorship of Iraq.

"TWO AMERICANS AND AN AZTEC WARRIOR"

By
RAOUL LOWERY CONTRERAS

Before I became a radio talk show host and television news commentator, I was a talk show guest. Once, while on a top rated talk show the show host blithely insulted me with a question racist Mexican-haters always ask. It is a question no one asks of Irish or Italian or British Americans.

"If Mexico (the country of my birth) and the United States were fighting each other in a war, which side would you be on," he smugly asked. He didn't realize that such a question was and is an insult to me and thousands like me who have served and do serve in the American armed forces.

Among people like this, we find a commonality of views about Mexicans, illegal aliens from Mexico and other points south—they hate them. They hate each and every one of them. They also have another commonality, few, if any, of them have ever served in the United States armed forces.

One of their shared views is that illegals (and all Hispanic immigrants) come to America to suck off the public trough; to suck up welfare; to steal jobs, and to otherwise simply live off the fat of the land. Why, they are the first to jump on the fact that Hispanics are "underrepresented" in the armed forces they never served in.

In a recent report, the Pew Hispanic Center reported that 9.5% of our armed forces is Hispanic. The 2000 Census concluded that 13% of the U.S. population is Hispanic. Thus, critics howl, Hispanics aren't carrying their own weight.

That is not true. First, a huge number of Hispanics are less than 18 years old, thus, the percentage of the general population that military age Hispanics comprise is far lower than 13%. Moreover, over half are women.

Secondly, Hispanics comprise a huge percentage of the armed forces that are defined as "combat arms," AKA fighting men.

In fact, Hispanics are 17.7 percent of the personnel who most directly handle weapons, according to Pew Hispanic report based on 2001 Department of Defense statistics. Hispanics make up 14 percent of the Marine Corps, 10.5 percent of the Navy, 9.7 percent of the Army and 5.6 percent of the Air Force. Subtracting out the Air Force and Navy, where few people other than pilots have hands on weapons, the 17.7 percentage mentioned in the report grows to something on the order of 25%.

These statistics and presence have been brought home to America by the deaths of three young men, all United States Marines, all in Iraq, all foreign-born Hispanic immigrants.

Jesus Suarez del Solar was born in Tijuana, Mexico, and was brought as a child to the United States. He was legally immigrated. Jose Angel Garibay was born in Mexico and brought her, legally, as a baby. Then, there was Guatemala-born Jose Antonio Gutierrez.

Gutierrez came to the United States, an orphan who lived on the streets of Guatemala City, by way of Mexico, by hitchhiking rides and riding Mexican freight trains headed north for almost two years. He came to the United States, alone, illegally, at 16, with no English, no family, no friends, hunted by the Border Patrol and "la migra".

Helped by Los Angeles social workers, Gutierez found himself in a foster family that took him in as a son and changed his life forever. They found a way to make him legal, to finish high school, to enroll in college and, then, to proudly watch him become a United States Marine.

It is said that he joined the Marines to give thanks to the United States of America for what it had permitted him to do, to become a solid contributing human being.

These three immigrant men died for us, regardless of whether or not we support the Iraq war. They died in combat, they died as Americans. The father of Suarez del Solar told us his son was an Aztec warrior.

Marines Garibay and Gutierrez may have died as "green card" immigrants, but they are being buried as American citizens, as United States Marines who gave their lives for this country, not Mexico, not Guatemala. They made the ultimate American sacrifice.

Compare that to vehement critics of immigrants, legal and illegal, who bravely give out interviews about how they are protecting America from those dirty illegal aliens. Especially illegal immigrant ones like Jose Antonio Gutierrez, United States Marine, born a Guatemalan in1977; died an American in Iraq in 2003.

◆   ◆   ◆

--Reader Letters in response to this article in Jewish World Review--

HERE IS AN EXCHANGE WITH ONE JEWISH WORLD REVIEW READER WHO, AS IT TURNS OUT, WAS THE ONLY CRITIC OF THE ARTICLE THAT WROTE THE AUTHOR.

Why, oh why, did jwr ever publish this column Americans and an Aztec warriors? What the hell does the "timothy mcveighs" of this country mean? as if there was more than one. And why does the author so smugly label anyone who asks a totally legitimate question, a "superamerican?" Is it because they know which side they'd be on if they went to war with a foreign country? I don't see people from these other countries the author mentions (ireland, england, etc.) flooding into the usa ILLEGALLY! As if one or two dead soldiers is worth the drain of this countries resources that these ILLEGAL parasites bring. while the writer illustrates one case of one illegal immigrant dying for the usa, there can be no question of where this young man's loyalties were located since his native land, Mexico, does NOT support the usa in its justified war. this is one soldier, or 3's deaths, where you have MILLIONS of ILLEGALS in this country. i don't see the > authors point. he seems to hate those that question ILLEGAL immigration, which is this countries biggest problem along with education. just a side note, i am an ANGLO (perhaps one of those "timothy mcveighs" or "superamericans" the writer refers to?) who lived for a short period of time in Puebla, Mexico. To this day, I still speak spanish and take classes in the language. The other day I asked my mexican co-workers what i should do my oral >presentation on in my class. I thought these people were my friends for over a year. These "friends" told me that i should do it on how hispanics are going to reconquer the usa. geez, i wonder where there loyalties lie? The soldiers proved their loyalties. MILLIONS of others do NOT! The author of this column is a smug, cowardly prick who should just come out and say it if he hates americans and america and loves mexico instead of using irrelevant human interest stories like they do on the network news and in public school classrooms. I can NOT in good conscience support JWR when they run racist trash from a racist trash writer like this. goodbye.

sdraoul@att.net wrote: Just a quick reply. Italians invented illegal aliens. Irish have flooded the country illegally over the years. Estimates are that up to 25% of the Irish American population in Boston is here, or their parents came, illegally. Irish immigrants raise millions to support the IRA. English women have come in by the thousands on visitor visas and never returned. You obviously have never served in the military. If you had, you would NEVER write the tripe you did. Because of these three and hundreds of thousands of others, you can read what you want. The only thing I ask is that you understand what you read. The young man I featured came from Guatemala, not Mexico, and he was legal when he died. The point was that illegals can and do become legal. It is only people like you who do not recognize that the only consistency in the world is change and circumstances changing. Raoul Lowery Contreras Semper Fi!

He wrote again:

People like me who fail to see, huh? What I see is MILLIONS of ILLEGALS waltzing into the country calling us "superamericans" and "timothy mcveighs". First, they are taught that americans are racist and from that point, THEY are the racist ones investing the usa by the MILLIONS whereas the other groups you mentioned collectively are only a fraction of this. The irish and italians and others aren't claiming to conquer this land in the name of their native country of origin as the racists within the hispanics proclaim with a straight face not believing themselves to be wrong. You may call this "change and changing", I call it what it is, permitted racism by the powers that be in this country. That being said, your reply was surprisingly civilized in contrast to your article. Thanks. I never served in the military, unfortunately. I wanted to enlist in '93 and my dad begged me not to since Clinton was in office and yeah, i may have had a problem butchering serbs while you may have seen them as timothy mcveighs like all anglos/gringo/hueros are seen these days, right? My very first girlfriend and high school sweetheart had a father from Paraguay and a mother from Uruguay and she was born in brooklyn. we still speak although she has since married a spaniard and become a bigot. we went with separate parties to the Shakira concert in las vegas and she was insulted by Shakira's use of english and rock cover tunes in her act. So, yeah, this country is changing and there's nothing I can do to stop it. I don't think it is changing for the better when this country is importing racism and bigotry. Sorry to take up your time and i DO respect your military service. thank you.—

--ALL OTHER LETTERS TO JWR WERE LIKE THESE--

Dear Sir;

I have often thought these same things myself although my ancestors started coming to what became the United States in 1635 and the last immigrants descend from came in the 1870's. I cannot understand why anyone would believe our country or it's people, would be better off without these new immigrants. Without the determination and energy of these new Americans; and I think that the best ones don't wait around for years to make sure all the paperwork is properly filled out, America would be poorer. So I say to you and all the rest, as an American citizen from birth; WELCOME.

Come ahead and be as great as you can; we'll all benefit from your presence. Come, and enjoy what we have here, and re-inspire the rest of us who've come to take it too much for granted. Whether your grandchildren work for mine, or mine for yours, we'll all gain from the experience.

Mark Goodfellow
West Jordan, Utah

◆   ◆   ◆

I wish to say "thank you" to our Spanish imports who chose to be Americans. Thank you for your participation in defending America. Thanks also goes to the families who loved and supported our brave defenders. May our Loving God comfort and bless all of you.

Mildred Barnes

◆   ◆   ◆

Sir, Your column published in Jewish World Review on 8 Apr 03 struck a real cord with me. As a member of the US Navy I have nothing but the highest respect for the three men your column highlighted. They are true American Heroes. During the eighteen years that I have served in the Navy, I have known numerous Hispanic young men and women serving in all branches of the military who are some of the most dedicated and hardest working people in our military. Some were US citizens, some were not. All are great Americans. Thank you for pointing out the fact that these young men were willing to give everything for their country. They make me proud to be a citizen of the "Great Melting Pot."

Paul B. Mitchell Wahiaw, HI

◆   ◆   ◆

Raoul,

I very much enjoy reading your columns. This last one on the three young Marine "citizens" who gave their lives was excellent.

I have a son, Matthew, who has been activated and will be shipping out for Kuwait shortly. I thank God for the efforts and the courage of those who proceeded Matt so that his job may be safer and less perilous. Matt (25 years old), his older twin sisters Erika and Stacy, and his younger brother Andy (22 years old) are the children of me and my wife, Naomi (formerly Naomi Oralia DeLeon).

We met in San Antonio, TX, thirty two years ago. I was a 22 year old Army draftee going through Medics training at Fort Sam Houston. I provide this information as explanation for an insight that I feel I have obtained that many others, especially other "gringos", may not have. Naomi's parents both came to the US as teenagers with their families. I often tell people I have a great relationship with my mother-in-law, Maria DeLeon. She speaks limited English and I speak limited Spanish and we get along great.

We really do, because we both have a great appreciation for each other. I look at my wife's family and I see a microcosm of what makes this country great. In 2 generations it has made the transition from immigrant parents; her Mom still speaking little English and very comfortable in one of the barrios of San Antonio; her Dad (who died of cancer in 1969, I never got to meet him) was a successful businessman and a man who had a real presence. Naomi has 2 brothers and 3 sisters. She is the youngest. I don't believe the 3 oldest siblings finished high school. the 3 youngest did.

Spanish was spoken most of the time at home. All of them speak fluent English and Spanish. All of them married and these marriages resulted in 16 children. Of their spouses, the 2 oldest sisters married Hispanics, the two brothers married wives who were both Hispanic and Anglo heritage, and the two youngest sisters married Anglo's. All six of them have lived the American dream of building a productive life in this country and raising children who have successfully continued this pursuit. Of the 16 offspring, I believe 13 are married. Husbands and wives of this generation are very much a reflection of the broad palette that makes up our great country.

Educationally, all in this generation completed high school and most got some post high school training. 3 have earned engineering degrees, one of them as a graduate of West Point. My son Matt earned a degree this past year in Science Education (he was teaching Junior and Senior High School Science before being activated). He is going to be an excellent teacher. My youngest son Andy graduates in one month from college with a degree in business and a minor in computer science. He already has a job lined up with American Express as a Financial Planner. He has always shown an entrepreneurial spirit like his Dad and his Grandpa DeLeon. Both of our daughters got post high school training, business school and Licensed Practical Nurse training.

All of Maria and Aiphonso Deleon's grandchildren are active and successful participants in this wonderful endeavor we are all a part of. I look at this family, my family, and I see the fiber that binds us together. I see the resulting fabric that makes us great. I may be a blond and blue eyed Swede, but I look with pride and love at my dark haired, brown eyed kids and nieces and nephews.

My family has pretty consistently supported conservative and Republican causes. Our youngest, Andy has shown a lot of interest in politics and was an alternate delegate to the Minnesota State Republican Convention. The point you made about "One of their shared views is that illegals (and all Hispanic immigrants) come to America to suck off the public trough; to suck up welfare; to steal jobs, and to otherwise simply live off the fat of the land" is one that I have encountered not only in the general population in Chicago County Minnesota, but also within the Republican caucuses. But I know better and I don't accept this attitude when I see it, no matter how it is couched (i.e. protecting our borders, national security, etc). It always is based on ignorance and bias. I know, because I have been fortunate enough to participate in and to observe this process that has been occurring over and over again in our country for over 200 years. It is where our strength and our greatness comes from.

The story of these 3 brave and heroic Americans is the story of our country. God bless Jesus Suarez del Solar, Jose Angel Garibay, and Jose Antonio Gutierrez. And God bless America, their country, the country they gave their lives for.

Sincerely,

Mark P. Thelander

◆   ◆   ◆

Excellent article. Hispanic men such as these need to be recognized and remembered. As I live in So. California, I am well aware of the feelings of many toward the many immigrants in our area. I even admit to some prejudice in that area myself but I have worked with many Hispanics and know that you cannot judge all by the acts of some lawbreakers. Once again, a good article and one that needed written.

Paul Vandivort
Lakewood, CA

◆   ◆   ◆

---

thank you for your great article it has made me take a hard look at my self and my opinion of illegals i just wish that we could come up with away that they could come as legals. please write article on how we can make it so they do not have to come in that way. i also wish to thank all of your people for what they have brought to this country and for the live's they have given for her!! thank you for moving my heart.

bob boltz
Marion Ohio

◆   ◆   ◆

Dear Mr. Lowery:

Re "Two Americans and an Aztec Warrior".

Bravo! A wonderful article. I am a Cuban-American with three brothers who served in the U.S. armed forces: One as a chemist at the Dugway proving grounds, one in the US Airborne in Okinawa, Thailand and other unmentioned places during the Vietnam War and a third in the Army Reserves. I just missed Vietnam, but I was 4F, as I was deaf in one ear...Your article really resonated with me. Many Americans don't appreciate the degree to which Hispanic-Americans have contributed to our armed forces and the many who have given the ultimate sacrifice for our country.

I like your work and read you regularly on JWR. I also plan to read your book.

Growing up in a conservative Republican family in California (We moved from Miami when I was 7 years old) has been an interesting experience for me, both in my academic experience and professional life. I really appreciate your views on many issues.

Saludos

Julio Garcia

◆　　　◆　　　◆

Dear Mr. Contreras:

Thank you for reminding me of what was stated on the news networks only once or twice following the deaths of the wonderful young men.

I am first generation American, father born in Liverpool on way to US from Poland and Germany in late 1890s. I still have his birth certificate and papers when he made the choice to relinquish UK citizenship and be an American (or as grandma would say "Yankee Doodle").

Just as the bigots worried that JFK would be more loyal to the Pope, these same folks worry that Jewish Americans would be disloyal to America in favor of Israel.

Yes, in post WWII, when Israel was fighting the Brits and the Arab legions, Jewish and non-Jewish American war vets and others did go there and volunteer. When Hitler backed Franco was stealing power in Spain, many Americans, including some of my uncles went to fight fascism. How many younger people still recall the Abraham Lincoln Brigade?

How many recall the Flying Tigers in China?

However, when the fighting was over, those alive all returned "home" to the USA. They went as Americans and came home Americans.

I have traveled, lived and worked in many parts of Europe, Asia and the Third World. I have been in those places at various stages of life......as a student with no money, as a "hippy", as an adult with reasonable earning ability, and as one no longer needing to work for my well-being.

Without any doubt, despite the shrieks of the Anti-Americans, both domestic and foreign, we are as a nationality, the people on earth with the greatest potential for individual achievement, freedom and happiness because of our core beliefs, balanced government institutions, and the young persons like those you reminded us of.

Not perfect, but still the best show in town.

Thank you once again.

Jim Furman

◆   ◆   ◆

Thank you for writing this article.

I went into the Army in 1965, served in VN and am home, most likely because of the skills passed on to me by men with Hispanic surnames. I, for one, will never question where were the loyalties of those NCOs that led from the front in my outfit.

Oran Woody,
Houston, Texas

◆   ◆   ◆

Dear Mr. Contreras,

A great article and damn poignant, too. I find it fascinating that the "evil wet-back" is still being run, though the Pat Buchanans have not gotten it right yet. The no brainer is the number of Leftists who carp on Hispanic rights and bilingual education, i guess to ensure that the gated communities the anointed live in won't be besmirched, except by gardeners and other "right kinds"...Keep kicking ass on this, Remind people that a Puerto Rican kid once commanded the 1st Marine Division. By the way, I'm not Hispanic, just sick of seeing the left try to hijack an entire culture with lies, Glad to see that my Spanish speaking brothers are not buying into it.

Yours,

Dave Bruton

◆   ◆   ◆

Dear Mr. Contreras:

Whether these boys were formalized American citizens or not, they were American warriors. I honor them and their families, and I am sorry and mourn for their sacrifice. I live in Colorado, where migrant workers are an important part of the economy. If anyone who works as hard as those people wants to immigrate, I more than welcome them. But legally immigrate. And some illegals do only use this country for the social services, without the commitment to being one of us.

James Tooley

◆   ◆   ◆

Dear Sir,

After reading your column on the deaths of three great Americans I was moved to write you to express my sorrow for their deaths and my disgust for those who would question their (and your) loyalties. Do these people not remember that we ALL came here as immigrants to begin with? Do they not understand that America is not an ethnic identity nearly so much as it is a common heritage based on a belief in liberty, justice, and > equal opportunity for ALL regardless of race, creed or national origin? People have been coming to this country for hundreds of years seeking the freedoms that some here take for granted. Those who come here for these reasons typically make some of the best and most committed citizens because they KNOW what it is we enjoy here. As a fellow veteran, I thank you for your service and for the service of many like those three brave young men who only sought to give back something of what they received.

Semper Fi!

S. Orr

◆   ◆   ◆

---

wow.

gracias.

i, for one, needed to read that.

Judah Rosen

◆   ◆   ◆

Mr. Contreras,

Those of us that have smelled the smoke know of the contributions Hispanics have made to our Armed Services. It was my experience that young Hispanic men gravitated to the Rifle Companies in my old branch, the Corps. To this day, anyone questioning the patriotism and bravery of our Hispanic immigrants has to fight a tired old man. Screw the racist sons of bitches, we know what's up.

Best regards,

Peter W. Davis,
Wills Point, Texas.

◆   ◆   ◆

Dear Mr. Contreras:

I grieve for the three young men you describe, just as I do for every fallen soldier. Unfortunately, I was very disappointed with the interview with one of the fallen soldier's mother. She spoke Spanish through an interpreter. I believe that, if this lady is to come to really understand what America is all about and what her son died for, she must learn English. Perhaps this lady has not yet had the time to learn English to the level she wants, but I really hope she will.'

Sincerely,

Frank G.Zavisca, M.D., Ph.D.
Director, Obstetric Anesthesiology
LSUHSC

◆   ◆   ◆

Sir,

You were, if anything too kind in your column. Pat Buchanan was the first thing to pop into my mind when I read your column. You should have called him and a few more of his ilk out. (I know Pat didn't serve in Vietnam, I'd be willing to bet few of the VDARE and American Renaissance crowd so much as served in the Boy Scouts.)

Kevin Shannahan

◆   ◆   ◆

Dear Mr. Contreras,

Thank you so much for your column "Two Americans and an Aztec warrior." My family immigrated to America from the British Isles in 1699, the key word here being "immigrated." My direct line has had members serving in every war this country has fought except for Viet Nam. We, too, are so grateful to this nation for it's blessings of freedom and opportunities. We, too, know that without adherence to and reverence for our Constitution, but also without the immigrants from every other nation on earth, we would not be so great, nor so prosperous, nor so rich in customs and traditions—not even counting the richness of our language!. We are not a nation truly unless we have protected borders. I think Mexico is a special case for us. We desperately need a legal mechanism for Mexicans to come here and work and return home, or to apply for residence and potentially citizenship. Tolerating the illegal status of so many among us is stupid and dangerous, both to the aliens and to citizens, and is a serious blow to our 'rule of law'. I am not familiar with your talk show and this is the first of your writings that I've read, but I will be looking for more. The situation for Hispanic immigration needs common-sensical and respectful resolution.

Cordially,

Peggy Whitcomb Salem,
Oregon Contributing Editor
Oregon Magazine

◆   ◆   ◆

War protesters are Anti-American in that they hate the idea of America: capitalist yet prosperous & free. It is UN-AMERICAN to ask Asians (and Mexicans) where they are REALLY from. I am just as American as the Navajo-Marine who came here 12,000 to 50,000 years ago and the first generation Chinese-American.

I am a California Native Son, and I say G-d bless the contributions of Mexican nationals & more recently Central Americans. When my mother got cancer & died I was 8 years old. My father was engulfed in grief and distant; our housekeeper was a beautiful older woman of 14 or so. She did more than cook our meals, mend my clothes, at her young age she was like a 2nd mother; my prayers always include her.

Our vineyard never had Anglos or Blacks clamoring for work. I love California wines above all others so how can I turn on the workers who cane the vines, trellis the vines, pick the grapes, crush the grapes, make the barrels, make the wine? I have to add that I have had the privilege of being friends with and slaughtered at chess by University of Mexico alumni. Our gain is Mexico's & Central America's loss; E PLURIBUS UNUM!

LBCALEX

◆   ◆   ◆

Raoul,

This is a very compelling piece. Although I have considerable problems with illegal immigration, this column makes me stop and think about the human side of the issue and the contribution that many illegals make to our nation, despite not being legal citizens. I was also appalled by the question of which nation would you defend.

Ward Connerly

◆   ◆   ◆

One of the most exciting experiences I've had as a professional writer is the educational role I play in discussing history that many simply don't know because the American educational system is plain hooliganism in disguise. Teachers and administrators seem bent on destroying the millions of inner-city children, whether they be Black or Hispanic.

Living, fighting and dying for freedom is not new to Mexicans and Mexican Americans. Here are several articles about how these men have fought for America since the Revolutionary War. There is also an article that describes the great battle of the 5th of May, 1862, in Mexico that directly affected the course of American history by keeping the French from substantially helping the rebel Confederacy before the issues were settled by the great battle at Gettysburg.

How we have fought for this country is just part of what Mexican Americans are; they are a unique people that have brought food, language and tremendous values to the American table. Courage—coraje—is one ingredient they have brought to the country like few other groups ever to come to America.

◆   ◆   ◆

"WE FIGHT, THEREFORE WE ARE"

Who was Maximiliano Luna? Who was Rafael Chacon? And, who was Bernie Galvez? Street guys?

These are just some of America's Mexican Americans and others of Hispanic heritage that have marched off to fight America's wars from the very beginning, before they were even Americans and before there was even an America.

In honor of the end of Hispanic Heritage Month, Congress' little gift to the country's swarming brown masses, we must take notice of Hispanic Americans who have fought for this country.

First, we must examine one of the great heroes of the American War of Independence, the Revolutionary War: Bernie Galvez, actually Governor General Bernardo Galvez, a Spaniard, born in Spain, who came to America t o make his fortune.

Governing much of North America from New Orleans, General Galvez itched to fight the British when war broke out between Mother England and her colonies in 1775. When Spain declared war on England in 1779, General Galvez struck with lightening speed at what is now St. Louis, Mobile bay and laid siege to the British base at Pensacola.

That's straightforward history, the details are more interesting. General Galvez' four warships joined up outside Pensacola Bay with a fleet from Cuba under the command of a real Admiral. Treacherous sandbars and heavy-duty British guns caused the timid Admiral to beg off attacking the British forts. General Galvez, however, already the victor over the British in other places, ordered his four ships into the Bay, guns blazing.

This shamed the Admiral and he came in also, firing. The British collapsed and with their loss at Pensacola, the British were done in America, forever. The Battle of Yorktown came as almost an afterthought, two years later. And, General Galvez was there, also, complete with brown-skinned Indians and Mestizos from Mexico and Creoles Spaniards and Blacks from Cuba and Puerto Rico, plus money donated by the women of Havana to pay Washington's troops and his French allies.

Bernie Galvez? Look him up. He's on a first class United States stamp. He has a city named after him, Galveston, Texas. And, in Washington D.C., you'll find a fine statue of Governor-General Bernardo Galvez, given the United States by the King of Spain in honor of the great General's contributions to American independence.

The only place you won't find General Bernardo Galvez is in your child's history books.

Then came America's first full Admiral, David Farragut, a true hero, a true American Hispanic hero. After his heroics in the Civil War he went to Spain to investigate his family history and wrote his family's genealogy, tracing it back to a Spanish knight in the 13th century and a great warrior against the Moslem invaders of Mother Spain.

Nine-year-old David Farragut, the son of famous Revolutionary War Spanish-born Admiral Jorge Farragut, was appointed a United States Navy midshipman at New Orleans. David Farragut commanded his first vessel at the tender age of twelve. Ladies and gentlemen, this man was a sailor's sailor.

When the Civil War broke out, Tennessee-born Admiral Farragut pledged his loyalty to the Federal government and led the United States Navy in it's two greatest victories of the war, the capture of New Orleans and of Mobile Bay. It was at Mobile Bay that Admiral Farragut standing high on his flag ship's mast watched as his battle group was held up by torpedoes and cannon fire. Over the din of battle, Admiral Farragut bellowed, "DAMN THE TORPEDOS! FULL STEAM AHEAD!"

Admiral Farragut became a national hero and has statues dedicated to him in New York, Washington, D.C., in Tennessee and at the United States Naval Academy. He was even offered the nomination of the Republican Party for President, for President of the United States. He turned it down and went to Spain to study his family's roots.

When he died in 1870, President U.S. Grant and his entire Cabinet attended Admiral Farragut's services. No other man would be a full Admiral of the United States Navy for eighty years. Admiral Farragut, America's first native-born Hispanic war hero, is well known for his "Damn the Torpedo's, Full Speed ahead," but not for being a Hispanic or that he was proud of his heritage.

You won't find that important part of Admiral Farragut's personal history in your children's history books.

Ever hear of Rafael Chacon? Well, Major Rafael Chacon led Mexican American cavalry against an invading Confederate army at Val Verde, New Mexico in February, 1862 and slowed them down enough that Mexican American infantry from New Mexico could stop the Confederates cold at Glorietta Pass in March, 1862. The Confederates retreated to Texas and never again tried to invade western Union territory and the gold and silver mines of Colorado.

You won't find these battles, the Gettysburg of the West, in your children's history books.

Maximiliano Luna, who's he? Well, Captain Luna, commanded Troop F of Teddy Roosevelt's Rough Riders in the charge up San Juan Hill. Luna, a Mexican boy from Santa Fe, leading his men up San Juan Hill challenges the idea of a bunch of white boys off on a Cuban lark, doesn't it.

You won't find him in your children's history books.

In San Antonio, there was a mother who sent six, count them, six sons to fight in World War Two and who told the world, that if she had had a seventh son, she would have sent him off to war, also. There's the story of Medal of Honor winner Marcario Garcia who stopped in a Richmond, Texas restaurant in 1946 to eat with six United States Navy men and was told that everyone could eat but the "Mexican". The "Anglo" sailors destroyed the restaurant.

A university study concluded that Hispanics from just five states (Texas, California, Arizona, New Mexico and Colorado) accounted for 20% of all killed and wounded in Vietnam, but contemporaneously accounted for less that six percent of the American population. And, more than 17% of the names on the Vietnam war memorial wall are those of Hispanics, even though they only were 6% of the country's population during the war.

You won't find any of these facts in your children's history books.

We don't need Hispanic Heritage Month to honor our men, or our country, do we? Every day we survive as free people honors those men named Galvez, Farragut, Luna, Chacon, et al., doesn't it? ###

Author's note—Despite a decade of huge growth throughout the country of the Hispanic population, most people in the educational establishment are so ensconced in an attitude that Hispanics are new to the United States and are poor little sheep without history, without pride and without dignity.

Few, if any, of these historical facts about Hispanic fighting men are taught by teachers who are ignorant of these facts, or, worse, intentionally ignored by teachers who do not wish to build community and collective self-esteem, teachers who wish to keep the Hispanic community of youngsters ignorant of their deeply-rooted tradition of fighting all enemies, "foreign and domestic" of the United States of America, even before there was a United States of America.

◆   ◆   ◆

THE BEST OF AMERICA—MEMORIAL DAY

He was just another 1940's kid from the Barrio, the neighborhood; wearing baggy pants, shirts to big, a zoot suiter. He spoke Spanish; didn't do well in school and looked forward to a job, car and girlfriend. He was a typical Los Angeles CHOLO (CHOH-low, half-breed, half-civilized).

So why is a US Navy ship named for him? The USS Pfc. Eugene Obregon.

"In Korea, on the 26th of September 1950, United States Marine Pfc. Obregon observed a fellow marine fall wounded...Armed only with a pistol, he dashed from his covered position to the side of the casualty. Firing his pistol with one hand as he ran, he grasped his comrade...and dragged him to the side of the road. Still under enemy fire...when hostile troops of...platoon strength began advancing toward his position...Seizing the wounded marine's carbine, he placed his own body as a shield in front of him and lay there firing...accurately and effectively...until he himself was fatally wounded..."

It was my good fortune to come to this country as a little boy from Mexico during World War II. The first thing I noticed was no young men in our Mexican neighborhood. No, all were at war. Our women contributed to the war effort, by packing tuna, by pounding rivets.

We cheered Saturday newsreels showing Americans smashing our evil enemies, the Germans, the Japanese. We cheered our fathers, brothers, uncles, and cousins. These were the grunts, the swabbies, the gyrenes. Mexican Americans were fighting, really fighting, for our country.

That we understood. Later, we realized they were fighting for freedom, for good and against evil.

"Army Technical Sgt. Cleto Rodriguez was born in San Marcos, Texas. On the 9th of February, 1945 in the Philippines, Sgt. Rodriguez (then Private) and his full-blooded Indian friend left their pinned down unit behind and killed 35 hostile soldiers and wounded many more...Moving closer, they killed 40 more...Rodriguez crept forward...threw 5 grenades into a building killing 7 more Japanese and destroying a 20-millimeter cannon and a heavy machine gun. Rodriguez and his companion killed more than 80 of the enemy in 2 hours before his buddy was killed...Two days later, Rodriguez performed similar deeds in another battle."

By 1953, a couple of dozen men with Spanish surnames had earned this country's highest military honor; The MEDAL OF HONOR. Two were Puerto Ricans, the rest Mexican American, like me. Cleto Rodriguez, for example, was America's second highest decorated soldier in WWII.

On my 18th birthday, I left college classes early and hustled downtown for an appointment made years before, on Guadalcanal, Iwo Jima, or Inchon—an appointment made for me by these men—then went home for dinner. Sitting at the table, with my policeman father and three younger brothers, my mother asked how my day went.

"Nothing special", I nonchalantly told her, "I just joined the United States Marines".

The last Monday of May honors those who have fallen in defense of this country. There are some, however, who pooh-pooh the day and what it stands for. These people do not usually have Spanish surnames, though some do. In fact, one told me, we Mexican Americans have earned only the right to die for the United States, not equality.

Baloney! We have every right any American has. Period. We don't have to whine or beg for them. They are not Affirmative Action gifts. We won those rights in battle—no one can deny us. Is that understood?

We have socio/economic problems, of course. All people do. Appalachia's poor white trash, Bronx Puerto Ricans, the Afro-Americans of Chicago's South Side all have the same complaints as los pobres (the poor) Mexicanitos of the Rio Grande Valley, of East LA.

But, problems of the poor have always been with us, throughout history, in all countries. They're not unique to the United States of America. What is unique to the United States is that individuals and groups can work through problems and burst out of poverty.

With effort, everyone can be educated for free at least through high school; anyone can succeed, with hard work. Everyone can speak out on political issues, without fear of death squads. They must, however, share that right.

We don't have to carry national I.D. cards, nor have our Social Security numbers tattooed on our arms. We can all vote. And, we owe all this to soldiers, in part to Mexican American soldiers.

Former California Congressman, Marine infantry officer and winner of two Silver Stars, Pete McCloskey says, "Mexican Americans make the best damn infantrymen this country's ever had."

Many have paid the ultimate price for America and for freedom. In the recent Persian Gulf War (#1), one of the first Americans killed was Marine Eliseo Felix of Arizona. Marine Sgt. Candelario Montalvo and Soldiers Andy Alaniz and Luis Delgado all of Texas also died in action, in the desert of Kuwait and Iraq.

On this Memorial Day, to all those who served before me, with me and since, as well as those in the future, and especially those who died for the USA, regardless of color or national origin—Gracias Muchachos. ###

AUTHOR'S NOTE—JULY, 2003—As this is written Lt. General Ricardo Sanchez is the commander of U.S. Army ground forces in Iraq. Daily firefights occur and Americans still die, weeks after major combat operations ended with victory in the form of the Hussein regime imploding and disappearing.

Once again, Mexican Americans and other Hispanics rose to occasion and stepped into combat and, though some died, most enjoyed the fruits of victory of American arms like the world has never seen. Never in history has an armed force traveled so far, so fast and defeated an army that was touted as the toughest in the Middle East.

As for my United States Marines, their forces attacked deeper into a country and away from the sea than ever since the North African campaign in 1809. As a self-contained army of their own, the Marine Expeditionary Force traveled faster than their Army colleagues and reached Baghdad at the same time, but were awarded by historical forces the honor of capturing the center of Baghdad City. They secured most of the oil fields and pacified the Southeastern provinces of Iraq that are Shia-controlled and face Iran along hundreds of miles of ill-defined border.

Thanks to the superb accomplishments of the Marines and the reporting of those by embedded journalists, the United States citizenry was finally exposed by positive reporting of the contributions of Hispanic soldiers and Marines.

One only has to read the letters my article in the Jewish World Review provoked to see how thankful many Americans are to learn of the contributions of Hispanics in America's wars.

2

Chapter introduction—One retired Border Patrol agent brags that he can spot an illegal alien by just looking at them. That, in fact, is the working method Border Patrol agents use every hour of the day to arrest people. The courts, on the other hand, are constantly slapping the Border Patrol and its agents about the legal head and shoulders because the method reeks of racial profiling.

Nonetheless, like the Border Patrol agents, many Americans observe the Hispanic community with stereotypical disdain, not out of informed opinions, but from opinions based on uninformed stereotypes fueled by lies and misrepresentations from bigots and racists who abound in California and other states.

◆　　◆　　◆

INVISIBLE NO MORE—THE EARLY 90S

For many years, Mexican Americans worked in agricultural backwaters, in mines, in packing houses and wherever railroads went. We lived in secluded, segregated towns and neighborhoods, mostly by choice, sometimes by force and law. Though we were around, no one saw us. We performed work which was the foundation of the Southwestern/Western economy, only our labor and its fruits were seen, we were not—we were invisible. No More.

Our national presence is such, our food is relished by millions, our music appreciated in sold out concerts around the country, movies about some of us, made by some of us, overheat ticket machines and win critical acclaim. If the country of our origin, Mexico, economically hiccups, everyone notices. Some people are even paying attention to what we write, or say, in mass media.

Moreover, with three million more of us in the amnesty pipeline and with the 1990 census and its attendant reapportionment of state legislatures, the U.S. Congress and Electoral College, our political power will soar.

With all this, why are we the least known Americans? Is the mantle of invisibility still on? Let's do a quiz, 20 questions—True or False.

1. All Mexican Americans snuck across the Border and were (are) illegal.

2. All Mexican Americans speak only Spanish.

3. All Mexican Americans refuse to learn English.

4. All Mexican Americans have dark skin.

5. All Mexican Americans live in California and Texas.

6. Massive numbers of Mexican Americans protested the Viet Nam War by leaving the USA, avoiding Selective Service, the Draft.

7. Many Mexican American prisoners of war defected to the Communist side in Viet Nam to protest conditions in America.

8. Mexican Americans were not permitted to fight in World War Two because they were considered cowardly and/or treasonous.

9. Mexican Americans cannot attend college because their test scores and grades aren't high enough.

10. Mexican Americans aren't good at mathematics/physics or any sciences, thus they are worthless in a technological society.

11. Most Mexican Americans work in agriculture and live in rural areas.

12. Most Mexican Americans are poor.

13. Most Mexican Americans are on welfare.

14. Many Mexican American children are born illegitimately.

15. Mexican American women have large numbers of abortions.

16. Divorce rates among Mexican Americans is high.

17. Mexican Americans never live in neighborhoods other than their own.

18. Mexican Americans are outnumbered by Puerto Ricans and Cubans.

19. AIDS has a high incidence among Mexican Americans.

20. Mexican Americans are lazy; they haven't the Protestant work Ethic.

FALSE is the answer to these 20 questions. Yes, all false.

We didn't just sneak across the border. Some of us trace back to 16th Century settlers in what is now New Mexico and Colorado. As to our language abilities, while many of us do speak Spanish, most speak English, though some never learn it. By the third generation, most can't speak a word of Spanish. Stereotyping by skin color is inaccurate as Mexican Americans come in all shades and sizes; blondes, redheads, dark-haired, short, tall, brown-eyed, blue-eyed, green-eyed. You name it, we got it. We live in every state of the Union, as well as Europe, Asia and Australia.

To find a Mexican American who fled to avoid Viet Nam service, or defected to the Communist side, one has to invent one, because none did. This was not a new phenomenon. In World War Two, our fathers, uncles, brothers and cousins fought America's enemies with great ferocity and won tons of medals.

Drop-out rates notwithstanding, those of us who do get through high school test, more or less, on par with the general population. As to technological competence, the computer this is written on was manufactured by Mexican Americans and, is used by one.

Where we live has escaped everyone's notice as attention has been focused on our rural cousins by Farm Worker Union leader Cesar Chavez. Fact: Almost 90% of us live in cities and suburbs. Chicago, for example, has half-a-million of us, a fact even Chicagoans don't know. Every major mid-west, southwestern and western city has large Mexican populations. After all, we number over 12 million, four times Puerto Ricans, 12 times the number of Cuban Americans.

Every day there are less and less of us officially poor. 25% are, 75% are not. Mexican Americans detest welfare, ridicule those who take it and sometimes refuse unemployment compensation because some label it welfare.

Our children are mostly born legitimate, though to an inordinate number of teen-age parents. Nevertheless, our children are mostly born, as abortion is not considered a viable alternative, or a form of birth control. Divorce rates, though rising, are lower among us than the general population.

Health wise, we offer interesting comparisons to the general population. Our basic diet, corn, rice and beans, is high on fiber and low in cholesterol. We do smoke too much. We drink too much beer. Yet, our cancer and heart disease levels are lower than the general population. Why? Because were not as stressed out as most Americans. If, for example, it's not worth doing tomorrow, it's probably not worth doing at all.

AIDS in the "Hispanic" community has little to do with us. Puerto Ricans have an AIDS rate ten times higher.

As to our work ethics, I'll beg off answering that one as it's two o'clock in the morning and I have a breakfast meeting with my tax man at 7:00 a.m. We'll discuss it next opening on my schedule, say two weeks from Tuesday. ###

AUTHOR'S NOTE—JULY, 2003—Reaction by bigots to articles like this are humorous. Generally speaking, they write how racist I am to even ask questions like these. They are particularly incensed because they answer like they do then are pegged as bigots by me for their answers. They do not face reality or the truth.

"THEY ALL LOOK ALIKE TO ME"

Too bad, Vice-President Dan Quayle allegedly remarked, that he didn't speak Latin in order to speak with Latin Americans during his many trips south of the Rio Grande. The alleged remark is reported by an anti-Quayle French-speaking Congresswoman from Rhode Island. She's serious, Quayle wasn't.

If the Vice-President had been serious, it would not have been shocking, however, as most Americans don't know their tush from the culture and history of 300-million Spanish-speaking people. Moreover, many of the Spanish-speaking know little of their own history and culture.

Last year, a high-ranking television editorial Director from San Francisco, who claims to be a "Hispanic", with a Mexican-born mother, wrote a widely distributed article on Cinco de Mayo, the 5th of May, which stated the Mexican holiday commemorated Mexican Independence and that it shouldn't be celebrated anyway because it glorified war.

She went on to state that a day in September should be celebrated as the Hispanic holiday, so Hispanics could join on a day together. Hispanitude, if you will.

The article was distributed by a normally competent news service, The Pacific News Service, which specializes in Pacific Rim and Latin American news and features, written by "experts".

The article was dead wrong. Cinco de Mayo commemorates a Mexican victory over invading French forces in 1862, forty-one years after the last Spanish troops were driven from Mexican soil in Mexico's War of Independence (1810–1821). But, what's forty years and a different war have to do with one "Hispanic" woman's opinions on war, peace and freedom.

I wonder if the lady's television editorials are prefaced with a disclaimer, "Don't confuse me with facts, my mind is made up."

Another example are individuals who claim there's a land called "AZTLAN", the ancient homeland of the Aztecs in what is now Arizona, New Mexico and, perhaps, Southern California.

The facts are, the Aztecs were like any other Indian tribe, or shall we say "Native Americans", who crossed a Bering Sea from Siberia to Alaska, then moved south. They finally settled in the Valley of Mexico just a hundred or so years before the Spanish arrived in 1519.

In fact, the Aztecs settled Culiacan (on the Pacific Coast) in 1325 on their way south, thus what time they spent in what is now the Southwestern United States was limited and probably about the time the Magna Carta was signed in England, circa 1215.

These facts don't justify claims of territory for a southwardly nomadic Indian tribe which moved through the real estate in question a thousand years ago. And, the facts don't justify a claim of "AZTLAN" even being a bona fide homeland for the Nahua-language speakers of Mexico. A more logical extension of territorial claim would be for Siberia, and who would want it.

A more egregious example of lack of knowledge, or sheer stupidity, however, is not among my Spanish-speaking colleagues. It lies with the Anglo/Black educational establishment of Philadelphia.

As reported in the Philadelphia Inquirer, a reputable newspaper, an essay was prepared by the highly paid educational administration of the Philadelphia schools to help understand the many Puerto Rican children in their public schools system.

According to this brilliantly researched essay, pinatas are a Puerto Rican Christmas custom; tacos, enchiladas and tamales are Puerto Rican delicacies.

Actor-singer Ruben Blades is Puerto Rican, as are the famous baseball Alou brothers, Felipe, Matty and Jesus, according to these brilliant school administrators.

The essay also states that the rumba, merengue, calypso and samba are Puerto Rican dances.

One, of course, has to commend the Philadelphia schools for attempting to bridge cultural gaps between themselves and their students, and among their various student groups. One would wish, however, that accuracy would mean more to these public school teachers and administrators. Why?

Because tacos, tamales and Enchiladas are Mexican, as are piñatas; because Ruben Blades is Panamanian, and the Alou brothers are from the Dominican

Republic. Because the samba, mambo and merengue are dances from other countries and islands of the hemisphere, as is the calypso, not from Puerto Rico.

Seems the authors didn't include anyone from Puerto Rico, or descendent from Puerto Ricans, and the essay wasn't passed by any Puerto Rican teachers for review and comment. The essay was printed and distributed to all Philadelphia teachers as fact to be used as a resource in teaching children about America's multi-cultural diversity.

Good intentions, however, mean little if the lord and masters are so ignorant as to confuse entirely different peoples from different parts of the world.

Black beans come from Puerto Rico, pinto beans from Mexico. But, I guess, a bean is a bean, a beaner a beaner, cause we all look alike, don't we? ###

◆   ◆   ◆

Author's Note—July, 2003—The news media in America is sorely lacking in its understanding of the Hispanic population and phenomenon. There are two reasons for these deficiencies: 1. The hiring class of the American media simply hasn't hired Hispanics in numbers great enough to count; 2. The media doesn't want to understand Hispanics for understanding Hispanics requires a non-parochial view of the world and the ability to enjoy a passionate people willing to die for a job.

"BIMBOS, GIGOLOS AND TELEVISION NEWS"

I made a serious mistake the other night. I watched an hour of local news on San Diego's local CBS outlet. During the hour, I watched and listened to the most biased, anti-Mexican, fact-lacking, unprofessional news bites ever presented in a single news cast. By Whom? The graduates of the Bimbo, Gigolo school of TV News Broadcasting.

Unfortunately, most Americans get their news from television. Not only is local television news incompetent, commercial and Public broadcasting also suffer from cuties and stud handsome young men, quintessential airheads, all.

In the local news, where handsome anchor men make $200–300,000 bucks (really!) a year, three stories caught my eye. First, in a panicky voice, a pretty co-anchor reported American environmentalists were frightened a toxic-waste burn-ing incinerator in Mexico, five miles south of San Diego city limits (the Border), would spew toxic materials into the sky with winds carrying them over San Diego. End of her 30 second story, but not the real story.

As reported in the San Diego Union and The Los Angeles Times, the Ameri-can built complex, which is partially American-owned, is "state of the art", cost $15 million, is supervised by American engineers, training Mexican engineers and, according to Environmental Protection Agency (EPA) people, is as modern as current technology. They (EPA) know because they've inspected the facilities.

And, if these pseudo-journalists had bothered to check with weather people, they would've discovered prevailing winds over San Diego blow into Mexico, not from it. This condition, by the way, leads to American smog choking Tijuana, immediately southeast of San Diego.

Finally, one has to ask why no mention of the distance from the plant to the border, or show a map pinpointing the incinerator location, five miles south of the border.

The second item related to the opening of a Japanese plant in Tijuana's boom-ing MAQUILADORA (mah-key-lah-door-ah, twin-plant) district. These plants assemble and manufacture a myriad of products, including clothing, electronics, computers, televisions, intravenous medical products, etc., using American mate-rials shipped, duty free, from the U.S. into Mexico for final assembly and returned, at low U.S. duties, for worldwide distribution.

On and on, the TV newsman intoned, pointing out how much better the life of 50 Mexican employees would be working for a Japanese company. Implying: the average wage of $55.00 a week would make life better for these Mexicans; that Mexico couldn't do it, that these Mexicans can't do it; that only munificent businessmen from Japan can improve the lives of these poor Mexicans.

Not once did this "newsman" tell his audience this plant was one of less than 20 Japanese facilities in Tijuana, or what The New York Times called "Mexico's Silicon Valley". Moreover, he didn't tell his audience there are over 1400 Ameri-can companies active in Mexico's Maquiladora program (less than two dozen Jap-anese companies in a program 23 years old); he didn't tell us there's over 300,000 Mexicans working in maquiladora plants along the border; he didn't tell us half the wages paid these workers is spent in the United States, in San Diego's shop-ping malls, where customer Spanish is heard in every store, where Mexico's hard-earned dollars are spent with great gusto.

No, he didn't tell us any of this. He didn't, because he doesn't know.

Thirdly, the pretty co-anchor reported the Tijuana Coroner's office had royally screwed up and misidentified two bodies of non-Mexicans accidentally killed in a car crash. The bodies were shipped, according to the pretty co-anchor, to an American mortuary which, compounding the grievous Mexican error, shipped the wrong bodies to the respective families for burial. Only then, was the mistake discovered.

Great story. But, alas, not true. A highly respected American personally witnessed the Mexican body identification, personally witnessed identification tags being placed by Mexicans on the correct bodies and told any newsman who asked, exactly what happened in her presence. The American mortuary switched bodies. But, unless you read newspapers, you'd never know it.

Local television "news" people strike again, with no retractions, of course. Not to be outdone, however, national television news hemorrhages ignorance or prejudice in massive doses during the News.

Examples: NBC's Connie Chung not bothering to check on the pronunciation of a commonly used Spanish word, which has been co-opted into America's English. The word—Junta (Hoon-tah), meaning a government by people who've forcefully seized power. How does Ms Chung, who earns in excess of $800,000 a year, pronounce this widely used word? Chuhn-tah.

Charlene Hunter-Gault, who shares billing on the acclaimed McNeil-Lehrer News Hour, committed an even more grievous error and one truly insulting to those of us who speak Spanish and have Spanish names. In referring to the Archbishop of Manila, Prince of the Church, Jaime (hi-meh) Cardinal Sin, she called him—Jay-mee.

No matter where we turn, therefore, whether it's with pretty local anchor women, gigolo handsome co-anchormen or national TV folks, we're assaulted with incompetence, with infidelity to truth, and with dumb, stupid coverage of Mexico and Mexican Americans. Is it plain stupidity? Or could it be the "B" word, Bigotry? Giving them the benefit of the doubt, it must be stupidity.

Though there's no room for it, there's nothing we can do about their stupidity other than turn the set off. If it's bigotry, however, that's another story, as television stations are Federally licensed. Licenses can be denied. Personally, I choose not to support stupidity with my television viewing. I think I'll just turn bimbo-gigolo news off. I wish I could turn bigotry off as easily. ###

AUTHOR'S NOTE—JULY, 2003—Unfortunately for us, local bimbo and gigolo reporters become network anchors and reporters.

"I Know Who I Am"

The world is full of social and political misfits and we Americans of Mexican descent have our share of them.

In Colorado, 69-year-old Francisco Coca refused to appear in court on various charges by stating, "I, Francisco Coca, of Aguilar, Aztlan (sic), do not recognize the jurisdiction of this court because the laws have been made by the European to suppress the poor, straight, and innocent native."

His troubles stem from his picking up a dead wild turkey from a mountain roadside. Apparently the bird had been dead for awhile. He and his 16-year-old son wrapped the bird to take it home.

A couple of miles away a Fish and Game officer pulled them over and asked the Cocas if they'd been hunting. No, they answered. He asked to see their rifle. It wasn't loaded, nor had it been fired recently. Seeing the dead bird he called for back-up.

When a second officer arrived, the elder Coca says he walked up to the officer and told him, "Gringo, why don't you go back to Europe and leave us alone."

Coca took the bird out of his truck, walked 50 yards and threw the bird as far as he could. He and his son drove away. One officer followed them. Young Coca was issued a citation days later while in school and the elder Coca was arrested three weeks later. A $2,000 bond was set, but American-born and raised Coca refused to speak English at his hearing and as the court couldn't provide an interpreter for seven days, he was held until they could. He refuses to cooperate with an appointed local public defender, nor with the regional or state public defenders.

Interestingly, Coca is a plaintiff in a law suit against the State of Colorado to keep it from implementing a voter-approved English-Only statute. He cooperates when he wants.

In direct contrast to Coca's position of being an "indigenous" person, we find Theresa Gonzales and Laurinda Fragaso Owens of San Diego who would do away with the terms Hispanic, Chicano, Brown and "people of Color".

They write, "Mexicans are Caucasian (white), unless more than fifty percent of their heritage is Indian, in which case the race thus becomes Mongoloid (yellow) (a.k.a. 'Asian')."

"Some Mexican Americans have popularized the term 'Brown'…The fact is, that there isn't such a race as 'Brown' race", they maintain.

These ladies top their demands with, "We want respect and equal justice." That is, officially they want to be called white. If, of course, the race police can prove they have more than 50.1% white, Caucasian blood. Sort of like South Africa, I guess.

The facts are, there are a lot of "Brown" people.

On the one hand, we have Indians (descendents of migrating Asians), who were here when Columbus arrived in 1492. On the other hand, we have the Spanish who came to colonize and intermarried with these same Indians. Questions of cultural and human "Genocide" aside, a new people was created, unlike North America, or India, Asia or Africa where whites did not, for strictly racial reasons, intermarry with local women.

Neither white nor Asian, the new people are something, they are mestizos—mixed bloods.

Protestations to the contrary, the combination of Spanish and Indian created a new skin color—Brown. I know, I see it every time I look in the mirror. So do a hundred million other Mexicans and Americans of Mexican descent, plus millions of others in Central and South America.

Modern Mexico has been forged by these Brown people. California, Texas and the rest of America have been built, in part, by these Brown people, who are increasingly more important in the American social, political and economic fabric.

We, who trace back to the union of Spanish Conquistadors and Indian women, can choose one of three paths. Like the ladies, we can insist on being white if, of course, we can prove at least 50.1% white blood. Or, we can ignore our white blood and be "indigenous" and refuse to participate in America like Mr. Coca.

Or, we can assert ourselves as a new people, we of brown skin, of Spanish and Indian blood. We are a very unique blend of cultures and races. We are Mexicans and Americans of Mexican descent. We are a very special people, a singular people with cultural and historical ties on both sides of the Atlantic.

There is little, if any, room for angst in our collective future. I'll leave that to Mr. Coca, Ms Gonzalez and Ms Fragaso.

For, I, KNOW who I am. ###

AUTHOR'S NOTE—JULY, 2003—Among the Hispanic community, there are many who simply can't accept what and who they are. In the 2000 census, almost half of Hispanics checked off the box "White" for race, while also checking the Hispanic box, Hispanic, of course, not being a race. Most of the others checked off the "Other" box for race. The brilliant people who put together the Census reports seem to have difficulty in interpreting the results of box checking.

Actually, those Hispanics who are Black like baseball's Sammy Sosa, for example, would check off Black for race and the Hispanic box as well. Nothing wrong with that. The problem seems to be that those with Spanish-European and Indian blood checked off "other."

WE'RE NUMBER ONE!

Slamming the screen door behind her, the 19-year old prostitute walked over to the porch edge and screamed, "Jasmine, get over here or I'm going to kick your ass."

Jasmine is two-years old. Neither Jasmine nor her mother are Mexican American.

A young man I saw the other day is, however. He was wearing a black overcoat, a black pork pie hat, dark glasses, and a wispy mustache and chin whiskers. In a word, he was dressed and looked like a CHOLO (an uncivilized half-breed). Dashing across an intersection, he pushed a baby carriage with his year-old daughter in it.

On the corner, he stopped, bent over the little girl and made sure her bonnet was on right so the sun wouldn't shine in her face. It was obvious for the world to see that he loved his little girl. He exemplifies one cultural trait we Mexican Americans offer America that seems to be lacking in some other Americans.

The trait: True and unmeasured love for our children.

As reported by the National Center for Health statistics, we Mexican Americans have the lowest infant mortality rate in the US of A by half the Black rate and even lower than the white, Anglo infant mortality rate. Specifically, Blacks have an infant mortality rate of 18.7 of every 1000 Black births; white Anglos a 9.1 rate; Puerto Ricans a 12.9 rate; and, we have a rate of 9.0.

Yes, for once we are number one at something and that something is good. More of our babies live. There appears to be no scientific explanation, at least the National Center for Health Statistics doesn't have one. Dr. Joel C. Kleinman of the Center states this astounding statistic is a "real anomaly" considering that poor Mexican American women have as meager pre-natal care as poor Blacks. How is this possible?

Poor Mexican American women without pre-natal care have their babies and smother them with love. It's an anomaly when they don't. Watch any Mexican American baby or child and you'll see someone—the mother, the father, a brother or sister—is always touching or holding the baby, always.

Pre-natal care hardly plays a role in how we raise and take care of our children, and while the low mortality rate is a mystery to Dr. Kleinman, it's no mystery to us. There are, however, some among us, who take exception to our proven methods.

Professional Mexican American poverty-types, those on public payrolls downgrade the mortality rate study, as it does nothing to keep them on a payroll. For example, Anna Diaz, program director for an LA County-University of Southern California family health program, pooh-poohs the good statistics because of Mexican immigrant women who, "are more prone to lead a more wholesome lifestyle and haven't gotten into the culture of drugs and alcohol."

Further, and with not a scintilla of scientific proof, she maintains that if "more acculturated" Mexican mothers were studied separately, their infant mortality rate would be the same as the Blacks. Baloney!!

These professional poverty employees, "Poverty Pimps", if you will, haven't the foggiest notion why our children live and others die. They would argue for more pre-natal funds from the Government so more people like Anna Diaz can get Government-funded jobs. Yet the study refutes this argument.

As too whether or not "acculturation' leads to higher infant mortality rates, what happened to the 75% of Mexican Americans who are not, I repeat, not in poverty and have access to pre-natal care. Does their mortality rate go up because they have a glass of white wine? Of course not!

Years ago, a scientist named Harlow conducted experiments known as the Harlow Study, which tried to determine if motherless infant monkeys sought food over comfort or sanctuary. In it infant monkeys were observed in two separate sets of circumstance. One had only a food feeder apparatus to run to when it was terrorized; the other a ball of fur and no food.

Invariably the infant monkey with nothing but food to run to would cringe in terror and fear, but would not run to his food. The other would run to, clasp and hug the ball of fur when frightened. The famous Harlow Study shows us why Mexican American children die less often than Blacks, white Anglos and Puerto Ricans.

It's love and touching; it's love and cuddling; it's love and laughing and bonding. It is love, something we are very good at.

Dr. Kleinman scratches his head and offers "a number of hypotheses" why Mexican American infants survive better than Blacks, Puerto Ricans, and Anglos. Two come to mind.

He thinks that Mexicans have "a lot more social support than other comparable groups," and "maybe (there are) some dietary factors we are not aware of..."

Until science comes up with better explanations, allow me to offer two: Love; and, Beans, tortillas and Jalapeno chile peppers.

An unbeatable "Mexican Combination"? Of course, it's why WE'RE #1. ###

AUTHOR'S NOTE—JULY, 2003—This essay needs no comment, it stands on its own.

"A HISPANIC IS..."

Among racists there are two common phenomena that are glaringly obvious to us yet are blind spots to them. First, is their denial of their racism and of racism in general. Secondly, there's their propensity to define their terms of reference despite their wrong-headedness.

In denial, for example, are many who simply deny that anyone but white Northern Europeans, have accomplished anything in history. Their use of code words in discussing problems they attribute to race is widespread and their own particular form of denial.

They make no effort to disguise their dislike of minority groups and seem to go out of their way to stereotype and to concurrently show their ignorance of the subject.

Pointing out this state of denial does no good, for they don't think they can do any wrong and aren't squishy on the question of race and ethnicity, at all. They aren't racist, they insist, despite evidence to the contrary.

Racists, you see, are like that.

They also have another side, and that is that they insist on trying to define others.

For example, San Diego's oldest bi-lingual newspaper, La Prensa, published an article by Dan Munoz in which he wrote about "Hispanic" contributions to America's defense and used a Department of Defense publication as a source. He wrote that Civil War hero, Admiral David Farragut, was one of the country's first "Hispanic" war heroes.

They came out of the woodwork with vicious attacks, the racists did, against the writer, the publication, Mexican Americans in particular and Hispanics in general.

One, who claimed to be a PhD in Economics and Statistics, wrote, "You should be aware that when you make outlandish and silly claims, you reduce your credibility and integrity. Several points you make are merely grotesque exaggerations, while others are whole cloth falsehoods…Union Vice-Admiral David Glasgow Farragut was not a Hispanic."

The United Daughters of the Confederacy (Falls Church, Virginia) weighed in with, "The Union Admiral David Glasgow Farragut was not a Hispanic…(he) was neither from Latin America nor did he speak Spanish…You must understand that people such as Daniel Munoz (the writer) base their entire lives on historical revision which makes them feel fulfilled in their otherwise vacuous history…Perhaps Mr. Munoz is mentally ill."

A local fanatical anti-Mexican bigot wrote, "(Farragut) did not speak Spanish, his surname was not Spanish, he did not emigrate from Latin America. Those three items define what a Hispanic is."

And, then, a man claiming to be the great-great-great-grand nephew of Admiral Farragut wrote, "That (Farragut being Hispanic) is ridiculous…I've had a difficult time correcting some idiotic political (sic) correct literature distributed by the Department of Defense since the early 1980's when President Reagan's officials were seeking to increase the Hispanic vote for Reagan…you are accurate about everything except Farragut was not Hispanic…I must demand that you retract and correct your statement…immediately."

Despite this obviously orchestrated campaign, the facts are that Admiral Farragut was Hispanic, assuming the definition of one is someone who comes from or is descended from people in Latin America or from Mother Spain. It matters not if they speak Spanish, for few do in America after a generation or two; and it matters not if they, themselves, have emigrated. And, it matters not if their birthplace or the birthplace of a parent was real estate that traded hands between incestuous European royalty from time to time.

What matters are the facts and how the individual, in this case, Admiral David Farragut himself interpreted his background.

We find some interesting original material at the University of Tennessee, Knoxville, in the Special Collections Hoskins Library.

For example, we find handwritten letters from Admiral Farragut about his trips to Spain to "discover more about his heritage, spending most of his time in Barcelona and the Balearic Islands (of Spain)." Further, we find contemporaneous(1864) published genealogical material that contains "A description of the Farragut family of Barcelona coat of arms as described and pictured in Adarga, Catalana, by Don Francisco Xavier Degarma Y Duran, Barcelona, 1753."

We also find a mimeographed page from "The Life of David Glasgow Farragut describing his ancestor—Don Padro Farragut—13th Century noble warrior."

Facts are stubborn things, President Reagan told us and we have his Department of Defense to thank for "Hispanic Contributions To America's Defense".

The United Daughters of The Confederacy and other racists notwithstanding, Hispanics can and will define themselves—that's one of the prerogatives of having a culture and ethnicity and of being proud of each, and not living in perpetual denial. ###

AUTHOR'S NOTE—JULY, 2003—Rebutting these idiots was more fun than sex. Funny thing, after LA PRENSA and I offered up our evidence in subsequent editions, we never heard from these people again. Oh, my, how the truth hurts. Sunshine truly is a disinfectant.

3

Chapter introduction—We may be Mexican Americans, Puerto Ricans, Salvadorans, Guatemalans, Hondurans or Peruvians, et al., but most us are a combination of Spanish and Indian blood.

It was that combination of blood that led the revolution against Spain in Mexico. Few full blooded white Spaniards or their sons, the Creoles, joined the revolution for the sake of equality, they joined the revolution to grasp power for themselves, not the nation.

The largest percentage of those who fought and died were pure blooded Indians or mixed blood Mestizos. Nonetheless, no Mestizos or Indians led the new nation of Mexico until full-blooded Indian, Benito Juarez became President of Mexico.

◆　　◆　　◆

FROM WHITE FATHERS AND INDIAN MOTHERS: A NEW PEOPLE, A NEW NATION

After three hundred years of Colonial Spanish rule, a Roman Catholic parish priest struck the first blow for Mexican independence, with a lie.

September 15, 1810. Spanish authorities were enroute to arrest the respected, Creole priest of Dolores, a well-to-do town north of Mexico City, for conspiring against Spain. Alerted by co-conspirators, he called his parish together, by church bell, at midnight (the 16th), exhorting them to join him in resisting and ousting atheist Napoleon Bonaparte's puppet regime in Spain. He lied.

The good priest, surely crossing himself while asking God's forgiveness, explained to his Indians and mestizos that Spain's King Ferdinand VII had been arrested and forced to abdicate by atheist Napoleon.

To protect their Faith from the Godless French, he, Friar Miguel Hidalgo y Costilla, would lead them to reclaim what was rightly God's, and King Ferdinand's. As one, his parish rose to their feet, cheering; cheering God, King Ferdinand and their beloved Fr. Hidalgo.

Rushing out of the church en masse, they jailed Spanish residents of Dolores, as well as any Creoles (Mexican-born of Spanish parents, 100% white) who did not join Hidalgo. Spanish-owned shops were sacked and burned. Prisoners were freed from Spanish jails. On this night in the early morning hours of September 16th, 1810, the revolt-to-be was bloodless—no one was killed.

The struggle for Mexican independence, the true objective of Fr. Miguel Hidalgo y Costilla and his aristocratic Creole co-conspirators, started that midnight, in a church with cries of VIVA EL REY! (Long Live The King); VIVA AMERICA! (Yes, America. They called themselves Americans, not Mexicans and Fr. Hidalgo was an ardent admirer of the United States); and MUERA EL MAL GOBIERNO! (Death to Bad Government).

DEATH TO THE GACHUPINES! (gah-choo-peen-ehs, white men), chanted the good Friar's dark-skinned flock. Ignoring their deadly chant, he focused instead on their religious zeal, zeal he could and would manipulate for independence for Mexico, independence from Colonial Spanish rule.

Responding to Fr. Hidalgo were long-oppressed Indians; Mestizos (mixed Spanish and Indian; and a few idealistic white-blood Creoles. From towns, villages and cities in Central Mexico, they came to Dolores to join his "Army." To them, it was an army to save the church and Spain from atheists; to Hidalgo, it was an army of liberation, an army of independence.

At the head of the motley army, a mob, by any objective definition, flew banners of LA MORENITA (lah—more-eh-neet-ah). La Morenita, Our Lady of Guadalupe, was and still is the dark-skinned patroness of Catholic Indians and Mestizos. Carrying a Morenita banner and leading the mob, the Catholic Priest, Miguel Hidalgo y Costilla.

The army carried machetes and faith, but few guns and no cannon.

They had a great deal of courage, and, as Hidalgo was to find out, much hatred for whites. These Indians and Mestizos knew little about Napoleon, other than he was white, but, they knew the difference between white and dark skin. This, they knew because white Spaniards and Creoles never let them forget the difference.

After the 1519 Spanish Conquest of the Indian empires of Mexico, some Indian religious symbols were incorporated into the Catholic mass, as were some

Indian words into Spanish, but for all intents and purposes, Indian culture disappeared.

After the Conquista (cone-kee-stah, the 1519 conquest), almost everything Indian disappeared in Mexico—except the Indian.

With this, vanished a toughness bred by hundreds of years of harsh desert existence. A struggle to survive-another-day-Indian, was supplanted by a docile SI SENOR Indian who paid tribute to Spain, and, whose women produced a whole new race and ethnicity from white fathers and Indian mothers—The Mexicans.

As described by Hidalgo's Bishop Quiepo, 1810 Mexico was, "…composed of 4-million inhabitants who may be divided into three classes: Spanish, Indians and half-castes (Mestizos). The Spaniards consist of a tenth of the total population and they alone hold almost all the property and wealth of the realm. The Indians and mixed breeds take care of domestic, agricultural labor, and ordinary offices of trade, arts and crafts. That is, they are servants, menials or day laborers for the first class."

Father Hidalgo's mob didn't change these conditions or much of anything. Hidalgo founded a newspaper, EL DESPERTADOR AMERICANO (The American Awakener) in which he published his independence program and called for better treatment and equality for Indians, Mestizos, as well as abolition of slavery. This platform was rejected by the predominantly white Creole landowner class.

Mexico City and other principal cities remained loyal to Madrid and the ersatz Royal House of Napoleon's brother. Of the many mistakes Hidalgo made, the worst was not marching on Mexico when his mob army numbered 80,000. During this equivocation, Royalist troops attacked Hidalgo's languishing army at Guadalajara and totally defeated and dispersed the mob. The triumphant Spanish commander wrote: "A great expense of powder and shot was saved by cutting the throats of prisoners…"

Captured by Royalists while dashing north to a safe United States, Hidalgo was tried on the spot by the Royalist military on July 30, 1811, convicted of treason and shot. Not content with a dead Hidalgo, however, the Spaniards, being Spaniards, cut off his head and hung it publicly at the Guanajauto granary where the first blood was spilled in the War for Independence, 11 months before when Hidalgo's followers butchered Spanish troops.

The Spanish Commander notified Madrid that the revolt was over.

But, in the South of Mexico, another parish priest, a part Creole, Indian, Negro, and former muleteer, Jose Maria Morelos, had been commissioned by

Hidalgo to organize an army in the South. Unlike Hidalgo, a quiet man of peace and faith, Morelos was a soldier.

His campaign was effective and endured until his capture and execution in 1815. Besides occupying southern Mexico, Morelos' greatest achievement was organizing an eight-man Independence Congress in 1813. He also commissioned another Creole-Indian-Negro freedom fighter, Vicente Guerrero.

After Morelos' execution, it was Guerrero (Spanish for warrior) who kept freedom's torch smoldering by leading Royalist troops a merry chase around the mountains north of Acapulco for six years. The Royalist troops were commanded by Agustin Iturbide, a Creole officer, who had been previously cashiered for financial irregularities, but called back into Royalist army service and sent to chase Guerrero's rebel guerillas in the South.

Hatred, however, for those who earlier had disgraced him and opportunism caused him to turn on Royal Spain. After convincing Guerrero he was serious, he took his troops and joined up with the rebels, stealing, in the process, the war from Los Morenos (the dark ones).

Now, with the war being led by one of their own, Creoles everywhere supported him and on September 27th, 1821, 11 years and 11 days after Hidalgo shouted "Death to Bad Government" in his church at midnight, Iturbide entered Mexico City at the head of a victorious Army of Independence. An independent Mexico now stretched from San Francisco (California) in the north, to Nicaragua in the south. After Imperial Russia, Mexico was the second largest independent country on earth.

Unlike the idealistic Hidalgo, Morales and Guerrero, Iturbide was not a democrat. He promptly declared himself Emperor of Mexico. His Creole empire lasted nine months. But, no matter, Mexico was free of her colonial master, Royal Spain.

With independence, Mexico, like its neighbor to the north, rid itself of European royalty. South America, following Mexico's lead, also rebelled leaving only Cuba and Puerto Rico Spanish in America. Their liberation would await 80 more years and would come at the hands of United States troops, not indigenous rebels and freedom fighters.

Not a real nation at independence, Mexico was a disparate racial conglomerate of Spaniards, white Creoles, Indians and Mestizos. this was so for almost a hundred years, into this century (1910–1920).

It was the victorious Mestizo armies of Mestizos Pancho Villa and Emiliano Zapata that forged the true Mexican nation, the Mexico we know today, the

Mexico Friar Miguel Hidalgo y Costilla dreamed of—The United States Of Mexico.

Conquerors and colonists alike left Spain Spanish, and arrived in Mexico Spanish, but, their Mexico-born children weren't, they were Mexican. As Victor Alba wrote in his The Mexicans; The Making of a Nation, "Mexico had her will of the newcomers in the end, for the Spaniards were transformed into Mexicans."###

AUTHOR'S NOTE—JULY, 2003—September 15–16 is celebrated as Independence day by all the countries south of the Rio Grande River, though there were few, if any, real rebels in those countries, countries such as El Salvador, Honduras, Nicaragua, Costa Rica, Guatemala and other South American countries.

In recent years, the proclamation of Hispanic Heritage Month in September by the United States Government is cued around Mexican Independence Day. Most Americans, and some Hispanics, however are confused because another celebration, that of Cinco de Mayo (the Fifth of May, celebrating a Mexican victory over French troops decades after independence from Spain), is thought by many to be Mexican Independence Day.

◆　　◆　　◆

CINCO DE MAYO, THE 5TH OF MAY

A great deal of blood drenched Mexico's soil to uphold the political principle of the United States of America on the 5th of May, Cinco De Mayo, 1862, and none of it was American. It was mostly French, and it was the first defeat of the French Army in almost 50 years.

The victors? Mexicans armed with half-century old rifles last used at the Battle of Waterloo; and, Mexicans armed with machetes and cattle. These Mexicans had thrown out their Spanish masters forty years before in a decade-long War of Independence that ended 300-years of Spanish domination of the ancient Indian nations of Mexia.

The beneficiaries? Mexican self-determination; Latin American self-determination; and, American pride, dignity and position in world affairs. When American Secretary of State James Monroe bravely proclaimed that European powers could not re-impose their monarchical or other systems on any country in the Americas, neither he nor the thirty-year-old United States could do anything to back up his "MONROE DOCTRINE".

Nevertheless, the Doctrine was respected by European powers until Communists took over Cuba in 1959, with one glaring exception, the 1862 French invasion of Mexico.

More beneficiaries? Abraham Lincoln and his struggle to keep the Union whole as the great Mexican victory prevented European royalty from flooding the American Civil War with munitions for the Confederacy. And, it benefited victorious Union American soldiers who swiftly made their way to Mexico when the Confederacy had been defeated to join the Mexican Army; it also benefited as well every American who savors freedom today.

Freedom won, in part, by Mexican teenaged soldiers in the mountains 100 miles east of Mexico City 138 years ago on the 5th of May, Cinco De Mayo.

Cinco De Mayo does not celebrate Mexican Independence Day; it commemorates the Battle of Puebla between 6,000 French soldiers and 2,000 Mexican allies and 4,850 Mexican soldiers under the command of Texas-born General Ignacio Zaragoza.

Following the same route Spaniard Hernando Cortes took in 1519 from the Gulf of Mexico towards Mexico City and American General Winfield Scott took in the Mexican American War (1846–1848), French General Charles Ferdinand Latrille, Count of Lorencez, marched his soldiers into the Mexican mountains hoping to engage the Mexican soldiers of President Benito Juarez in one decisive battle. He did and he lost.

On the 4th of May, General Zaragoza ordered Colonel Porfirio Diaz, later Mexico's President and dictator for thirty years, to take his cavalry several miles away from the city of Puebla to be used as a battle reserve.

The Count divided his forces and sent one column to chase Diaz's cavalry and his main column to attack two forts guarding the city of Puebla. The evening of May 4th was used by both sides to prepare for battle.

Confessions were heard by priests, letters written, rifles cleaned and prayers uttered by Mexican citizen-soldiers who knew the army they faced hadn't lost a battle since Waterloo, fifty years before (for purists, 49 years and some months). The French prepared for battle as only professionals can, for they knew they hadn't lost a battle since Waterloo and, brimming with professional confidence, they prepared to win.

The rains came. Heavy torrential rains. Then, before dawn, came the Indians, the Indians for whom there were no rifles, only machetes. They also brought their cattle with them, cattle they stampeded through the French troops causing the professional soldiers to scatter, giving Zaragoza time to better position his cannon and troops.

The Mexicans waited. Dawn came. Onward came the French through the mud, to be slaughtered. Porfirio Diaz and his cavalry, probably some of the best cavalry in the world, attacked the French sent to hunt him down.

When the sun went down, that 5th of May, 1862, almost a thousand French soldiers and allies were killed or wounded. Diaz was chasing French ostrich-plumed cavalry-men late into the night. The Indians scoured the Killing Fields and retrieved French rifles, then melted back into the hills. The Hills from which they would wage a guerilla war for the next five years.

With tails between their legs, the French retreated to the coast to await 30,000 more men; to wait for a year. They would return, and they would win the second battle of Puebla. They would chase Benito Juarez to within yards of the American Border. They would bring Prince Maximilian from Austria and crown him Emperor of Mexico. They would occupy most but not all of Mexico.

They came, they told the world, to collect legal debts. The reality was, however, they came because the United States of America was busy disemboweling itself and couldn't enforce its Monroe Doctrine. But when America defeated its domestic enemies it turned a jaundiced eye towards the French interlopers on its southern border.

Combat-veteran Americans, answering Juarez' 1864 call for volunteers, rushed across the border to help the very army and country they had fought less than twenty years before in America's bloodiest war ever. Armed with weapons covertly supplied by the U.S. and protected by U. S. soldiers in Texas, Mexicans and their American volunteers took the offensive. It was now only a matter of time.

When the war ended in 1867, Juarez led his Army into Mexico City, an Army which included an American Legion of Honor. Though long and bloody, the war's end began on the 5th of May 1862 at the Battle of Puebla and continued through victory because, as one French General put it, "Bah! Every Mexican is a guerillero, either he has been or he will be".

True, General. Every Mexican…every American…is a "guerillero" for freedom. The 5th of May, like the 4th of July, is proof. ###

AUTHOR'S NOTE—July, 2003—American beer companies like Budweiser and Coors have had much to do with the rise of Cinco de Mayo observances and celebrations around the country. There is much confusion among Americans about Cinco, because many think that Cinco is Mexican Independence Day, it is not, as we have read above.

Nonetheless, it appears that the United States takes more notice of Cinco de Mayo than Mexico does in recent years. For example, in Los Angeles, the Cinco celebration is usually held the Saturday before Cinco de Mayo, the 5th of May, and draws over 400,000 people to the streets of Downtown Los Angeles for music, dancing and just plain having a good time.

In San Diego, Cinco is celebrated all over the 3,000,000 person San Diego County but is particularly celebrated in "Old Town" where the original Spanish settlement in the entire Western United States was founded in 1769. Somewhere between 100,000 and 200,000 regularly join together to celebrate Cinco.

Schools observe it, churches observe it, thousands of non-Mexicans observe it, it being Cinco de Mayo. When I first started writing professionally, I distributed two Cinco de Mayor stories, one was 2,000 words long, the other 750 words in length. The country was so hungry for information on Cinco that I sold so many newspapers one of the two versions that I thought I was going to get rich as a writer.

In later years, I wrote that I had a major impact on raising awareness of Cinco by my annual articles on it. My then editor at the North County Times, which is a large daily in San Diego County, rebuked me by declaring that a well known California historian had discussed Cinco in one of his books in the 40s or 50s. My reply to the former high school English teacher, a man in his late forties with a long pony tail, was, so what?

The proof of the matter was in the fact that over a hundred newspapers bought my Cinco articles including most major newspapers in large cities. If that historian had informed so many people about Cinco, why were so many people hungry top buy and read my Cinco articles.

The Pony-tailed editor simply was an argumentative liberal who fought me on many fronts, many times. Nonetheless, circumstances had seriously changed since the historian wrote his books in the 40s. In those years, Mexican-origin people were not so numerous, thus their celebrations and observances of Cinco were simply ignored. However, in the 1990s the Mexican-origin people numbered in the millions.

Just as important, is the historical view that by stopping the French on the 5th of May outside the City of Puebla, Mexico, and sending the French invaders reeling back to the coastal harbor of Vera Cruz, the United States was able to hold off victorious Confederates long enough to build the world's largest Army, an Army that finally defeated the Confederacy at Gettysburg, just 14-months after the Battle of Puebla.

Many military historians observe that had the Confederates more cannon and gunpowder and cannonballs to use at Gettysburg, they might have won that battle and the United States would have ceased to exist.

I broached that theory in early articles in the 90s and by 1995 it had been picked up by others and is now mentioned from time to time by journalists and historians.

Cinco de Mayo reflects many things to many people, but recognition that Mexicans could defeat a highly touted foreign invader is a collective self-esteem item that helps modern Mexicans grasp their place in today's world.

◆　　◆　　◆

"OF GREASERS AND WETBACKS…"

Richard Rodriguez enraged militant Chicanos and guilt-ridden white liberals a decade ago with the publication of "Hunger of Memory". In it he belittled affirmative action and bilingual education. He has recently published an Act of Contrition in "Days of Obligation: An argument With My Mexican Father".

In this collection of ten essays Rodriguez struggles to identify the origins of the dark face he sees in the mirror every morning. Taught to be an Irish Catholic by nuns and priests who took vows on the Emerald Isle to escape the living death of Ireland, Rodriguez didn't know he was Mexican.

What am I, Rodriguez asks, over and over. Am I Indian?: am I Spanish?; am I both? Every dark-skinned Mexican has, at one time or another, asked the same questions.

There are Mexicans of every skin color and hue of hair.

But a real Mexican looks like Rodriguez, for Rodriguez is Mexican, a combination of Indian and Spanish.

"Mexico is littered with the shells and skulls of Spain, cathedrals, poems, and the limbs of orange trees. But everywhere you look in this great museum of Spain you see living Indians," writes Rodriguez.

"Where are the CONQUISTADORES?", he asks; he demands to know.

Rodriguez continues: Liberal white politically correct America "pities the Indian the loss of her gods or her tongue. But let the Indian speak for herself. Spanish is now an Indian language. Mexico City has become the metropolitan see of the Spanish-speaking world...Mexico City has captured Spanish".

I once wrote that the Mexican Indian pulled the mantle of Spanish civilization around him as just another layer, as an addition to the many layers of civilization that he was.

The PhD in Renaissance Literature, Rodriguez, phrases it this way: "the Indian stands in the same relationship to modernity as she did to Spain—willing to marry, to breed, to disappear in order to ensure her inclusion in time; refusing to absent herself from the future. The Indian has chosen to survive, to consort with the living, to live in the city, to crawl on her hands and knees, if need be, to Mexico City or L.A.

Rodriguez has discovered who he is, and he is proud. In Mexico City, he writes, "Everywhere I look. Babies. Traffic. Food. Beggars. life. Life coming upon me like sunstroke.

"Each face looks like mine. No one looks at me.

"Where, then, is the famous conquistador?

"WE HAVE EATEN HIM, the crowd tells me, WE HAVE EATEN HIM WITH OUR EYES.

"I run to the mirror to see if this is true.

"It is true."

Through his eyes, Rodriguez searches and sees others who look like him. He watches them prepare to cross into the United States at twilight along the Tijuana River, those whose misfortune it was to be born in some distant mountain village in southern Mexico rather than Los Angeles.

Of those men who crossed the Border, alone, he writes, "they were men without women. They were Mexicans without Mexico." On Saturdays, they "flooded the Western Union office, where they sent money...all the way down into Mexico. America was a monastery. America was a vow of poverty. They kept themselves poor for Mexico."

Rodriguez discovers who he is in these thousands of thoughts and observations transferred to words onto paper, and he has discovered who they are, the Mexicans, the 90-million people south of us, as well as the 16-million who look like Rodriguez in the United States.

"I take it", he declares, "as an Indian achievement that I am alive, that I am Catholic, that I speak English, that I am an American. My life began, it did not end, in the sixteenth century."

Like Rodriguez I searched for who I was, also. I made my discovery as a young man on the day I climbed the Pyramid of the Sun at Teotihuacan, just outside the city of 16-million people, Mexico City, the city of my birth.

After an exhaustive climb, I stood at the top, facing the sun, just as the first Spaniard did in 1519. Like him, I turned slowly to face west. Ruins and trees is what I saw.

Then, in a flash of inspiration, like a bolt of lightening, I realized that what the Spaniard saw was the largest city in the world in 1519. A city built by people who looked like me (and Rodriguez).

I knew then I was not a "wetback', a "beaner", a "greaser" as the white boys (Anglos) derisively used to call me.

My mother was the Indian who built that magnificent city; my father the Spaniard who conquered it. I am the child with the best of two worlds.

Of the billions of people in the world, only a few can say that, Richard Rodriguez and I are but two. ###

AUTHOR'S NOTE—July, 2003—Many among the bigot community refer to Mexicans and mixed blood Mestizos as "mud people," or half-breeds, or Colored people. Many among the Hispanic community, the more leftist among us, call themselves "people of color" and Chicanos. That is their right, but it is pure baloney (the reader may read this as BS).

Those that call themselves these deprecating terms are simply "professional victims" existing, they say, at the feet of a White population intent of keeping "people of color" subjugated. These "professional victims," these whiny incompetent, usually uneducated people, are simply Poverty and Victim-hood pimps, without shame or dignity and without honor. They are people as bad as it gets in American society.

Richard Rodriguez and I know exactly who we are; neither of us suffers from angst, neither of us are criminals raised in middle class suburbs and educated by nuns; both of us are educated eclectic students, observers and reporters of what we see about and among us. We do so with our own backgrounds as prisms to filter what we see through; thus, our views are certainly more valid on national issues Hispanic, while certainly more valid than those views on the same issues of less educated and experienced people within our Hispanic population.

◆   ◆   ◆

STUPID, LAZY MEXICANS...

Mexicans are stupid, lazy, indolent, whiney, thieve'n rogues. Everyone knows this. It's a fact. You can look it up.

Some are, of course, as you can find in any ethnic group. Disappointed as their detractors are bound to be, however, most Mexicans do not fulfill these bias-ascribed characteristics. Most of these people are simple trabajadores (trah-bah-haw-door-ehs, workers).

Recently, we forayed into my old neighborhood to rehabilitate a three-bedroom house, a house totally wrecked by the evicted former residents and practically destroyed by narcotics raids. Kicked in doors, wall holes used to hide drugs and money, filth and cockroaches knee-high in size and depth greeted us and the armed marshals assisting us. The Mexicans who lived there were gone. We groaned at the task before us.

We decided that the first order of business was to drive to the nearest Catholic Church to ask the pastor if he knew of a deserving family man he could recommend to help us repair the house. As we were leaving, however, several neighbors and their children approached us. Mexicans, real Mexicans, amnesty candidates from the state of Michoacan from where many Mexican immigrants come from. We introduced ourselves.

They tell us how happy they are to be rid of the human cockroaches who lived in the house. We tell them we're headed to the Church to seek a helper. The leader, a strong Indian woman, raised her hand and said, "Senor, we have someone here who can help" and motioned towards her house.

"Hijo (ee-ho, son)), vengate (vehn-gah-teh, come here)!" A slightly built teenager walked toward us.

"How old are you, and what's your name", I asked, in Spanish. He answered, "Manuel, I'm sixteen."

I explain that we're here to clean up the house. He tells me fine. I ask him how much he wants to help us. Both he and his aunt respond, "Whatever you want to pay". We settled on $4.50 an hour. A good summer wage for any sixteen year old starting high school.

For the ten straight days it took us to rehab the house, he did everything we asked him to do, including truly dirty jobs, all without complaint. He worked hard; he never asked for time off. Every day I asked him if he wanted to work manana, and every day he responded "si." He earned every cent. When I asked him what he was going to do with the money, he answered, "I'm going to use it for school."

One day, we left for awhile, forgetting to tell him to take a lunch break. When we returned and finished for the day, we realized he never had lunch. He didn't take one, you see, because we didn't tell him to.

Some of his family have been here for years, he himself snuck across the border in the dead of night, pursued by border bandits and the Border Patrol. He was twelve-years old that night. Happy Birthday.

The whole family is legal now, thanks to Ronald Reagan's Amnesty. Aunts and uncles, he and his parents, brothers, sisters and cousins, all reside within blocks of each other. In his house live ten people.

"Ten people?", I ask incredulously.

"It's a big house!", Manuel exclaims. It is a big house.

Manuel reminds me of another young Mexican, who arrived several years ago in Los Angeles without a word of English and no skills other than being able to throw a baseball. Though a rookie, he opened the baseball season for the LA Dodgers, pitching in front of 50,000 skeptics who questioned Tommy Lasorda's sanity in starting a rookie.

He won and ignited "Fernandomania", sweeping all before him, mowing down batters like Little Leaguers. Fernando Valenzuela became the best known Mexican in the world. We saw Fernando on television selling products, leading literacy drives in Los Angeles or rewarding Fernando certificates to children with good grades. He was everywhere.

Most striking, however, were his work habits. Until last year, he never missed a start in eight years. Never. If he had the flu, or a fever, or was so weak he could barely walk, he worked. Reporters wrote that even when it was obvious he was sick, when asked how he felt, he would answer, "Fine", and go out and pitch. This, while other teammates snorted cocaine and missed assignments, or complained their backs ached, or the sun was too hot. "Another lazy Mexican" this Fernando.

Fernando is, of course, a millionaire who set the standard by which all pitchers have been judged since his rookie year. But what of less famous Mexicans, do they live up to Fernando's work standards?

In several articles for the San Diego Union, reporter S. Lynne Walker wrote of an exodus of newly-legalized farm workers to the city for higher paying jobs in construction and other industries. One former strawberry picker comes to mind, one Rudolfo Ledesma.

Ledesma left the strawberry patch last December to join a shopping center grounds crew. Starting work early in the morning allowed him to apply for a night job, as well, at a huge restaurant in the same shopping mall, working as a baker of rolls and muffins. When hired he told the manager the job was temporary. He's still there. He's still on both jobs.

"We keep asking him,' the manager says, "when he's going to leave and he just smiles." Yes. "Lazy Mexicans."

Several years after my divorce, we were in court arguing money and my ex-wife complained that when we were married I worked 14 hours a day, seven days a week, in my own business. The judge looked at me and asked, "Is that true?"

Casting a glance at my attorney, he whispered, "Answer the judge." I looked back at the judge and asked, "You mean, I wasn't supposed to?" ###

AUTHOR'S NOTE—July, 2003—Fernando was so popular among Mexican and American baseball fans that whenever he pitched, no matter the city, the home team drew an average of 5,000 more fans than their average with the same teams.

Once in San Diego, Fernando was announced as the pitcher two days before the Dodgers came to town. Not only did the fans fill the stadium, but they were pouring in even after the scheduled start of the game.

The game was delayed for 20 minutes because the California Highway Patrol had radioed in that they were escorting 50—count them—50 busloads of Mexican fans through the San Diego mountains that were headed to San Diego Stadium for Fernando's game. This was the only game I ever recall that was delayed because thousands of fans were still making their way to the stadium.

Mexican fans they were, coming to root for their national hero. Fernando lost the game that night, but no wonder, the San Diego Padres ran away with the division, set a for-all-time record by coming back from 2 losses to whip the hapless

Chicago Cubs three games in a row to win the League Championship Series and go on the World series for the first time ever.

Ironically, the San Diego Padres brought Fernando back after several seasons in the Mexican League to pitch with a very young staff. Old man Fernando had enough to help the Padres win two division titles and play a World series against the New York Yankees. Despite being in his late thirties, Fernando still brought them in, Mexican and American fans.

◆　　◆　　◆

"HISPANIC, HISPANO, LATINO, CONFUSION"

Well, what do you know? Despite the language and style police in America's newspaper editorial suites, Mexican Americans like to be called Mexican Americans, some even Mexican; Cubans like to be called Cubans and Puerto Ricans prefer to be called Puerto Ricans.

Not all of us prefer to be called Hispanics. Certainly most of us refuse to accept the very derogatory handle of "Chicano."

Yes, Virginia, we are not all little brown robotic creations of editors, journalists and the Census Bureau. We, whose roots lie in the lands of the conquistadores, are as different from each other as are any other people in America.

So concludes any objective reader of the Latino National Political Survey conducted among 2,800 "Hispanics" under the direction of (then) University of Texas Professor Rodolfo O. De La Garza. After years of confusion, several foundations funded the first-of-its-kind survey.

The survey concentrated on the three major Spanish-speaking groups, those with roots in Cuba, Puerto Rico and the largest group, those with Mexican roots. It should be noted that within sight of Los Angeles City Hall there are more people of Mexican origin than all of Cubans and Puerto Ricans in the United States, combined.

Many surprises can be found in the survey's final report. It should be noted that most of the surprised were Anglos, radical fringe New York Puerto Ricans and Chicanos (radical Mexican Americans).

Surprise No. 1: The majority of "Latinos" surveyed prefer to be referred to specifically as Mexican Americans, Cubans or Puerto Ricans. Despite this, major newspapers such as the Los Angeles Times continue to lump everyone together as "Latinos".

Surprise No. 2: Mexican Americans and Puerto Ricans agree that there are too many immigrants from each other's native lands coming to the United States. In other words, Mexicans don't want more Puerto Ricans to come here and Puerto Ricans think too many Mexican come here. Quite simply, they don't care much for each other.

Surprise No. 3: About a third of Cubans and Mexican Americans think that abortions should "always" be available, as do 28% of Puerto Ricans. Though this was reported widely in the American press, few newspapers pointed out that 67% of Mexicans and Cubans and 72% of Puerto Ricans stated that abortions should not be allowed. Reporters and editors forgot to do their arithmetic.

Surprise No. 4: More than 80% of the survey's interviewees back bilingual education as a means of learning English; more think that English is an absolute necessity to advance in the United States.

Surprise No. 5: Few, very few, call themselves "liberals. Among Mexicans, fewer than 5% call themselves "very" liberal; 11.6 percent "liberal" and 12.1 "slightly" liberal. To the shock of most big city newspapers the remaining 71% consider themselves to be "moderate" (35.4%), "slightly conservative" (14.8%), "conservative" (15.4 percent) and "very conservative" (5.8%).

These figures prove once and for all that Mexican radicals, otherwise known as Chicanos, have little currency in the almost 20-million Mexican American community. In fact, assuming that all of them are "very Liberal", they don't even match the percentage of us who are "very conservative."

Most of us are good solid moderates and conservatives who believe that English is absolutely necessary to make it in the United States; who provide the American military with an abundance of our men; who believe that abortions should not be available and who (except for me) believe by 75% that too many immigrants are coming to America.

Most of us reject the notion that we are "Hispanics" or "Latinos", except in a very general sense. Unfortunately, major newspapers, their reporters and editors, continue to shove those labels down our throats. As to why, could it be because 98 percent of them are white, middle class?

Maybe this study will make a difference in how the 26-million people with Spanish-surnames are treated by the press, but I doubt it. It's easier for lazy editors and reporters to use Hispanic and Latino, than to use Mexican American, Cuban or Puerto Rican.

It's even easier to not bother knowing the difference between Mexicans, Mexican Americans, Puerto Ricans and Cubans.

They all look alike, you see. ###

AUTHOR'S NOTE—July, 2003—The survey that motivated this article was, perhaps, not only the first of its kind that the public became aware of, by was shocking in its conclusions—to some. Many Hispanics are quite aware that there is a pecking order within the community that is more than economic. Mexicans don't like Puerto Ricans…Cubans don't like Mexicans, Dominicans don't matter to the rest, except when they are baseball players.

Economically, most Mexicans are far better off than Puerto Ricans. Another essay in this collection pins that fact down to the number of telephones owned by each group. Especially reviled by Mexicans are the Nuyorican of New York City. The Nuyorican welfare dependence is revolting to hardworking Mexicans who have a much higher labor market penetration. Puerto Rican drug use and AIDs incidence (according to the Center for Disease Control) is as much as ten times higher than among Mexicans. Prison populations of both groups is no where near the same, with the Puerto Rican rate higher than among Mexican-origin people.

Mexicans are quite aware that almost the entire island of Puerto Rico is on food stamps that Mexican workers (and others, of course) pay for in taxes they pay, taxes Puerto Ricans don't pay.

As for Cubans, most of those in Florida are best described as not happy with Puerto Ricans because many have black blood and black blood is unpopular with white anti-Castro refugees, just as it is with Fidel Castro's government itself.

Cubans, also, don't particularly care for Mexicans. Mexicans respond with disdain for the Florida Cubans.

Voting patterns also display differences among these various Hispanic groups. Generally, Florida Cubans vote Republican, though they didn't in 1996, when they voted for William J. Clinton's reelection. Mexicans generally vote for Democrats, though 35% of them voted for George W. Bush and 40% voted for Republican congressmen and Senators in the 2002 off-year elections. Contrast those figures with only 9% of Blacks voting for George W. Bush. For those mathematically challenged, Hispanics voted for President Bush four times more than Blacks did.

Puerto Ricans generally are the most loyal of Democratic voters, even more so than Blacks. Despite that record, Puerto Ricans, joined by Democratic Dominicans in New York City abandoned Democrats and voted in large numbers for former Mayor Rudy Giuliani and gave almost half their votes to the current Republican Mayor, Hizzoner Mr. Bloomberg.

The worst case of Hispanic bigotry remains that of my childhood in Mexico. Spanish refugees from a triumphant General Francisco Franco and his victory in the Spanish Civil War (1936–1939) escaped to Mexico, arriving as invitees of left-wing President Lazaro Cardenas. Most were penniless when they arrived and received Mexican government help, and the help of many sympathetic Mexicans. Mexico officially helped the government of Spain, as did many Mexicans.

Unfortunately, Spaniards are Spaniards and haven't changed since their racist asses were run out of Mexico in 1821. Spanish men and women who came with only the clothes on their backs in Mexico, immediately tried to take over Mexico. They ordered Mexicans around in their own homes as if they were servants. They demanded government help to buy existing businesses. They demanded jobs from the government, mostly executive level jobs because, they declared, they were so much better educated than and socially superior to "mongrels" with Indian blood—Mexicans.

These Spaniards were Communists, mostly. Communist Cubans are no different, today, in Cuba.

All in all, many Hispanics don't like many other Hispanics. Economics has something to do with it, as does education. Cuban American have little problems with graduating from high school and entering the American economy. Mexican Americans born in the United States are graduating from high school in record numbers and flooding into college. Currently, in California, for example, 575,000 mostly Mexican American Hispanics enrolled in California public colleges last fall. Puerto Ricans outside New York City mirror the communities they live in irrespective of ethnicity.

One of the strongest supporters of the Republican Governor of New York in his last reelection was a Dominican labor leader in New York City.

Hispanics come in all shades of color and with all shades of ideas and opinions, period. They are human, not robots.

PART II

4

WHO AND WHAT THE HELL ARE WE?

Chapter introduction—During the Nineties, it was this writer's pleasure to have been one of a tiny number of Hispanic writers that anyone published in the mainstream press. From my unique perspective I was able to reach out and educate many as to who Hispanics were, Latinos were, Mexicans and Mexican Americans were and are. I recall how an editor now and then would call to caution m about being too confrontational, about not setting up "us against them" scenarios.

Sensibilities of Anglo editors about my issues didn't and don't guide my work. Over a decade ago, I strongly wrote about the coming bankruptcy of Social Security and how Hispanics would take the brunt of higher taxes to support a retired Anglo group of retirees who never paid in enough to pay for their own Social Security. My editor at the Oceanside Blade-Tribune called to warn me that the publisher was extremely unhappy, as were dozens of letters to the editor.

That was and is but one issue of many among which I explored areas ignored by the mainstream media and social commentators who only saw and see problems in the United States as Black and White. The following essays discuss the growth and growing influence of the Hispanic/Latino community in the United States during the 80s and 90s. No one, not even this writer, could forecast the huge growth that actually would occur during the 90s, mostly from immigration, legal and illegal, mostly from Mexico, but also from Central and South America.

Also discussed are various questions about who Hispanic/Latinos are in the United States and whether they are, in fact, Hispanics or Latinos.

"The All-Conquering Jalapeno"

Is the United States in danger of losing its cultural-socio-political identity its 32-million Hispanics? There are many who believe this to be true. They are wrong, and they are right.

That is, some Hispanic cultural and social traits will crowd out some tired, traditional American ways and social mores. Why?

Music? Try Los Lobos and their distinctive 1990's East LA rock. Or, try Linda Rondstat's Spanish renditions of "Canciones de mi Padre" (Songs of My Father). Try, also, Julio Iglesias for an international adventure.

Dance? Count the sold out houses when Mexican Folklorico troupes tour the United States. Count the Anglos who pay upwards of $50.00 to see traditional Mexican dances.

Work ethic? See the Census Bureau reports that note that 82% of Mexican American males work in contrast to only 74% of the rest of American males.

Food? Count the number of Mexican restaurants springing up around the country. Watch the sales of Mexican food products climb in America's supermarkets.

Language? Federal law requires bilingual education in school districts that have 20 or more students with a language other than English as their home language. Thus, millions of kids who enter school speaking Spanish-only are supposed to be taught in Spanish, then switched to English.

This, however, is not happening and when it does, it creates problems. Protests come from those who believe America is being hijacked by Spanish-speakers. They confuse language with culture. In this, they are not alone.

Militant Mexican-Americans, self-styled Chicanos, insist that the use of Spanish is a manifestation of their Mexican cultural background. In doing so, they give their detractors ammunition.

Let's see what such ill-informed militancy—on both sides of the question—can nurture. We have two examples, one Canadian and one Israeli.

Famed Canadian author Mordecai Richler writes in "Oh Canada! Oh Quebec! Requiem for a Divided Country", how he watched a middle-aged man photographing restaurant signs to turn in violators of Quebec's ban on English-language signs and menus. The man, Richler writes, is a "tongue trooper" a "self-appointed vigilante" who will turn in his "evidence" to Quebec's Commission for the Protection of the French Language.

Sounds like US English and other English-only organizations, doesn't it?

Other language restrictions in the Province of Quebec are that indoor signs can have English on them as long as they have twice as many French words. Richler suggests that French be spoken twice as loud as English, as well. Additionally, Quebec is spending over half-a-million dollars on removing bilingual traffic signs and replacing them with French-only signs.

Does this sound like those Americans who object to California's publishing traffic regulations and educational material in Spanish and some Asian languages?

Lastly, Richler describes how French-speaking hardliners organized undercover language cops to enter department stores to see if clerks used English or French with their customers. If English, would the clerk turn "curt or disagreeable" when asked to speak French?

Does this remind anyone of English-only speakers who file complaints when employees of companies or government agencies speak Spanish in their presence? Are we destined to have language cops also?

Our other example comes from the democratic theocracy that is Israel and concerns one of the highest cultural contributions any group can make to a society—food.

Pizza has come to Israel. In ultra-Orthodox towns and neighborhoods, pizza, according to rabbis is dangerous, decadent and decidedly un-Jewish. This according to Chicago Tribune writer Tom Hundley.

He quotes one rabbi as saying, "Pizza is goyish food. It will lead us to become like all goyem. It is cheap, not respectable and not nice to eat like that in public." Goyem, Goy and Goyish are Jewish-Yiddish terms for non-Jews. It carries a disparaging meaning, much like gringo used to when used by Yanqui-baiting Latin Americans.

Despite rabbinical opposition, pizza is hot. Ask Benny Fakash. When he opened his first shop in an ultra-Orthodox neighborhood, he sold over a 1,000 pizzas in the first three days.

"It was crazy", Benny told reporters, "Two thousand people came to the opening. People got so excited they fainted".

What can we deduce from these experiences of our Canadian and Jewish friends? Smile when you speak Spanish around English-only speakers, and smile when you see burgeoning Mexican food sections in supermarkets.

And, note that one more American cultural bastion has fallen to the onslaught of 32-million Hispanics. To wit: Salsa has just surpassed catsup in sales, in America.

Conquering the world with Jalapenos, what a people we are. ###

AUTHOR'S NOTE—JULY, 2003—There are many symbols from Mexico that have been incorporated into American culture. Tacos, the "whole enchilada," burritos, tortilla chips, "La Bamba," calaboose, savvy, nada, "Send my bail to the Tijuana Jail," mission churches in California, California, itself, and leaf-blowers and cars that bounce up and down—but the jalapeno chile towers above them all.

A large jalapeno chile is about three or four inches in length and over an inch around at its thickest point. Properly pickled in "escabeche," the heat it can generate in one's mouth is spectacular. It raises one's metabolism. Of course, there are other chiles in the world that may be as hot, or even hotter, but Mexican chiles like Serranos and Chipotle and the jalapeno represent culinary, political and social cultures like no other such items in the world.

In the words of a rookie Californian (newly arrived from the Midwestern mecca of Cleveland) whose mouth was inflamed by an especially hot jalapeno, so much he could barely speak—to the question of why does he continue to inflict such pain on himself by eating jalapenos—"Because they taste so good."

◆   ◆   ◆

TREASON OR LOYALTY

What is it with certain Americans who can't seem to understand the English language and how words are constructed and used? Specifically, why do we have to listen to the wailing and complaining by people who object to: African Americans, Black Americans, Asian Americans, and, most specifically, Mexican Americans?

Recently a Border Patrolman publicly stated that he objected to such terms because they forcefully implied dual loyalty and he thought that is disloyal to the United States. The complaints are usually directed at Hispanics and, in particular, against Mexican-origin people. One rarely hears a rebuttal to the asinine complaints and the generalizations that are usually uttered concurrently by these people who define themselves with these complaints.

Black Americans, or African Americans, use those words to distinguish themselves as prideful individuals with a common ground with millions of others who share their blood and heritage. Because of this blood and heritage, these people were and are discriminated against since they stepped off the boats in chains in the 1600s. Thankfully, no one proclaims that their own characterization implies disloyalty to the U.S. or dual loyalties to other countries.

Hispanics, on the other hand, use the term Hispanic American to self-identify as an American with a Hispanic background, be it Mexican, Cuban, Dominican, Puerto Rican, et al. After all, they are different, culturally and sometimes racially. This is a general application that shouldn't imply anything but cultural identification. There is no such thing as disloyalty or dual loyalty to the United States involved, just as enjoyment of a drag queen's night club act doesn't imply a propensity to cross dressing by men in the audience.

Most of the complainers make their complaints against Mexican-origin people and this confirms this writer's theory that the complainers tend to be people ignorant of history and of the centuries of interaction between people of Mexican and Spanish origin and those of English origin in North America. They also tend to be racist by definition. For they have no logic or evidence on their side when they charge Mexican Americans with disloyalty to the U.S. Evidence, what is their evidence?

Has any Mexican American ever been charged with treason against the United States? Has any Mexican American ever been charged with spying against the United States? Has any Mexican American ever been charged with desertion in the face of the enemy and shot as punishment (Private Slovak, where are you?)? Has any Mexican American ever been charged with stealing official secrets and selling them to foreign nations? Has any Mexican American ever been charged with terrorism, like the Oklahoma City mass murder by bombing? Has any Mexican American ever been charged with terrorist bank robberies or murders? Have any Mexican American "militias" been formed to train disloyal potential terrorists?

Are there any Mexican American Jane Fondas? There is a simple answer to all of the questions—it is NO.

So where is the proof that Mexican Americans have dual loyalty to Mexico? There is none. It exists only in the mind of people who find themselves being left behind by the fastest growing demographic group in the USA-Hispanics as a whole and Mexican Americans in particular.

Almost without exception, the complainants are non-Hispanic White. They overlook Irish Americans, Italian American, German Americans, etc., groups that have countless clubs and organizations designed to perpetuate their cultural backgrounds into the 21st Century. I do not hear complaints about these groups.

Where, for example, were the complainers when the German American Bund was running rampant throughout the country in the Thirties fostering hatred and racism towards Americans and loyalty towards Nazi Germany? They were nowhere to be found.

Enough, however, is enough. There is no evidence to show Mexican Americans are loyal to any country but their own, the United States of America. Even when a few apply for the new "dual nationality" that Mexico offers it's natural born who have emigrated and changed their citizenship and their children, this is not a display of loyalty. It is an emotional move to some, but mostly a property rights business decision for most.

The complainers can take their complaints and sashay into the sunset. More importantly, they might, perhaps, study the English language. They might learn the difference between an adjective, a descriptive adjective and a noun. "An adjective serves as a modifier of a noun to denote a quality of the thing named" is how my Webster's Collegiate Dictionary defines an adjective.

The word Mexican, when used with American, modifies the word American to describe the person's ethnic or national background, while the noun American is the nationality.

In other words: ethnic or national origin/nationality. Besides, we have to call ourselves Mexican Americans because there's close to a hundred million real Mexicans just minutes south of this writer's home. If we didn't, all Anglos, non-Hispanic Whites, would think we are Mexicans, real Mexicans, when we are Americans, real Americans.

In fact, some Mexican Americans can trace their presence in America (1540s) to long before the first Russian, German, Italian, Romanian, African, or even Englishman etc., ever dreamed of coming to Amerigo Vespucci's "America". Complain about that.###

AUTHOR'S NOTE—JULY, 2003—Mexican haters abound in America though the vast majority of Americans aren't so inclined. Enough, however, are so that we have to be ever vigilant that their lies don't overwhelm the public discourse. Or the public perception of the country's fastest growing ethnic group.

The very debate about "hyphenated" Americans is silly. It totally reflects a continuum of the early national discrimination and bigotry that led to "Irish need not apply" in the 1800s and "Catholics need not apply" when President Bush nominates a believing Catholic to the federal appellate bench.

The strain of White bigotry reflected in the abhorrence of "hyphens" is interesting because those people somehow think they are more American than, say, Mexican American Cleto Rodriguez, Master Sergeant, United States Army (ret), who was the second highest medal-winning American fighting man in World War II, after Texas hill person Audie Murphy.

People who object to the "hyphen" in Mexican American are missing something in their being and personality. Strictly speaking, they don't have all their oars in the water, as yachtsmen are wont to say.

◆   ◆   ◆

AMERICA'S BEFUDDLED MASSES

These words appeared in a report prepared by Vanderbilt University's Dr. Roy L. Garis for United States Congressman John Box (D-Texas) sixty years ago; to wit:

"Their (the Mexicans) minds run to nothing higher than animal functions—eat, sleep, and sexual debauchery. in every huddle of Mexican shacks one meets the same idleness, hordes of hungry dogs, and filthy children with faces plastered with flies, disease. lice, human filth, stench, promiscuous fornication, bastardy, lounging, apathetic peons and lazy squaws, beans and dried chili, liquor, general squalor, and envy and hatred of the gringo. These people sleep by day and prowl by night like coyotes, stealing anything they can get their hands on, no matter how useless to them it may be. Nothing left outside is safe unless padlocked or chained down. Yet there are Americans clamoring for more of this human swine to be brought over from Mexico."

After watching and listening to Pat Buchanan run for President and Ross Perot preparing to do so, is there any doubt that they believe in the observations of Dr. Garis and Congressman Box? Moreover, does anyone not believe that candidates and current office-holders throughout the Southwest believe in the Garis descriptions.

Item: Congressman Elton Gallegly (R-CA) sponsored a successful amendment to bar "illegal alien" children from schools, if the host state desires to do so. Who are most illegal aliens? Mexicans, of course.

Item: He tried to bar American citizen children from school if their parents are illegal, much as Prop. 187 tried to do on the 1984 California ballot. Who are most American citizen children of illegal alien parents? Brown-skinned children of Mexican parents, of course.

Item: Under intense pressure from such groups as the Center for Immigration Studies (CIS) and the Federation for American Immigration Reform (FAIR) and myriad other anti-immigrant groups and bashers, Senators have been pressing to lower legal immigration or to impose a moratorium on immigration altogether. Who are the largest number of legal immigrants into the U.S.? Mexicans, of course.

In fact, Pat Buchanan campaigned for a moratorium and pointed to national surveys that showed that most Americans want a cut in legal immigration, or a moratorium. And, during the North American Free Trade Agreement (NAFTA) battle two-and-a-half years ago, Ross Perot went out of his way in his anti-NAFTA book (written mostly by Pat Choate) and speeches to criticize the work permit immigration allowed in the NAFTA of up to 60,000 Americans allowed to go to Mexico and to the same number of Mexicans permitted to enter the United States to work.

Lower wages, cut-throat job competition and a general lowering of living standards were the words that flowed from Perot, Choate and Buchanan. Because Americans would be going to Mexico to work? No, because Mexicans would be coming here.

Again, Mexicans, Mexicans, Mexicans.

Things haven't changed much since Dr. Roy Garis wrote his golden words sixty years ago, have they? Congressmen (Gallegly and Hunter) and political candidates such as Orange County's State Assembly candidate Barbara Coe continue to use code words to cover their belief in the Garis Golden Rule and try to sound respectable in the process. They, and Buchanan, claim grass roots support in their push against immigrants in general and Mexicans specifically.

Interestingly, none of the Congressmen were originally elected on anti-immigrant platforms. And, so, it has come to pass that few political candidates have won office with anti-immigrant platforms, Governor Pete Wilson being the exception, of course.

Take for example, Orange County's Barbara Coe, an original sponsor of 1984's Prop. 187. She was handily defeated in the primary election (March 26) by a Republican indicted for election fraud and perjury four days before the vote. In fact, she managed only 27% of the Republican vote against the indicted politician.

Better yet, take Pat Buchanan. Despite his hysterical campaign against immigrants, legal and illegal, in California, allegedly the most immigrant-sensitive state in the Union, and despite his radio ads and rhetoric saturated with misstatements of fact and outright lies, he lost; he lost big-time.

His 17% of the Republican vote, untainted by cross-over Democrats and Independents, was almost half of what he received in the 1992 primary against George Bush. In other words, Senator Dole smashed Buchanan. Why?

Because, as Barbara Coe and every other anti-immigrant candidate found out the hard way, only one in nine California primary Republican voters cited, according to the exit polls, immigration as their "prime concern".

In other words, immigration is a phony issue, promoted by phony politicians and, in 1996, is a loser at the polls.

I'll bet Dr. Garis and Congressman Box are turning over in their graves. Pass the salsa, please...###

AUTHOR'S NOTE—JULY, 2003—Though the immigration problem seems to be a large one, many Americans don't seem to care. The critics, however, cry loud and often, so people like me have to be wary and ready to counter-attack all the lies, emotion and paranoia.

The ultimate rejection of the lie of anti-immigration came in the Presidential election of 2000. Pat Buchanan ran again, but didn't even raise a Republican eyebrow, so, hijacked Ross Perot's old party, the Reform party, stole its nomination and ran off to run for President with $12-million in public funds. He was rejected, as was his anti-immigrant platform of hate-Mexicans and Mexico. He received less than 1% of the vote.

On that Election Day, 2000, the attempted Gore theft of George. W. Bush's victory by the use of quasi-criminal partisan judges in Florida overshadowed one of the big stories of that vote count. That story was Pat Buchanan's pathetic showing on the national ballot. His tiny 1% proved for all time that immigration is simply not the problem he and others say it is.

His placement of an anti-Mexican, anti-immigrant retired Black schoolteacher best known for her defense of organizations like the John Birch Society didn't even get him a "dozen" Black votes.

Buchanan continues his anti-free trade, anti-immigrant, anti-Mexican tirades on little-watched MSNBC and in a new magazine he started no one reads, and in World Net Daily.

Seems that the manifest racism he demonstrated his entire life by, among other things, calling Black maids out of his house to hose them down, by throwing rocks at segregated Washington D.C. buses and by attacking Washington police officers, being charged and found guilty of those attacks, plus being booted out of college has finally roosted on his shattered career.

Add to that his obvious avoidance of the draft that all other young men of his and my era had to face and be subject to and his total lack of military service during the Cold War and Vietnam and we can report that Buchanan is done, and so are many people like him and people who followed him.

◆   ◆   ◆

HISPANIC OR LATINO?

For years I have campaigned against the Los Angeles Times-imposed word, "Latino," in describing the country's fastest growing ethnic "Group," those with Spanish-surnames, those who speak Spanish, et al. The LA Times set it's feet in concrete on the use of the word "Latino" and nothing has cracked that concrete since. Worst of all, other newspapers have followed the Times' lead and news coverage, accuracy and the community have suffered.

Now, I am not alone. In Agustin Gurza's November 30th LA Times column, he describes an in-house Times controversy about the use of the Times-imposed word "Latino." He quotes pioneering Times columnist Frank Del Olmo from a 1981 column in which Del Olmo wrote that he had convinced the Times to not use the word "Hispanic" because it is "that ugly and imprecise word." He added that "Latino" was less bureaucratic and that "nobody" actually called themselves "Hispanic."

Gurza's Del Olmo reference is fairly accurate, but lacks details. Frank Del Olmo had several reasons to object to the word "Hispanic." And, as he was the management favored Mexican-origin reporter at the Times, if not the only one at the time, he had great influence with Times management. The public had no input, only Del Olmo did.

Del Olmo had three specific reasons to oppose the word "Hispanic." One was that the Coors Brewery company of Colorado was using the word "Hispanic" to sell beer in the "Decade of the Hispanic."

Coors was then being boycotted by radical Mexican-origin people—Chicanos—and unions for perceived slights against them by the ultra-conservative Coors family. Del Olmo bought into the boycott because he was more than left-of-center, if not a "Chicano," himself.

According to him, he grew up in a blue-collar union family that was the antithesis of a "free market" Republican household.

The second reason was that the word "Hispanic" was coined by the Administration of Richard Nixon in the early Seventies and became the "official" word used to describe people like Del Olmo and me. Contrary to conventional wisdom, the word "Hispanic" was not invented for use by the Census in 1980, but rather, was developed at the Department of Housing and Urban Development (HUD). Del Olmo's passions were such in 1981, that any Richard Nixon legacy was to be rejected.

And, lastly, as Gurza writes, "By their choice of language, journalists not only describe people, they define them for others." The third reason Del Olmo objected to the word "Hispanic" and championed the word "Latino" was that "Chicano" had been roundly rejected by all Mexican Americans but the most radical, blue collar, less educated, under-class people of Mexican-origin. Del Olmo pushed "Latino" as a substitute for the rejected "Chicano." Unfortunately, he was in a position to push this substitution into the language of the "Newspaper of Record" in the West. Other papers and broadcast stations took up the word because it was the "style" of the LA Times. Frank Del Olmo single handedly branded millions of people.

Del Olmo was wrong in 1981. The Los Angeles Times has confused the entire reportage of the fastest growing group on the country by insisting on following Del Olmo's blue-collar bromide. Other than the Times, very few people in the real world use the word "Latino." I recall a very confused New York Newsday reporter asking me the difference between Hispanic and Latino. Her confusion is interesting because Newsday and the LA Times are owned by the same company.

I tried to make the words clear to her by stating that Hispanic usually meant educated middle-class people who work hard, yearn to live in good neighborhoods, want their children well-educated and depend less on government than the working or non-working poor. Latino, being a substitute for Chicano in California, means less than well-educated, less than well employed, if employed at all, more dependent on government and a tendency to blame others for their lot.

Hispanic is used everywhere (except the LA Times) and is now ingrained in the language by usage and by dictionary definition. The people have voted with their usage and Latino is not the word of choice. It doesn't sound right when used with American—Latino American has no ring to it. As far as formal recognition, "Anglo," for example, is defined in dictionaries as "non-Hispanic white," not non-Latino white. Besides, Latino can mean Italian, or Romanian, or any group with Latin as the basis of their language.

As for "Americans" who object to the use of either term, when Irish Americans quit using Irish Americans to identify themselves, we will quit also.

In twenty years, when the population of California has mostly Spanish-surnames, few people will remember the wrestling match between Hispanics (Contreras) and Latinos (Del Olmo) and that most Hispanics wore coats and ties and most Latinos didn't. They will also know that Hispanics won the match.###

AUTHOR'S NOTE—JULY, 2003—in this very year, the issue of the official use of Chicano, Latino and Hispanic is being contemplated by committees of the University of California Board of Regents and other institutions in California.

Chicano is simply unacceptable when referring to the entire community of the Spanish-speaking, heritage ethnic group which is the subject of this particular attention. People can call themselves Chicanos if they wish, but they have no right to call anyone other than themselves that ugly made up, no-basis-in fact or history word that came out of the Sixties when the entire country was propagandized by the media to the use of the word. Anglo-writers and reporters loved to use Chicano because it manifested underclass connotations applicable to the entire multi-million person population involved.

Del Olmo, the blue-collar background, union household, liberal Democrat, house Mexican of the Los Angeles Times swayed the right people early in the game, but his day is past as demonstrated by the Gurza challenge. Gurza, of course, was terminated, but the will of the people will prevail.

Del Olmo is like the proverbial Dutch boy with his finger in a leaking dike, holding back a flood. But like dikes everywhere, there is always a weak spot and water finds it. As I noted in the above column, in another generation no one will remember Del Olmo or his silly anti-Republican, anti-Nixon passions that led to the mislabeling of millions of people for an entire generation.

◆　　◆　　◆

AN IDENTITY FOR 400-MILLION PEOPLE

The reporter from a New York newspaper asked me: "What's the difference between a Hispanic and Latino"? That stumped me, not because I don't know the difference, but because this sophisticated, Ivy League, New York City national politics reporter sipping a martini didn't know.

Hispanic? Latino? Chicano? Nuyorican? Cuban? Puerto Rican? Dominicano? Mexican American? American of Mexican descent? Of Mexican-origin? Which is it?

The term Hispanic is totally appropriate, in my view, for describing the totality of our people, some 400-million of them. It fits when one discusses a people that inhabit the pampas of Argentina, the shanty barrios of Peru, the teeming ghettos of Panama, the peaceful towns of Costa Rica and the hugeness of Mexico City. It fits the people of the desert towns of Chihuahua and Sonora, the hi-tech factories of Tijuana, the Eastside of "los", Los Angeles, the fields of Watsonville and the laundry rooms of Las Vegas hotels. It fits the people of the slaughter houses of Iowa, the hot, dusty plains of Spain and Texas, the South Side of Chicago, San Juan, and the Spanish Harlem of Manhattan. Hispanic fits them all.

Nuestro Gente, Our People, may look like me, brown skin, tall, lots of hair with a good dose of "Indian" blood; or short, dark, no beard, with jet black, coarse hair; or redheaded like my daughter and Hernando Cortez, or blonde and blue-eyed like my nieces and nephews. Some speak many languages, some speak only one. Most speak two, the language of romance and Cervantes (my California-Mexican Spanish) and the language of commerce and individual liberty (my American English).

We are everything. We look like everybody. We are different.

It is silly, defensive and a cop-out to say we are of one race, the human race, for that is true in a biological sense, only. Socially and politically, it is not true. If you think it is, tell that to the Jews of Germany, Poland, Russia, etc. They thought they were of the human race. Adolf Hitler and the German people thought not.

We are not one race, politically and socially. We are different, so we should say so, organize so, speak out so and stand on our own. To do that, we either must wear uniforms, be armed, have a flag or—have a name. A name is best suited to our needs here in America, for we are not enslaved, suppressed, or oppressed. We are, however, not as politically powerful as we can be, strategically placed as we are. A name legitimizes us politically, for a name implies a mass or people.

Should that name also include Italians, Romanians, French, Swiss and other people whose language is also based on Latin but have no American indigenous bloodlines? Or should it be more concise? Should such a name be based on language or geography, natural or political, or should it be based on culture, race or ethnicity, mixed or unmixed?

It should be based on many factors, I think, Country of origin, ethnicity, language-group, culture and cultural and historical heritage.

Latino? No. I have nothing in common with the Swiss who speak Latin-based words. Spanish? No. Not all of my blood is Spanish. Spanish-speaking? No. I speak Spanish, but without the silly lisp of the Castillian. My Spanish is of the Americas, based on that of the mother-land but made rich with colloquialisms and additions from the language of the Nahua, the Aztec and Maya Indians. Many of our people still speak Nahua.

For example, the White European Spanish call the Mexican bird, the turkey, a PAVO, a short version of peacock. How boring! Try the Nahua word for turkey, the word most Mexicans use today—GUAJALOTE (WAH-HAW-LOW-TEH). Now, that's language!

We are as different as we are the same. Call yourselves what you will, but use an all-encompassing term for us all. A name indicates numbers, numbers are power.

Hispanic, then, is a good name to use. It was not invented by White Anglo bureaucrats, but by one of us on a Federal government committee. It is a useful term which is easily modified by specifics. For example, in general I'm a Hispanic, but specifically I'm an American of Mexican descent; or, a Mexican American and sometimes, of Mexican-origin.

Chicano? No. I am not a Chicano, for I do not speak Chicanese, nor do I eat Chicanese food, nor was I born or live in Chicanolandia. I am a Hispanic (culturally and linguistically), American (politically) of Mexican (culturally and geographically) descent, a Mexican AMERICAN.

The lady reporter now knows that Hispanic generally applies to me, to Cubans, to Argentinians, to Chileans, et al and Latino doesn't. It's as simple as that. ###

AUTHOR'S NOTE—JULY, 2003—This piece really needs no comment. It stands by itself. I really think it is irrefutable by any reasonable person. Only those who hate the White blood in their veins, or the White European blood they don't have will argue that Chicano is proper to use. They are wrong.

◆   ◆   ◆

"GOOD NEWS, BAD NEWS"

For California Anglos the bad news is that they will change places with the state's Mexican Americans and be but a minority in exactly 47 years (less, actually). The good news is that the same study released by the California Department of Finance concludes that "Hispanics" will be a majority of California's projected 2040 63-million population.

This, of course, is the proverbial good news, bad news story. This is especially bad news for the Asian and Black populations because they are not projected to grow in percentage. Asians will remain about 9.6% and Blacks will hold steady at about 7.4%.

For Anglos, however, the news is particularly depressing. Since the state was invaded by a small force of U.S. Marines and sailors in 1846, California has been alternately raped and developed by Americans who poured in from the East with land lust in their eyes.

From the moment gold was discovered at Northern California's Sutter's Mill, Americans (Anglos) went out of their way to steal land by legal means. Spanish and Mexican land grants weren't recognized by the U.S. Congress; heavy property taxes were levied on Californios who had never paid property taxes; lands had to sold to pay legal fees of lawyers.

The United States Congress sided with Anglo squatters after they descended on ranchos like locusts. In 1855 the new powers-to-be passed a "Greaser Law", an anti-vagrancy law aimed at "persons who are commonly known as 'Greasers' or the issue of Spanish and Indian blood".

Further, according to James Crawford's "Hold Your Tongue: Bilingualism and the Politics of English-Only", The legislature, owned by the nouveau riche racists recently arrived to California, proceeded to hamstring the Californian Mexican with odious laws designed to castrate him culturally, including English-only laws.

The legislature was not alone in its attempt to destroy the real Californians. By the Constitutional Convention of 1878 an entire generation of Anglo robber barons came to power in California, along with railroad tycoons loaded with cash. History records that their mission in life was to completely subjugate the conquered Mexicans. They weren't even nice about it.

The 1878 Convention didn't have a single native Californian Spanish-speaker as a delegate. The Convention was dominated by the Workingman's Party. Today's equivalent would be the anti-NAFTA Democrats of Congressman Richard Gephardt, Senators Max Baucus, Carl Levine, Barbara Boxer and Patrick Moyniahan.

The Party was obscene in its anti-Chinese and Mexican mood. The Convention's stench is memorialized in the words of a Party speechmaker.

"This State," he drawled, "should be a State for white men. We want no other race here."

And, so it came to pass. Anglos took over the state lock, stock and barrel. They developed industries and agriculture that became the envy of the world. California became the Golden Land; the land of dreams, the land of "Go West Young Man, Go West". Built, of course, by Mexican labor.

Those in power built fine schools for their children, while sending Mexican children to shacks. In the San Diego suburb of Lemon Grove, in the late Thirties, Mexicans had had enough of inferior segregated schools and incompetent teachers and sued (with surreptitious help from the Mexican government). The courts agreed and the anti-Mexican tide began to turn.

World War Two Anglo sailors and soldiers reacted against Mexicans by attacking them in Los Angeles in the misnamed "Zoot Suit Riots". This was the last time California experienced organized race violence and hatred imported from the East, Midwest and South.

Slowly but surely, California's Mexicans slipped out of the Anglo bindings they were wrapped in. By 1960 Mexican Americans in San Diego were the highest paid "Hispanics" in the country. That hasn't changed, they still are. They are the most educated Mexican Americans in the country, as well (They have double the college graduation rate of the country's other Mexican Americans).

Like long distance runners, Mexican Americans have rapidly closed the gap on better educated Blacks and passed them by in social acceptance and ability to live wherever they can afford to without problems. They may never catch up with the over-all Anglo community, but they can and shall narrow the gap. In the short term, the gap will widen between the California Hispanic and Anglo for the simple reason that many of the new immigrants will make less money, but that is not forever.

Their children, though not as well educated as Suzie Jones in Thousand Oaks, will be better educated than their parents and will speak better English, thus, they will earn more and live better.

This progress will continue, we hope and pray. It must, you see, because in 47 years (or less), we will outnumber everyone else in California and Texas.

Who are we? We are "the issue of Spanish and Indian blood". ###

"THE BROWNING OF AMERICA"

Turning $100 into $110 is a struggle, while turning $100-million into $110-million is inevitable, says a Canadian whiskey-heir. Nature turning the green leaves of summer into the brown leaves of autumn is also inevitable.

And, now, the ultimate inevitability—the "Browning of America"—as derisively portrayed by national newsman Paul Harvey.

By the year 2050, according to Gregory Spencer of the Census Bureau, "If you want to sell things and go where the growth is, about half your market will be people in their 50's and the other half will be the Hispanic and Asian populations."

There are 262.8 million people in this country today and that will increase, conservatively, to 393.9 million in 2050, according to the Census.

The population now is 73.6% non-Hispanic white, 12% Black, 10.2% Latino (Mostly of Mexican origin), 3.3% Asian and 0.7% Native American (formerly known as American Indian). In 2050 the percentages are projected to be 52.8%

non-Hispanic white, 24.5% Latino, 13.6% Black, 8.2% Asian and 0.9% native American.

The growth of the Latino community is predicated on two factors, immigration and birth rates. Immigration is currently under attack by elements of both political parties but nonetheless provides a net population growth of 325,000 Latinos yearly which, when added to 550,000 Latino births adds 900,000 to the Spanish-surnamed population each and every year.

Asians, on the other hand grow more by immigration than by natural births (235,000 immigrants and 135,000 births).

The non-Hispanic white population continues to shrink and get older, while the Latino and Asian groups are younger. The Black population is stable and is getting older as well. The most immediate result of this huge demographic change will be that Hispanics will become the nation's largest (and still growing) minority group in 2009 (It actually occurred in 2003, six years before 1990s projections), when they will outnumber American Blacks.

Currently, the median age—half are older and half are younger—of non-Hispanic whites is 35.3, for Asians 30.6, 29.2 for Blacks, and an astoundingly young 26.3 for Latinos. Projections are, that by 2030, one in five Americans will be 65 years-of-age or older and most of them will be non-Hispanic whites.

California, by the way, is the harbinger of the these national projections. The state is currently 52.5% non-Hispanic white, 29.8% Latino, 10.7% Asian and only 6.9% Black, according to the most recent estimates of the California Department of Finance.

The same department estimates that by the year 2040 the state will be comprised of 49.7% Latinos, 32.4% non-Hispanic whites, 11.8% Asian and 5.9% Black.

Combining, then, the huge numbers and younger age of Latinos, the forthcoming "Browning of America", promises one of three things: The decline of America as a world economic and political power; a young stronger leader of the economic and political world of the future; or, a fascist, racist police state run by a declining number of white old people supported by Brown, Black and Asian worker bees.

Which will it be?

1994's Proposition 187 was and is solid proof that the non-Hispanic is quite prepared to institute police-state methods to retain control of the political apparatus and status quo. The California sponsors of the now legally-dead 187 have moved to Arizona to try another 187 there.

The fervent whites who pushed 187 onto the American political landscape were aided and abetted by the Black population, despite the obvious racial overtones of the proposition.

The status quo contains an undemocratic two-thirds legal margin to pass school and other bond issues thus depriving Latino children the one factor they painfully need to grow intellectually and economically—schools. The Black population, of course, helps in it's own destruction by aiding and abetting this political monstrosity.

But, in the end, these road blocks must fall, for sooner than later most Latinos who are legal residents will become citizens so they can vote and most will vote in their own economic and political interests. Most who are native-born will do the same. They will vote for schools to educate their children and they will swarm into the universities, just as every group in America has before them.

The result: America will continue to lead the world and it will do so speaking more than one language and with a world view tempered by a heritage of family and faith. In other words, the "Browning of America" is not a disaster in the making as the Paul Harveys and Pat Buchanans predict.

Light-hearted proof is in Neil Morgan's San Diego Union column: "At San Diego State, a political science lecturer was trying to illustrate the infusion of Mexican tastes across our border when he posed this question to his class: 'Do you know why more salsa is being sold in America than ketchup?'. The first student to answer blurted the real truth: 'Because it tastes better!" ###

AUTHOR'S NOTE—JULY, 2003—All numbers cited in this article were tossed out when the United States Census Bureau shocked everyone when it released its census figures for 2000. Then, in 2003, the bureau announced that their 2000 Hispanic population figures were not only obsolete, but shockingly larger than even the most imaginative and optimistic Hispanic could have dreamed up.

In 2000 the Bureau announced that there were 35-plus million Hispanic/Latinos in the country. That number had not been projected to occur until about 2010. Then in 2003, the Bureau announced that the Hispanic/Latino population had grown by 10% since 2000 and now numbered over 39-million.

What shocked many was the huge growth that occurred between 1990 and 2000. There were many explanations for the huge growth, none of them completely true and all of them partially true.

One school of thought is that there are millions more illegals from Mexico and Central America in the country than ever calculated before. Two professors at Northeastern University posit that there were 10-million illegals, four million more than the Immigration and Naturalization Service estimated. The professors offered no proof, only projections based on the Census figures and other records available to researchers.

Another theory was that the census Bureau had terribly undercounted the 1990 Hispanic population by a million or more. This theory makes great sense, for illegals prefer to hide, not fill out census forms.

Both theories make some sense. I would accept both.

In any event, the numbers shocked many in the country, no matter how they were arrived at.

Of course, population growth effects other areas of the locality, including schools, housing, job availability, tax collections, crime rates and income levels.

It is no secret that per capita income levels fell in Los Angeles between 1990 and 2000, the decade in which Hispanics grew in numbers and filled the void left by many Anglos who left Los Angeles and California when the California defense industry collapsed.

Critics of Hispanic immigrants shrilly point to the drop in income as a sign of times to come; they point to a huge exodus of native born California Anglos who left California during the 90s, but they are wrong.

Of the many reasons why these people left, Hispanic immigrants were not the basic reason. As mentioned, the collapse of the defense and aerospace industries suddenly threw hundreds of thousands of comfortable mostly Anglo men out of work. Those industries had employed these people in good paying jobs financed directly by the U.S. Government to the tune that jokesters called the situation middle-class welfare.

Another reason is that many men and women reached retirement age, or ages close to it, so when the defense industry collapsed, these people retired early and moved to Nevada or Arizona, two neighboring states with far lower costs of living and taxes than California. Some moved to Idaho like disgraced Los Angeles detective Mark Fuhrman to retire in another right-to-work state with low costs of living.

So, as these $50,000–$75,000 a year people left their jobs, or had their jobs disappear, they were replaced by Hispanic immigrants with far lower job prospects. Had those Anglos not left, the per capita of Los Angeles County might have dropped a bit, but nowhere near as much as it did.

5

Chapter introduction—WE ARE A CULTURAL ETHNIC GROUP, NOT A RACE; OR WE AIN'T ALL GANGBANGING TAGGERS AND DRUG RUNNERS!

Every day, somewhere in the media, we hear plaintive whining by many Whites, or Anglos, which are non-Hispanic Whites, complaining that Hispanics/Latinos aren't a race, that many consider themselves White, thus, they really aren't an ethnic group. This attempt at non-recognition by some Anglos and many Blacks is purely racist in context and pure paranoia by Blacks uneasy at being displaced as the largest minority in the United States.

To clarify the situation, the Census Bureau attempted in the census of 2000 to split ethnic hairs even more than they have in the past. They added dozens of new "ethnic" identities to the list and were surprised when the vast majority of Hispanic/Latinos marked off "White" and "Other race" boxes. Lagging far behind were the "Sammy Sosa" Hispanic/Latinos, Blacks, in other words who have their immediate roots in Latin America, mostly the Caribbean islands or countries like Panama with large Black populations.

When the results of the Census were released, a number of Whites complained that almost 50% of Hispanics labeled themselves White. So? These ignorant people still don't want to accept the concept of Hispanics/Latinos being am ethnic group, not a race. There is no Hispanic or Latino race. There is, however, a Hispanic/Latino ethnic group.

Ethnic group is defined as a nationality, a racial group or, a cultural group.

While many Hispanics/Latinos racially are mixed between Spanish and Indian blood, Mestizos, if you will, some are of pure Spanish blood, some of other European blood with longtime roots in Latin America. Some are of African blood mixed with Spanish, British, Dutch or even French blood. Some are mixed Indian and African blood. Some are pure African blood. Some are of pure Indian, indigenous, if you will, blood.

The glue that brings them all together under one ethnic umbrella is the Spanish language. Haitians, for example, are mostly pure Black and share an island home with the Spanish speaking Dominican Republic (Sammy Sosa, again), but are in no way defined as Hispanics or Latinos. They are African with a touch of French history and language. Haitians are not Hispanics, nor are those from the island nation of former British colonies of Trinidad and Tobago, or the Dutch island of Aruba. Nonetheless, there are other cultural aspects that make up Hispanics. The other aspects, however, are not by themselves definitive, though they add to stereotypes and characteristics unique, usually, to Hispanics.

Cultural aspects of the Hispanic community are generally perceived by most of the United States as "Hispanic gangs," gang sluts, drug dealers, drug smugglers, Tijuana whores, salsa music, mariachi music, baggy clothes, graffiti, and movie bandits with bad teeth. Unfortunately, we are what we are perceived to be by the establishment and its media outlets.

The University of Mexico was founded a hundred years before Harvard; Mexico City hosted a poetry contest in 1525. Mexico City's Frida Kahlo, the half Mexican wife of artist Diego Rivera, was, perhaps, the greatest female artist of all time. Her husband, Diego Rivera, was not only the best known Mexican artist of all time, but, perhaps one of the top ten artists in the world of the 20th century.

Culturally, Mexicans have done well over the years and have done so without kidnapping European culture en toto. Nobel Prize winners have come from Mexico, as have Congressional Medal of Honor winners in America.

Culturally, Mexicans sometimes are embarrassed to admit they are Mexicans, but, then again, so are some Americans who bow to Europe as the wellspring of all culture. Then again, some Mexicans and some Americans laugh at Europe and European culture, a culture some think is buried along with Dead White Men of the past who, while contributing much to what we are, did not contribute all of what we are.

Culturally, Mexicans have contributed much to America. At the base of American culture is the cowboy, and that cultural icon came north from Mexico to become a foundation of what we are today. The cowboy did not come from England.

Mexican culture is very special…it has delicious food, literary giants like Octavio Paz, piñatas at Christmas and birthdays, beautiful music of love in the language of love, the cowboy and the quintessential defiant "I don't need no stinking badges." It has bandit/hero Pancho Villa and peasant fighter Emiliano Zapata. It has fascists and communists, it has lots of newspapers and magazines, it has a deeply religious population while being anti-clerical for decades…it has Our Lady of Guadalupe.

◆   ◆   ◆

"AIN'T GOT NO CULTURE"

Once, at a cocktail party, a beautiful people person asked my name. Hearing it, she asked if I was Spanish. Reaching into my pocket, I pulled out my cash, counted $18.00 and replied, No. "I'm Mexican; I'd be Spanish if I had more than $20.00 on me".

This old "chiste" (chee-steh), though a joke among Mexican Americans, reflects for many of us a continuing conflict of what we culturally are. I know Mexican Americans who absolutely refuse to acknowledge their background. If, for example, they have one atom of Italian or Spanish blood, they proclaim themselves Italian, Spanish or sniff the word, European.

Before discussing the problem, let's define culture. My dictionary has several definitions which are applicable here; they are: The act of developing the intellectual and moral faculties; enlightenment and excellence of taste acquired by intellectual and aesthetic training; acquaintance with and a taste in fine arts, humanities and broad aspects of science as distinguished from ordinary trade and craft pursuits. Also included: The integrated pattern of human knowledge, belief and behavior that depends on man's knowledge and the capacity to pass on that knowledge to succeeding generations; and, finally, the customary beliefs, social forms and material traits of a racial, religious or social group.

That's the general definition. Those of us who live in Western Civilization, specifically we Mexican Americans, trace our socio-political and cultural roots back to Egypt, to the Greeks, Romans, the Roman church, the Spanish and their conquering Arabs, the thesis/antithesis of clashing Spanish and Aztec empires and the resulting synthesis we now call Mexico. There's also the interplay of hundreds of years of people, ideas and language blending along the border between Mother Mexico and Mother America.

By accepting what America has to offer, we Mexican Americans don't lose any cultural identity, we simply add one more layer of culture to all those before. We are better people for it.

Nothing irritates me more than hearing some foreigner proclaim cultural superiority to Americans (in the broadest sense, meaning all of us this side of the Atlantic/Pacific). Is an opera performed in a language we cannot understand, about people we've never seen, speaking/singing words which have no modern relevance, superior to one written by an American, in English, about people we see every day? "Summertime, and the living is easy…"

Is a painting by some long-dead European superior to one by Mexicans Siqueros, Rivera or Orozco? Are the cathedrals of Europe any more spectacular or architecturally splendid than pyramids at Teotihuacan or Chichen Itza, which were built hundreds of years before? Is there any European equivalent to the Aztec Calendar?

Are Shakespere's characters, say, the Merchant of Venice or Shylock, any more relevant to us than Arthur Miller's Willie Loman, or Allen Drury's Senator Seab Cooley in Advise and Consent, considering the recent Senate rejections of John Tower and Robert Bork? Is Othello more relevant than the characters in Carlos Fuentes' Old Gringo?

Vivid is my memory of 9th grade English and my assignment to read Charles Dickens. Having never seen little English boys in my neighborhood, I approached my teacher, confused, lost and told him I didn't understand Dickens. I couldn't define the characters, I told him. Could I, I asked, write a report on Leon Uris' Battle Cry? I could identify with boys training to become men, preparing for war; and, with Uris' Spanish Joe, a fellow Mexican American from El Paso. Please, I asked, don't make me report on an English book, I wouldn't know an Englishman if I tripped on one.

True, he replied. But that's how one learns and becomes cultured, by reading, studying and breathing someone else's culture, he said. No culture, he told me, is superior to another. Political systems, armies and economic systems may and can be superior. Cultures are not.

How wise my 9th grade teacher was, this WW II army corporal who earned his college education fighting Germans in the hedgerows of France. I read Dickens and Battle Cry, wrote reports on one for assignment and one for extra credit. And, though I still wouldn't have known a little English boy if I'd tripped on one, I had some idea what one was, albeit, he wouldn't have been as much fun as Battle Cry's Spanish Joe.

And, now, I put words on paper for others to read. I'm part of the culture of 1989 America. I still have less than $20.00 in my pocket, so I'm Mexican, not Spanish. I do have a confession, however. I've seen operas in languages I didn't know; I've seen some of Willie's plays; I've soared with music composed by Germans, Russians, and Polish men. I've examined the painted works of Dutch, Italian and Spanish masters. I've watched Russian men dance ballet. I've read many words of Europeans and Asians. My teacher was right, cultures are not better than other cultures.

Despite four decades exposure to the world's culture, I still like "La Bamba".
###

"Crews, Homies and Tagbangers"

They scurry about like cockroaches in the dark, leaving their marks where the world can see them in daylight. They don't do it to mark their tribal territory like the Aztec Indians used to, nor like the gangs do today. They do it to brag—they are graffiti taggers.

Unfortunately, most of the taggers are Mexican kids, though copycats have sprung up everywhere. Copycats may be Filipinos in Filipino neighborhoods, Blacks in Black neighborhoods, or whites in white neighborhoods. Whites, however, tend to be more mobile thus their tags can be anywhere. Mexicans get blamed for everyone's tags, of course.

Their little tagging groups have names. They must, for their marks, or tags, are usually the initials of the group.

Though they are secretive about their tagging and hide their work in the dark of night, they want the world to know they've been there, wherever there is. They brag to their friends, so that their friends dare them to pick more dangerous locations. They brag to girls about their exploits.

They brag at parties, parties they're invited to because they're taggers. They tag because its cool.

They wear funny clothes; that is, they wear cockeyed baseball caps, flannel shirts or extra-large white T-shirts and baggy, extra large pants. They also wear hoop earrings.

They call themselves a "crew", or "posse", "mob" or "tribe". They're each others "homies", because they're in the same "crew". A newcomer to the "crew" is called a "toy", and if he chickens out at defending his "tag", or graffiti signature, he's a "ranker". If one is caught by a rival crew without his homies to back him up, he's "slipping".

When the crew picks a place to tag, they "mob it", that is, they hit a place with graffiti. When in an industrious mood, they "seek and destroy", i.e., tag everything in sight. To really show what the crew can do, the "map the heavens", or tag extremely hard to reach overhead highway signs.

In a version of the Beach Boys "Be True To Your School", taggers are "to be down", dedicated if you will, true to his crew and vice versa. Or taggers are "to get up", to put your tag in as many places as humanly possible, the ultimate being a "landmark" where the tag can't be "crossed out" by rivals or "buffed" (erased or painted out) by authorities.

Then, there's the "hero" an adult who will turn in a tagger. That's me, I'm a "hero".

These kids are punks, or as we used to say in the old neighborhood, pachucos (paw-choo-kohs). Their stupid goals of having the world marvel at their craftsmanship and ingenuity are just that, stupid.

Even more stupid are the parents who are aware of what their little pachucos are doing and don't do anything about it. One mother told the LA Times, "I detest what he does. It's terrible. It's wrong to deface people's property. He told me it was an illness. Like smoking, hard to kick."

Another mother, in San Diego County, was sent to jail after being convicted of being her son's lookout while he tagged a building. Another mother, in San Diego, scrubs graffiti written by her 13-year-old son, while her husband, a retired 67-year-old, scrubs graffiti alongside his busted son, the tagger. These parents are working off their fine (at $6.00 per hour) after being convicted of vandalism, the vandalism committed by their son.

It does not displease me to see the 67-year-old retired janitor, or whatever occupational category the old man worked at for a lifetime, and his welfare-collecting wife work cleaning up their boy's mess. After all, he's only 13, he's a kid. They knew better.

Or do they? Is there something in a poverty Mexican's psyche which demands the vandalism or destruction of someone else's property? Is their something in their sexuality which demands they show some manhood by tagging, as well as getting some stupid teenaged girl pregnant.

Somewhere there must be an answer. Hopefully someone will find it soon, for the "crews" in Los Angeles are arming themselves with guns to shoot rival "crews". Worse, the taggers have girl friends—you know, sweet cuddly little girls who grew up.

"We're tagbangers, too. But I don't carry a gun. I carry a screwdriver. It's just as effective", brags someone's sweet little daddy's girl.

Los Angeles spends $15 million a year "buffing" graffiti. This does not count the amount of police budget used to combat "tagbanging", that is, the backing up of tagging with violence. ###

"IS AMERICAN CULTURE SUPERIOR?"

There is a school board in central Florida that believes that American Culture is "superior" to all others and has instructed its teachers to teach it as "superior".

Unfortunately for the rest of us, these super-American school board members are ignorant fools. No culture is superior to another. Political philosophies may be superior; so may technologies and industries; as may governmental systems and constitutions. But, cultures? No.

There are cultural elements that exist in every country that are admired by all and some that are not. More importantly, some cultural elements that are undesirable have been inherited by contemporary people to our community detriment.

Specifically, I note that recently a number of Mexican Americans objected to proposed laws that would outlaw the roping of horses' legs during the Charreada, a Mexican rodeo. They did so on the basis that this is part of the Mexican cultural heritage and that the propose laws were racist. Wrong, boys.

The law is designed to protect horses. That is as it should be. Culture has nothing to do with it.

Another example would be graffiti, the trademark of many of our Mexican American youth. The tradition began centuries ago with the Indians of Central Mexico. Despite the fact that the late Aztec empire was comprised of related Indians who spoke the same language, they marked off (without spray paint) their clan and tribal areas by colorful paintings on rocks, walls and buildings to let everyone know who owned the territory.

They killed anyone who crossed into their territory.

Recent laws have been passed limiting the sale of spray paint and felt markers and more are pending relating to graffiti artists (taggers) that some complain are racist because they target taggers who are mostly Mexican American.

Moreover, there are elements in the community who praise graffiti as art and as a way for young people to express themselves. They claim it's part of their culture. Yes, it is.

However, we are not Indians marking off our territory today and we don't kill strangers, do we? These cultural traits come to us from Indians who were communal in nature and had no private property. There were no private buildings, residences or otherwise flat surfaces to paint, in Indian Mexico—there was no private property, period. Thus, there was no respect for private property.

Even if graffiti is a cultural legacy of our Indian ancestors, it's not right. Another cultural legacy has replaced it, respect for private property and for the dignity of its owner.

And then there's clothes. Many among us have adopted the clothing fads of the pachuco (pah-choo-koh), the punk, which include baggy pants, over-large shirts, both woolen and T-shirts, baseball caps worn backwards and, in some areas, hair nets for boys.

The hair nets come from our men who have worked in restaurants and are required to wear hair nets as a matter of public health, i.e., keep hair from dropping into food. They're the Mexican equivalent of plastic shower caps worn by under-class Blacks.

The baggy pants and shirts come from the need and desire by the Los Angeles pachucos to hide their hand guns and other weapons of choice such as bicycle chains. Others joined them in wearing these clothes because they consider it to be cool to look like gangsters.

But, are these faddish clothes a cultural legacy, tradition or an actual ingredient of contemporary Mexican American culture? No.

If anything, due to our ranching and agricultural cultural background, jeans, cowboy boots and hats are more culturally correct than the urban hip-hop junk so many of our youngsters wear.

Yes, that would be more correct than, say, white boys from our South wearing Western gear and clothes. For, you see, there were no cowboys in Alabama, Georgia, et al. There were, however, thousands upon thousands of vaqueros (vah-ker-ohs), cowboys, in Mexico and out southwest and west in past years and throughout the history of America.

The cowboy culture of Northern Mexico survives to this day. In fact, the State of Wyoming actively recruits Mexican cowboys to staff it's ranches because Americans don't want to be cowboys any longer. The cowboy culture is dying in America, but it lives on in the country of its birth, Mexico.

I wonder if the school board in Florida knows that and if it will order its teachers to teach that the American cowboy culture is "superior" even though it no longer exists and was Mexican to begin with, anyway. (This article appeared in USA TODAY)###

AUTHOR'S NOTE—JULY, 2003—This article was published in USA TODAY and caused apoplexy among my critics and critics of Hispanics and immigrants. I recall one caller to my radio show questioned my observation that the cowboy culture came from Mexico. He simply said the cowboy came from Spain. He was wrong, Spanish soldiers on horses came from Spain, but they didn't know how to handle cattle because there were no massive cattle herds in Spain. Those didn't occur until the great open spaces of Texas and Mexico were ridden onto by Spanish soldiers.

◆   ◆   ◆

FELIZ NAVIDAD MEANS MORE THAN MERRY CHRISTMAS

A brilliant blue sky with no clouds and temperatures in the mid-sixties greeted me that Christmas morning. In the background was the clanging of the streetcar that for a nickel could take me downtown, to the San Diego Zoo or to the wild frontier on the eastern city limits. That day it would take my mother to work, leaving Christmas preparations to me and my great-grandmother.

Christmas Day, 1946, three years and three months after we came to the United States from Mexico. It was the first Christmas I remember and second in memory only to the first Christmas that my-now-grown daughter can remember.

After serving me a breakfast of CHILAQUILES (chee-lah-kee-lehs, a casserole of corn tortillas, tomato sauce and assorted onions, garlic and chiles), a fried egg and CAFE CON LECHE(cah-feh-cone-leh-cheh, a few drops of coffee and lots of milk for the kid), my great grandmother told me to go out to play while she ground corn on a stone METATE(meh-tah-teh, a stone with a hole worn in it with a stone pistel to grind with).

Sensing something special was up, I manifested my kid machismo and volunteered to my NANA that I would help her in the kitchen and promised not to get in the way. By 9:00a.m., six women relatives were scurrying about our kitchen getting in my way.

How my hands tired grinding dried corn into a fine flour-like consistency. TAMALES (tah-mah-lehs), I was told was the destiny of the corn flour, the MASA (mah-saw). So were the spiced pork and beef simmering in separate pots.

Then with a wooden spoon I folded lard into the masa until my arms almost dropped off. Nana brought out HOJAS (oh-haas, corn shucks) which had been soaking in water over night.

Smoothing each out, she spread our masa on individual hojas, placed a small amount of pork or beef on top, then carefully folded the masa around the meat and wrapped the hoja around the whole thing, leaving one end open. The tamales were then steamed.

There is no time certain for cooking tamales. To know when they are ready, they must be tested. Perhaps the best description of such an event is in John West's "Mexican American Folklore."

"After an hour of steaming, the tamales should be ready—and a taste-test is the only way to check. Off comes the top, then the blanket of shucks…the tamale is unwrapped and if comes free of the hoja, the prognosis is excellent. Then the tasting—and the rolling of eyes, and the pronouncement that these are the best tamales ever made—make it plain that the hours of work have not been in vain.

These, the ones made with my masa, were the best ever made, I assure you.

Attention then turned to making BUNUELOS (boon-whe-lohs) giant flour tortillas deep-fried and sprinkled with cinnamon and sugar. I preferred maple syrup from Vermont on mine, others preferred cane sugar syrup, the kind from Mexico. Then came Christmas cookies, BIZCOCHOS (beez-coh-chohs).

Surrounded by goodies, I couldn't wait for my mother to come home. But, before that and the Christmas feast, we would have to go on a POSADA (poh-saw-dah).

A custom passed down by our Spanish ancestors, the posada reenacts the original Christmas Eve in which Joseph and Mary went from house to house seeking shelter.

We went from house to house, inn to inn, seeking shelter and singing in Spanish: "Who will give shelter to these pilgrims who come tired from traveling the roads?"

Turned down, inn after inn, house after house with, "There is no shelter here", we finally came to our second story apartment, above the liquor store, where my Nana sang, "Enter, holy travelers, receive this corner, although the chapel is poor, I give thee from the heart." We entered salivating at the smell of food that I had worked so hard on.

I didn't really understand all this, because I was just a kid. Nor, because I was a kid, had anyone told me that this was a very special day. No one told me my grandfather was returning from the Middle East, from the oil installations of Saudi Arabia he was helping to build. No one told me my great-uncle was coming from Alaska where he had toiled during the war doing his part for Victory.

And no one told me my paratrooper Cousin Luis was coming home, triumphant from a defeated Germany; nor that my Uncle Johnny was coming home from Occupied Korea. All the men of my family had been scattered around the world by World War II, that I remembered.

I did not know that my family's warriors were coming home that Christmas Day. One by one they came home. Being only five and except for my Uncle who lied about his age so he could fight, I didn't know them, for they been scattered across the world by a war that started when I was but eleven months old.

Finally, up the stairs came my Uncle Johnny, at 17 the best looking and most handsome American soldier there ever was. What a glorious moment!

I jumped on him, almost knocking him over. He was home from the war, and he was alive. There would be no telegrams from the Secretary of the Army, no Gold Stars in our windows; there would be no Contreras men buried on some Pacific island, or under some hedgerow in Europe, or on the deserts of Africa or the Middle East.

Fiesta! Yes, a fiesta like no other; a Christmas almost as important to me as the very first one. And, as it has turned out, a Christmas that brought much to my family and my people, those of Mexican origin.

The world hasn't been the same since that Christmas of 1946, has it? The world as I know it began that day and so it did for my people, for they had received the best Christmas present of all, for the fighting men had brought dignity and pride to our homes and our families—gifts that even the three wise men didn't bring to the manger in Bethlehem. And, now, in contrast to a segregated America of 1946, is there anyone who doesn't know what FELIZ NAVIDAD means? In case there is, it's our way, all 350-million of us Spanish-speakers in the world, of saying Merry Christmas. ###

AUTHOR'S NOTE—JULY, 2003—The entire world knows of Mexican food. It is, perhaps, our greatest cultural contribution, Thousands upon thousands of Mexican restaurants open every day and serve hundreds of thousands, perhaps millions of tacos, burritos, enchiladas and various combination plates topped off with rice and refried beans and Jalapeno chiles and hot or medium salsa.

There are small family run taco joints that used to be hamburger stands, there are medium middle-class upscale sit-down restaurants that are a cross between fast food and sit-down and there are fancy sit-down restaurants with bars and fine wines, and, of course, Sunday morning Champagne brunches.

In 1941, most people hardly knew Mexicans existed. World War II changed much of that. Hundreds of thousands of American soldiers, sailors and Marines were trained in bases along the border from San Diego to Texas. Thousands others, like the famous old Buffalo Soldiers of the Black 10th Cavalry were stationed right on the Border to help protect California from invasion by Japanese always rumored to be landing in Mexico.

Mexican American men joined up to fight. Many of them had never been more than a few miles from home. Now they would fight across the Pacific, island to island; in Burma, In China, in North Africa, Sicily, Italy, France and Germany; in the Middle East, everywhere.

"What are you going to do when they see Paree…"

1946 was a seminal year for my community. Our men came home, many of them had earned high school equivalency in the service and they snatched up the free college that was theirs after the Congress passed the educational benefits bill for our fighting men, the G.I. Bill of Rights.

By the time I reached high school in 1955, many of these men were teaching and coaching. Unlike my immediate predecessors in the 30s and 40s I had real men to look up to in school. They were my teachers and coaches. One, Armando "Shadow" Rodriguez, would coach me in wrestling. He would go on to become a school principal, a Democratic politician, a Presidential appointment to the Equal Employment Opportunity Commission, then appointed President of East Los Angeles Community College.

He is retired now, in his Eighties. He was nicknamed "Shadow" because his moves on the wrestling mat were so fast that his opponents could never grab him, he was like a "Shadow."

I saw him one day a few years ago in our gym. He smiled and said, "I read you in the New York Times." We both had come a long way from the Barrio, from Logan Heights, "La Logan." That's what the smile meant.

◆   ◆   ◆

XMAS 1999

Like any other boy growing up I looked forward to Christmas with delight and glee. Church, singing, presents and food, lots of food made up my Christmas in what would later be known as the barrio. The singing was in Spanish, the food, Mexican. The Christmas—German, Scandinavian, Dutch and English.

Kris Kringle, Santa Claus, Christmas trees, "Deck The Halls" with boughs of holly, "Stille Nacht, Heilige Nacht," and myriad other European traditions make up the American Christmas and have since the 1600s. As we enter the 21st Century that is no longer totally true.

To the European facets, now come Mexican contributions, contributions of food and celebration. Tamales (tah-mah-lehs) and pinatas (peen-yah-tahs) have jumped the border and become part of the American Christmas for many. Is it because so many Mexican-origin people (22-million plus) now live in the USA or is it because these Christmas contributions are just plain good and appealing?

Plainly, the PINATA has entered the country's Christmas celebration, the country's lexicon and has even become part of the birthday party of many an American child. The PINATA is easily recognized despite myriad forms and colors. It might be Big Bird, a star, a small bull, a large parrot, the Titanic, Mickey Mouse, Donald Duck, or Richard Nixon. It might be yellow, green, red, blue, white, or any color. It might be a traditional clay pot in the middle full of candy and small presents, or it might be hand crafted paper strips from old newspapers and flour glue with a hollow center filled with candy and small presents. It might be hung from a tree, a clothesline, a garage rafter and it might be hung in stationary setting or on a rope so the PINATA can be moved about. A child may be blindfolded or not. A stick, a broom-stick, a baseball bat may be used by a child to strike and break the PINATA.

Striking a PINATA is not a violent act, it is a child's attempt to get the candy inside, it is a game.

I loved PINATAS when I was a kid. My daughter loved them when she was little, especially Big Bird, Kermit the Frog and Miss Piggy ones. Comics use PINATAS as part of their comic imagery with "pummeled like a PINATA."

We are told that pinatas were developed by priests to bring children into the Christmas celebration of the birth of Jesus. Thousands of Mexicans, mostly women, sit around all year making PINATAS in border cities like Tijuana for the American market. It might even be possible that more PINA-TAS are sold in the United States than Mexico.

PINATAS are one thing and they are for children, but TAMALES, now that's a subject we adults can savor.

Mexican food is, perhaps, one of the best gifts by Mexicans to American society. While it may be rare in Montpelier, Vermont, Mexican food is pretty much everywhere. Tacos, enchiladas, jalapeno peppers and even CHALUPAS are as well known as scrambled eggs and Green Ham, thanks to a little dog and a multi-million dollar television ad campaign. Only true connoisseurs of Mexican cuisine, however, really know tamales.

When I was a kid, I used to help the women hand grind corn kernels into a course wet mass, a MASA (mah-saw), while corn shucks were soaked in warm water. When the masa was just right, we spread it on wet corn shucks and rolled it with a rolling pin until the thickness was just right, say something between 3/8ths and half-an-inch. With fingers, we then created a depression in the middle and filled it with CARNE PICADA, spiced beef, or with shredded, spiced CARNITAS (deep fried pork), or with POLLO PIC-ADO, spiced, shredded chicken. Then we rolled the masa and filling into the shucks, enclosing the bottom and leaving the top open. Stacked vertically into a pot they are then steamed until the entire masa is cooked, done, the shuck unwrapped and the tamale is eaten with gusto. Millions of tamales will be consumed this Christmas, including those that I will prepare using my generations old recipes that the women of my youth passed on to me.

I didn't mention the best tamale. We always set aside some masa for dessert tamales, sweet tamales. The masa normally is made of corn flour, lime and water, but the best tamales have something else—sugar, and raisins, or pineapple, or both.

I prefer brown sugar and crushed pineapple. Lots of brown sugar worked into the masa and raisins and crushed pineapple in the middle makes the sweet tamale. **This is the perfect non-fat, high calorie food item than can make a grown man cry with ecstasy. I know, it does me every Christmas, as it does millions of other Mexican men, and, every Christmas that goes by, Americans, more and more Americans. Trust me.**

The Mexican PINATA and TAMALE have arrived. They are the latest significant immigrants from Mexico into America. Like all immigrants, the pinata and tamales are affecting American culture, positively I might add. Christmas (Navidad), you see, will never, ever be the same again. Gracias y Feliz Navidad. ###

THE MOVIES

If one goes to a favorite book store, the most diligent shopper will find a paucity of books by and about Hispanics. In music, most Hispanic progress is in the forms of singers like Rickey Martin, Julio Iglesias, J Lo, Serena and a few groups, but few Mexicans. In the movies, however, Mexicans and Mexican Americans have made impacts far beyond their numbers. For years, the Hollywood/Mexico City axis made thousands of movies that circulated throughout the world. Even today, Mexican NOVELAS (steamy soap operas) make their way all over the world, just like American movies do.

Mexican actors made their way into American movies at the genesis of Hollywood. In the opposite direction, American movie directors went south to make movies like Treasure of the Sierra Madre, the Wild Bunch and many others, or shot movies about Mexico and Mexicans, revolutions and great Mexicans like Benito Juarez, Zapata and the infamous Pancho Villa, about whom there must be a score of movies made about his exploits in the 1910–1920 Mexican Revolution and Civil War and, of course, his raid into New Mexico in 1916.

The motion picture, the great art form of the 20th Century, has been the greatest cultural contribution by Mexicans and Mexican Americans.

"FACELESS BUREAUCRATS AND THE HUNGRY SOUL"

Two years ago, in New York, I happened upon an exhibit of the Soviet Union's first star painter, the one who created the Soviet poster art. His name, like his ability, isn't important because his art—government art, propaganda art—isn't important. Government art usually isn't.

Government art is what became of the legendary Mexican movie industry forty years ago when the Mexican government took over the industry, lock, stock and film canister. Film directors became government employees intent on collecting pay checks from bureaucrats happy that their children had movie roles.

Talent meant little in the once proud film industry of Mexico, second only to that of the USA in style and production. Government financing went only to political lap dogs, just as in Nazi Germany and Soviet Russia.

The world ignored Mexican films for four decades—until now.

Suddenly, in the past three years, there's been an explosion of creativity in the long moribund Mexican film industry. Mexican films written, produced and filmed by Mexicans are appearing in American theaters and winning international awards for quality like never before.

Why? Why the sudden emergence of top quality, prize winning films from Mexico? Why have films such as "Cabeza de Vaca", "Danzon" and "Like Water for Chocolate" mowed down international competition like sugar cane stalks in a hurricane?

There's a very simple reason, according to Mexican movie director Alfonso Arau. He should know as his sixth film, "Like Water For Chocolate", has won 10 Ariel Awards, Mexico's Oscars, and 18 international awards ranging from the Chicago Film Festival to the Tokyo International Film Festival.

"Privatization", Arau declares, is the reason for the explosion of Mexican film creativity. President Carlos Salinas' historic move away from government control of Mexican industry and, in particular, the movie industry has unleashed a torrent of pent-up talent.

Quality Mexican films are crossing the border faster than migrant workers. They come here for two reasons: first, the US film market is the largest and best in the world; secondly, a good film will find its audience here, among our 250 million people, making a modest production very profitable if it does find an audience.

Profitable films beget more films and more films draw out new talents. Quality wins and so does the audience when talent pursues excellence. This, of course, is in contrast to art of the Soviet Union and Nazi Germany.

Creativity and artistic freedom died in those countries when the thugs took over. Creativity and artistic freedom died in Mexico when the bureaucrats took over.

Mexico's film industry was crippled like a forest after a fire. Today, through four decades of ashes, the industry is sprouting again and is more vibrant than ever and its leaders are a whole new generation of writers and directors.

Alfonso Arau, for example, brings years of acting experience to directing and has already won two Ariel Awards, Mexican Oscars. American film goers will recognize his infectious smile as that of the loveable drug smuggler who steals the show in "Romancing the Stone".

His wife, Laura Esquivel, wrote "Like Water For Chocolate", first as a prize-winning novel, then as a screenplay.

They made the movie for two million dollars. It's a hit. More importantly, it's an artistic success that pleases its director.

"A movie", Arau states, "is either good or bad."

It doesn't hurt that government officials are no longer looking over his shoulder as he makes the crucial decisions that result in a good or bad movie, either.

In the final analysis, then, individuals free from government shackles and control make quality movies and art. Their art and the statements that make up their art succeed or fail in the marketplace on merit.

Government art, like its creators, is not important because it is a product of faceless committees made up of faceless bureaucrats, pleasing only their superiors, not the hungry soul.

Freedom makes artists and their art important. Ask the Mexicans, they'll tell you this is so. ###

AUTHOR'S NOTE—JULY, 2003—Ah, Freedom. Ah, free enterprise. Ah, freedom.

◆   ◆   ◆

HOORAY FOR HOLLYWOOD!!

Jane Fonda's done it again. For her production of Carlos Fuentes' OLD GRINGO, for her casting Puerto Rican actor Jimmy Smits, for her using an Argentinian director, and for portraying Mexico's revolutionary years in a relatively accurate manner, Jane Fonda is picketed.

The pickets aren't her Viet Nam war antics critics, or conservative Republicans. No, they're in the Mexican American Coalition, a Los Angeles group, which objects to her production of the movie "Old Gringo".

According to Raul Ruiz, a California "Chicano Studies" teacher, they object to a double standard, "a heroic, courageous old gringo and...cowardly, violent Mexican males and whorish females."

Is there really a problem here? Yes and no. Hollywood has been very unkind to Mexicans and Mexican Americans in the past. The result, according to a ten-year study by Professor Carlos E. Cortez of the University of California-Riverside, is American school-children entering school with predetermined notions that Mexicans are lazy, stupid and cowardly.

Silent Hollywood produced and distributed these movies: THE GREASER'S GAUNTLET; TONY THE GREASER; THE GREASER'S REVENGE; and, THE GIRL AND THE GREASER.

Dennis Hopper portrays in COLORS that our Los Angeles brethren are murderous, licentious dopers who kill at the drop of a hypodermic needle; who sexually pass around their sisters and girlfriends; who are—animals.

Besides being portrayed as dumb and murderous, Dr. Cortes says, "Its not proper for male greasers—dark-skinned, usually Indianized Mexican or other Latino men—to have love affairs with Anglo women." He told the SAN DIEGO UNION, "Movieland's greasers certainly lusted for Anglo women, providing a constant threat from which Anglo heroes could rescue their damsels."

Dr. Cortes points to a new Hollywood theme, of Anglo women manifesting superiority over Mexican men. SUNBURN, with Farrah Fawcett-Majors; and, LOSIN' IT have American women outsmarting dumb Mexicans in their own country. This is aided and abetted by the tax-supported University of California at Los Angeles (UCLA) which recently allowed one of its film students to produce a film about Mexican whores which, charitably, is qualitatively terrible, at best, and totally racist. Anglo professors called it a work of art. Racism cloaked as art, is a technique imported into UCLA from Nazi Germany.

Before we boycott LA-LA-LAND, however, some of Hollywood has shed it's intellectual vacuity in allowing Edward James Olmos (STAND AND DELIVER); Luis Valdez (ZOOT SUIT, LA BAMBA); Moctezuma Esparza (MILAGRO BEANFIELD WAR); Cheech Marin(BORN IN EAST LA); and, Gregory Luna (EL NORTE), to produce and/or direct recent positive and critically acclaimed movies. LA BAMBA and BORN IN EAST LA, have even been box office hits.

Dr. Cortes commends long-ago movies: BORDER INCIDENT with Ricardo Montalban; the cult classic, TOUCH OF EVIL, with Orson Welles and Charleton Heston (playing a blonde, blue-eyed Mexican policeman); and, ZAPATA, which won an Academy Award for Mexican Anthony Quinn.

He mildly criticizes TREASURE OF SIERRA MADRE for featuring a dumb Mexican who casts aside gold dust, thinking it's sand. He neglects, however, to note Director John Huston's having the same Mexican say, "I don't need no stinking badges." John Huston: Mexicans don't have to prove themselves to anyone.

Cortes is silent on Sam Peckinpah's WILD BUNCH, in which American mercenaries are killed avenging the death of a Mexican PISTOLERO they love and respect as one of their own. Peckinpah: Americans and Mexicans are brothers, in war, in life, to live and die together in fighting oppression.

Cortes suggests Hollywood dishonors Mexico in depicting Benito Juarez (Paul Muni) carrying a portrait of Abraham Lincoln while running from the French army. Surprise, Dr. Cortes, he did. Dr. Cortes implies the movies "JUAREZ", and Charleton Heston's MAJOR DUNDEE, suggest Americans were pivotal in driving out French invaders.

The fact is, Americans served in Juarez' army, and organized their own brigade, the hard fighting Juarez-decorated American Legion Of Honor. They used American guns which didn't cost Juarez a dime. Lastly, Mexican guerilla fighters operated openly out of Texas under U.S. Army protection. Dr. Cortes' historical facts fall a little short.

As to the landmark 1934 VIVA VILLA movie, starring Wallace Beery, Dr. Cortes fumes, it was "violent, ludicrously macho…a greaser movie in historical drape." He does not comment, however, on the fact the Mexican Government of Lazaro Cardenas had final script approval, nor that the 1910–1920 Mexican rebellion was, in fact, very violent. Choir boys, Dr. Cortes, don't win wars.

Had Pancho Villa been alive when VIVA VILLA was made, he probably would have enjoyed it. After all, he was no saint. Pancho Villa was irrefutably a "violent, ludicrously macho," man. In fact, he'd been dead forty years before

Mexico declared him a Hero of the Revolution. Until 1966, officially—he was a thief, a bandit. No, Pancho Villa's objection would have been to an ugly Wallace Beery portraying him, not how he was portrayed.

Speaking of objections, are the Mexican American Coalition's complaints about Puerto Rican Jimmy Smits playing a Mexican Revolution general valid?

Did, for example, Greeks complain when Academy Award-winning Mexican actor Anthony Quinn portrayed ZORBA THE GREEK? Did Filipinos object when Quinn played a Filipino war hero in "Bataan" and "Back to Bataan"? Did Mexican Americans object when Anthony Quinn, Mexican, portrayed a Mexican American Marine in 1942's "Guadalcanal Diary".

No, of course they didn't. And, though Quinn won his Academy Award for playing the treacherous brother of Emiliano Zapata, he was also nominated for portraying a Jewish thief executed with Jesus. I don't recall Jewish pickets protesting his portrayal, nor Charleton Heston's Moses.

And, where was the Mexican American Coalition when an European American actor was selected to play Emiliano Zapata? The same European American who lovingly rolled the word "Greaser" from his lips a decade later in "One Eyed Jacks". Yes, Great liberal and defender of Indian rights, Marlon Brando.

Overt racism notwithstanding, its a complicated subject how we are portrayed in today's movies. Different historical and sociological interpretations of our past and present clash on the screen, some true and some untrue. In this, we are the same as everyone else. Furthermore, what makes it doubly difficult, I believe, is that we Mexican Americans are as complicated as are our portrayals. Or, is it our portrayals are complicated because we're complicated. Quien Sabe?

If we don't know, how's Jane Fonda supposed to know? ###

AUTHOR'S NOTE—JULY, 2003—When Irish Mexican actor Anthony Quinn died in his eighties a short time ago, his death was a big deal. This man who portrayed Mexicans, Filipinos, Jews of the Jesus era, Greeks, Italians and Mexican Americans was an actor of the century. A good actor can play almost anything on the stage or on the screen. One does not have to be a Mexican to play a Mexican, period.

◆   ◆   ◆

"NODS AND GESTURES"

When I met him I told him he had done more for the collective self-esteem of Mexican Americans than anyone ever by portraying teacher Jaime Escalante in the movie "Stand And Deliver," a role for which he was nominated for an Academy Award.

I told him I had seen every one of his movies and that I had even spotted him in a bit part on an old "Kojak" rerun. He became famous by playing a police Lt. on Miami Vice, a role for which he won television's highest honor, an Emmy.

He is a fine actor, and a bigger-than-life role model for anyone from the barrio, or from anywhere for that matter.

Edward James Olmos is his name.

A couple of days ago, I saw a new side of actor Edward James Olmos when I watched the most stunning movie I had seen in years. Edward James Olmos had invited me and the National Association of Hispanic Publications convention to preview his first directing effort, his soon to be released feature movie, "American Me".

Stand and Deliver" chronicled the struggles and accomplishments of East Los Angeles Barrio Mexican American kids who surmounted impossible odds to academically succeed. It did not do well at the box office.

"American Me", in contrast, is a superbly crafted, totally shocking, completely illuminating Amorality play featuring East LA Mexican Americans as they are absorbed by the gang world.

We watch little boys brought into the gang. We watch the women of the Barrio suffer the loss of their beloved sons to the gangs and to the justice system. We suffer with them as they continue to love boy murderers who become men in prison.

We enter the shocking world of prison, man-on-man rape, drugs, death and the founding of the most infamous prison gang ever, the Mexican Mafia.

Edward James Olmos creates Santana, a character who orders people killed with a gesture, a nod of the head. He displays no emotion as he builds his prison gang and manipulates the infamous Folsom Prison with head nods and gestures.

He is as powerful as the brute force he organizes and controls. Santana is king of the place he becomes a man in, prison.

He is a man who cries only when his mother dies, or when he visits her grave. He is a man who hates his father because the man hated him, the issue of a rape. He is a hard man, a prison man, who doesn't know how to dance with, or make love to a woman.

He is not really a man, as his girl friend points out force fully when her younger brother dies from an overdose of Santana's heroin. He is, she declares, "Nothing but a...dope dealer".

Edward James Olmos' Santana is more than a "dope dealer," he is at once a destructive and self-hating person, what we used to call a Pachuco (pah-choo-koh), a very specific type of Mexican punk.

As Mexican Nobel Laureate Octavio Paz wrote in "Labyrinth of Solitude", "...the (Los Angeles) pachuco cannot adapt himself to a civilization which, for its part, rejects him, he finds no answer to the hostility surrounding him except this angry affirmation of his personality." Olmos substitutes dysfunctional family for Paz' civilization.

Paz writes, "...instead of attempting a problematical adjustment to society, the pachuco actually flaunts his differences (clothing, speech, tattoos, etc).

"The pachuco", Paz declares, "has lost his whole inheritance: language, religion, customs, beliefs."

Olmos' gangsters have no conscience, no morality, no cultural or social inheritance, no language other than street patois. By rejecting family, they have only each other. For each other they will kill anyone, including family.

For gang loyalty and bonding, they destroy the one remaining cultural trait that holds Mexicans and other Hispanics together, the epoxy of family.

"American Me" offers one ray of hope in its depressing morass. Olmos portrays women as that hope. "American Me" hints at what Octavio Paz wrote decades ago, the Mexican woman "...is a symbol, like all women, of the stability and continuity of the race...she has an important social role, which is to see that law and order, piety and tenderness are predominant in everyday life."

Edward James Olmos gives life to these words in "American Me". He will be criticized and castigated by elements of the Mexican American community for this movie. He will be praised by others.

"American Me" is brutal, brutally honest, brilliant and truthful. For it, and the courage to make it, Edward James Olmos will be honored and remembered. It starts here. ###

"IT'S HARD BEING A MEXICAN AMERICAN…"

"We have to know about John Wayne and Pedro Infante. We have to speak English better than Americans, Spanish better than Mexicans. It's really hard being a Mexican American."

I wish I could say I wrote those lines, but I didn't. They come from the movie "Selena", produced by Moctezuma Esparza and Jack Katz, directed by Academy Award winning San Diego native Gregory Nava and co-starring the speaker of those lines, Edward James Olmos.

The story of Twentysomething Selena, the Tex-Mex–Tejano (teh-haw-no) superstar singer, who was gunned down by the President of her fan club and business associate, is well known. How she got to be a star is not. To fill the information vacuum, in steps this movie.

It has been out for a while and has grossed something on the order of $40-million and will probably double that when released overseas and in videotape. In other words, it's a hit.

When Director Nava called casting sessions around the country for a young girl to play Selena the child, 8,000 children showed up. When Nava searched for the adult Selena, women from all over the country showed up. He chose Puerto Riquena—New York actress Jennifer Lopez. Immediately there was controversy. Chicano radicals fussed that the role should go to a Chicana, not a foreigner. Nava, a self-proclaimed Chicano, cast aside their protests and stuck to his artistic decision. He was right.

Jennifer Lopez is spectacular as Selena. Jennifer Lopez grasped what must have been Selena's soul, wrapped herself in it and brought it out for you and me to see and feel.

Edward James Olmos plays her father and holds out the dream of success for his daughter and family with an obstinancy that must grate on some, but is typical of those who succeed or direct success for others. A Mexican American Col. Tom Parker is what he was; what Parker was to Elvis Presley, Abe Quintinella was to his daughter Selena.

I must say that it was a pleasure to watch a movie about Mexican Americans that had more Mexican Americans in the cast and production than anyone else. In other words, we didn't have to suffer through some Midwest Hollywood starlet wearing a black wig awkwardly trying to move and shimmy a la Latin. It is painful to watch such starlets move a la cumbia to music they've never heard and to sing words they don't understand.

There is no such problem with Jennifer Lopez. She's beautiful; she can move and can she smile. When she smiles, the earth stops. National movie Critics Gene Siskel and Roger Ebert have declared that this movie is a launching pad to stardom for Ms Lopez, and I agree.

It does wonders too, for Director Nava whose "El Norte" won every conceivable award a few years ago and whose "La Familia—My Family" made some box office ripples a couple of years ago. There will definitely be more Nava projects to come.

As to Moctezuma Esparza and his partner, Jack Katz, though they keep on producing movies that revel in Hispanic icons and culture, they made their reputation with one of the best movies ever made about the American Civil War, "Gettysburg". Their production of a couple of movies a year should keep them busy enough to draw more producers into the field of making films about Hispanic icons and culture, films that we now know can make money.

Jennifer Lopez, the talented, beautiful Jennifer Lopez? Who knows how high her star will climb. We can only look forward with great anticipation to her future films.

And, then, there's Edward James Olmos. Selena's movie father has played a Miami Vice cop, a Migra officer, Mexican Mafia kingpin, dope dealer, desert soldier and the country's best known teacher. Where will he pop up next? Anywhere he wants to, for this former rock and roll musician is a consumate professional, a deep thinking man. It can be said in these precincts that Edward James Olmos just might be a 1997 Renaissance Man.

"We have to know about John Wayne and Pedro Infante. We have to speak English better than Americans, Spanish better than Mexicans. It's really hard being a Mexican American." Olmos, the actor, spoke those words as Selena's father; Olmos, the man, deeply felt those words, for they have been so true for so long.

It is hard work being a Mexican American, but not as hard as it was before the movie Selena came out. ###

AUTHOR'S NOTE—JULY, 2003—Who knew Jennifer Lopez would become a megastar when she played Serena so well? No one did, but I recall what Siskel and Ebert, the famous movie reviewers, said about the movie and Jennifer Lopez. They thought the movie was all right, they gave it a Copyrighted Two Thumbs

Up, then both agreed that this newcomer, Jennifer Lopez was going to be a big star. Were they right, so right?

6

Chapter introduction—They really all don't look or act alike.

While many among us have difficulty in telling one Hispanic from another, a Mexican, for example, from a Puerto Rican, there are significant differences that even a Border Patrolman could see. Little things like the number of phones each community has, the number of businesses they form, the amount of welfare each group collects, the percentage of AIDS sufferers, drug addicts, labor market penetration, unemployment, voting patterns, etc., are benchmarks that are easily attributable to each sub-group among Hispanics. It seems, therefore, that Mexican-origin people are far more successful in the United States than native-born U.S. citizen Puerto Ricans.

"THE MEASURE OF CIVILIZATION-THE TELEPHONE"

The greatest con job ever perpetrated on the American public is that of a minority cabal within the Hispanic-Latino community with regards to the composition of the community.

It is not monolithic. It does not speak with one voice. It does not look the same. It does not come from the same place. It does not speak the same language. It does not live in poverty.

For example, because most of the important media in this country is based in New York, a false image has developed in the media fueled by professional ethnics in their midst. Most of the Eastern professional ethnics are Puerto Rican. The result, the American media tends to think that all Hispanics act, work, eat, play and exist like Puerto Ricans. Do they?

No. Using current Census Bureau Data published in "A Special Report: Second Edition" by the Census Bureau and the National Association of Hispanic Publications, we can make some interesting observations.

First, there are very few Puerto Ricans in the United States, a little over 1% of the total American population (2.8 million). They are mostly concentrated in the Northeast, in New York and New Jersey. Contrast that, if you will, with the 17-million Americans of Mexican-origin. In numbers, therefore, we have a huge difference in population, thus in socio-political and economic impact on American society, as well.

Then, there's population growth. Between 1970 and 1980, the Mexican-origin population grew by 93%, while the Puerto Ricans grew by 41%. Between 1980 and 1990, the Mexicans grew by 54% and Puerto Ricans by 35%. Thus, the impact of Mexicans in America is growing faster and larger than that of Puerto Ricans.

In political impact, we find a huge divergence from the myths perpetrated by the Eastern media and special interests; i.e., that Puerto Ricans wield heavy political influence. In 1990, the "Hispanic" population amounted to 9% of America. In the same year, 48.2% of New Mexico was of Mexican-origin. In California, almost 25%; in Texas, 25%; in Arizona, 18.8%; and, in Colorado, 12.9%. New York, on the other hand, shows up at the tail end of influence by numbers. It's Puerto Rican population of 12.3% which, with New Jersey's 9.6% Puerto Rican population amounts to little influence on a state or national level.

Projections for the future are significant from the myth view because influence is reflected by population. In 2020, the Census Bureau projects that there will be 14-million Mexican-origin people in California and 10.3 million in Texas. Puerto Ricans will number approximately 2.6 million in New York and 1.2 million in New Jersey. in other words, even in 23 years, Puerto Ricans won't have enough numbers to influence state and Federal elections in New York and New Jersey, while Mexican-origin people will provide the margin of victory in state and federal elections in California and Texas, states with 80 or more electoral votes for the Presidency.

Even age plays a role in the differences between Puerto Ricans and Mexican Americans. Non-Hispanic Whites have a median age (half above and half below) of 36-years-of-age. Hispanics as a whole have a median age of 26-years. Puerto Ricans have a median age of 27, while Mexicans have a median age of 24.

Education statistics favor Puerto Ricans in that 1990 numbers show that Puerto Ricans have a higher percentage of high school diplomas than Mexicans; the numbers are 59% in 1990 against 47% for Mexicans.

In percentage of native-born, that is, born in the 50 states, Mexican born people are fewer as a percentage than the percentage of Puerto Ricans born in the 50 states. Puerto Ricans are, of course, American citizens from birth, while Mexican-born are not.

In the labor market (March-1994), we find huge differences between the better educated, all-American citizen Puerto Ricans and Mexican-origin people. Only 66% of Puerto Rican men work; 45% of Puerto Rican women work, as against 59% of non-Hispanic White/Black women and 74% for non-Hispanic White and Black men. Mexican-origin men dwarf the labor market penetration of all others in the country. Mexican-origin men have a 80% labor market penetration; the women 52%.

In unemployment, Mexicans win again. March, 1994 statistics show an unemployment rate among Puerto Ricans of 14.2% against 11.2% among Mexicans.

In 1993 median family income, better educated Puerto Ricans at $19,700 are 25% less than Mexicans at $23,400. In 1993 poverty rates, the better educated Puerto Ricans have 35.4% of their own in poverty against the less-educated Mexicans with 27.6%. Among children, Puerto Ricans have a 54.3% in poverty, while Mexicans have a 40.5% child poverty rate. 1994 home-ownership rates reveal much about better educated Puerto Ricans and less-educated Mexicans. Among Puerto Ricans, only 24% own their homes; 47% of Mexicans, on the other hand, own their homes.

Lastly, in a final comparison, the better educated Puerto Ricans lag behind Mexicans in the ultimate measure of assimilation, wealth, economic and social standing—the telephone. In March, 1994, 76% of Puerto Ricans had phones; 81% of Mexicans had phones.

There are substantial differences between the Eastern Puerto Ricans and the Western and Southwestern Mexicans. They are quantifiable, they are important and they are obvious—obvious, that is, to everyone but the media and the minority cabal that benefits from misinformation, disinformation and the Big Lie. ###

AUTHOR'S NOTE—JULY, 2003—Puerto Ricans blew a fuse when this article was published. On many chat rooms and web sites they posted accusations of my being a racist, a bigot against Puerto Ricans. Nonetheless, the facts are facts. Mexicans are far better off and make more money than Puerto Ricans. Mexican Americans have less AIDS, commit fewer crimes and collect far less in government services and "benefits."

At the risk of sounding crass, tough breaks. You are what you are and you are pretty much molded by your community.

There are huge differences between Puerto Ricans and Mexicans. Puerto Ricans are all native-born U.S. citizens and many Mexican aren't because they were born in Mexico and have immigrated here. So, many ask, how is it that Mexicans can sneak across the border and find jobs, even in New York City, while Puerto Ricans whine and complain they can't find jobs even as Mexicans can.

The fact that only one of the 36 Medal of Honor winners is Puerto Rican is striking when one lays out the birthplaces of all Hispanic Medal of Honor winners side by side.

Telephone ownership and use is as good a benchmark as one can use in the United States.

◆   ◆   ◆

"BUDDY, CAN YOU SPARE A MILLION BUCKS IN NEW CAPITAL"

As the rate of immigration from South of the Border has increased, so has Hispanic accomplishment in one of the most visible aspects of American life. Welfare? Poverty? Criminality? Gang-banging? Guess.

There was a book published several years ago by a do-gooder, social worker mentality, liberal writer, Earl Shorris, who dismissed HISPANIC MAGAZINE and HISPANIC BUSINESS MAGAZINE as pure vehicles for advertising sales and for some Hispanics to strut around pretending they were prosperous, middle-class Americans.

Earl Shorris exalted the poor with anecdotes about the single, poor Dominican "single parent" mother with a covey of illegitimate children and her welfare grant. He wrote of the shacks and dirt roads of the "suburbs" of El Paso. He placed the poor on such an altar that anyone not familiar with the community would guess that every single Hispanic in the country is poor, lives in shacks and collects welfare.

Shorris was wrong, of course. His readers who bleed for the poor are wrong if they think the Hispanic community, approaching 30-million strong, is the poor relative of this America.

EXTRA! EXTRA! READ ALL ABOUT IT! Hispanic business ownership has grown at three times the rate of all American new business. The Census Bureau announced this week that between 1987–1992, the Reagan-Bush years, the number of Hispanic businesses soared like an eagle.

They grew by 76%. In 1987 there were 489,973 Hispanic-owned businesses, in 1992 they had grown to 862,605.

Gross revenue of these firms grew 135% during that period of time which was twice the growth rate of all American firms. In 1992, the revenues of the 862,605 businesses was $76.8 billion.

Yes. Much to the chagrin of the do-gooder social worker mentality people like writer Shorris and many, if not all, of the "social activists" in the Hispanic community, Hispanics are avoiding the welfare trap and rebuilding America from the inside, using American techniques of economic growth even better than non-Hispanic White, Anglo Americans.

And, they don't all mow lawns or make tortillas. In my county, for example, Hispanic business numbers increased from 10,373 (1987) to 18,983 (1992) and, surprisingly, covered every area of economic activity there is.

Of the 18,983, 9,485 were in the services; 2,852, retail; construction, 1,619; finance, insurance and real estate, 1,092; transportation, 641; wholesale trade, 632; and, manufacturing, 422. Yes, manufacturing.

Being in California, this writer is proud of the fact California has the highest number of Hispanic-owned businesses (249,717–1992). Florida is second with 118,208, Texas third with 155,909 and New York with 50,601.

But the future is better indicated and predicted by looking at New Mexico, where Hispanic-owned business are 20.1 % of the total number of businesses in the entire state. Of course, 38.9% of the New Mexico population looks like me and answers to names like Martinez, Garcia, Serrano, etc.

New Mexico, however, is so small that their 21,586 Hispanic businesses only gross $1.5 billion. In contrast, the mind-boggling 249,717 Hispanic businesses in California gross $19.6 billion.

Gross, net, business formations are words totally foreign to people like writer Shorris and the activists, which is why he is critical of HISPANIC BUSINESS MAGAZINE for even existing. People making money on their own, by their own sweat and ability, are concepts foreign to Shorris and the activists. More importantly, about the proposition that Hispanics are making money from mainstream Anglo-controlled corporations like General Motors, Ford, Bank of America, Citibank and myriad other such businesses.

Consider that the huge growth has occurred in the face of limited government intervention, the biggest recession in years and growing White, Anglo lack of respect for Hispanics, immigrant or native born. Hispanics have shown great economic accomplishment—greater economic and free enterprise accomplishment than any other group in America—during this period of time. This period of time has seen anti-immigrant and anti-Mexican sentiment expressed by Presidential candidates Ross Perot and Pat Buchanan, plus many little Know-Nothing type groups in California and the Southwest.

Unfortunately, there is one bit of negative news in all this. That is, the numbers stop in 1992, for that is the last year the Census Bureau has complete data available for analysis. The negative is that the numbers the Census Bureau reported are out-of-date because they are four years old.

If one applies the same rates of growth of the 1987–1992 five year period to the last four years, VOILA!, we have some real numbers. This is a legitimate exercise, for the recession came to an end in the last quarter of 1992 and the economy has grown each of the last four years, albeit, not at rates of earlier post-recession growth periods.

For example, at the same rate of growth experienced during 1987–1992, there are, probably, 1,290,457 Hispanic-owned business in America today. They probably gross $132.98 billion. They employ thousands upon thousands of fellow Hispanics, according to critics of the Hispanic community that bemoan the fact that Hispanic business people tend to employ fellow Hispanics.

In 1992, they had an average gross revenue of $89,000 per, in contrast to the average American company with $193,000. And, 47% of these firms had revenue of less than $10,000, with 9,200—of the 863,000—grossing a million dollars or more.

All this great stuff, these great percentages, and the Hispanic population increased by only 7% during that 1987–1992 period. EXTRA! EXTRA! READ ALL ABOUT IT!

We're Number One!! ###

AUTHOR'S NOTE—JULY, 2003—The progress of Hispanics working with and in the free enterprise system is astounding. For decades this writer has preached that free enterprise economics and business is the only choice Hispanics can make if they want to be something other than the Nuyorican model of welfare, crime and drug addiction in New York City.

It doesn't matter that all Hispanic businesses aren't General Motors, it only matters that working for oneself and growing business that needs employees us what is important.

Being a cheerleader for Hispanic business is so much more beneficial to the community than highlighting poverty and exalting single mothers with a gaggle of illegitimate children by different fathers.

I've said for years that, in the words of baseball philosopher Yogi Berra—"When you come to a fork in the road, take it." My version reads, when you come to a fork in the road, one welfare, statist(the Earl Shorris) fork and one of free enterprise, take free enterprise.

Only then can the community break away from the paths of failure and isolation that over a third of the Black community and over half the Nuyorican community have followed since Lyndon Johnson built his cage for these groups.

◆   ◆   ◆

NEIGHBORHOODS, COLONIAS, WHERE WE LIVE

Hispanics with a third grade education, making $2500 a year have a better chance of living in an integrated neighborhood than does a Black Afro-American PhD making $50,000-a-year, concludes a recent study by the University of Chicago. Really?

As I look around East L.A., Pomona, San Diego's Logan Heights and San Ysidro, Santa Ana, Colton, Chicago and the "Valley," the Rio Grande Valley, I see many Mexican Americans living in demographically and economically similar neighborhoods. Barrios—many call them, colonias (ko-low-nee-ahs), purists call them. They have always been there, just like we've always been here, we Mexican Americans (Mexicans who were Spanish citizens first settled in San Diego, California, in 1769, in about 1540 in New Mexico).

Our neighborhoods, like all neighborhoods, consist of buildings, houses, schools, businesses, restaurants, streets and alleys, some paved, some not, and, of course, people, lots of people. There is a difference, however. Our neighborhoods have life, a self-rejuvenating life of their own. A life at once, raucous, romantic, and hot (as in chili pepper) connected by an invisible umbilical to our Mexico in the form of music, newspapers and cinema.

When compared to other ethnic neighborhoods, say L.A.'s Koreatown, San Diego's Manila Mesa, or Watts, our neighborhoods sometimes suffer when upward money making experience is the criterion, but outdistance, by far, other communities in livability. Mexicans, for example, don't usually pack four or five families under one roof as occurs in other ethnic households, though family members are welcome. Mexicans are loathe to bar their windows and doors as others so quickly do. And, while other communities are depressing, our huge numbers of children make for anything but a depressing neighborhood.

Other noteworthy characteristics of Mexican American neighborhoods are the fluidity of their populations. Some residents count by decades their presence on a given street, but most are recent arrivals. These are well known for a deep seated desire to own their homes. As our population expands, our traditional neighborhoods are growing in area. In Los Angeles, for example, Mexicanos who scrape together three-four-five thousand dollars are buying up South Central L.A. (Watts) houses faster than the proverbial hotcakes. Nice, you say. Of course. However, there's one problem. They want to live in their "new" houses. In doing so, they displace Afro-Americans.

Every Mexican neighborhood, new and old, has its Spanish-language movie house (s), as well as a myriad of video rentals stores, neither of which can meet the insatiable demand for movies by America's greatest moviegoers and video renters, the Mexican Americans. Luckily, Mexico is one of the leading movie making countries. Additionally, every major Spanish-speaking market now has Spanish-language television liberally dosed with local advertising, proclaiming for all the world to see that even white, Anglo businessmen "Se Habla Espanol!"

Yep! Se habla Espanol. Tying up the bundle of homeownership (almost 50%), bilinguality, economic gains and explosive population growth is a dynamic Spanish-language and bi-lingual press. Written off during the fifties and sixties, the Hispanic press is, perhaps, the fastest growing element of America's communications industry, albeit still small. In San Diego, for example, there are four separately owned Spanish or bi-lingual newspapers; in Chicago, at least ten; in California's booming Orange County, two.

Mostly owned by non-journalists these publications sometimes leave something to be desired in terms of journalistic quality, but, nevertheless, they're trying and they have growing readership. Concurrently, as revenues increase, they hire professionals, resulting in more professional product.

The Spanish-language press has not gone unnoticed by national advertisers. At the recent second annual convention of the new National Association of Hispanic Publishers, major American corporations were strongly represented, spending mucho money and paying attention to publishers from Northeast New York, Southeast Florida, Southwest San Diego and Seattle in the Northwest.

As our population and neighborhoods grow, problems will develop with those we displace, friction will increase and, in some cities, blood will be shed. Nevertheless, on the positive side, also growing will be our business community, as well as the soon-to-be influential and powerful Spanish-language and bi-lingual media, television and newspapers.

As one highly placed corporate advertising buyer commented, "Hispanic publications are no longer a political buy. We buy results."

Results. Our neighborhoods are growing, as our population grows. Our means of communication are growing. We are being paid more attention. We are demographic stars, with houses and cars to buy, movies to watch, lots of money to spend and neighborhoods to build.

And, as the University of Chicago study proves, most of us can live wherever we want, and we do. As more of us make it, we leave the barrio-colonia sprinting to the suburbs, our places taken by newcomers from Mexico, a process which makes the old neighborhoods more Mexican, more Spanish-speaking and more spicy, salsa-fied, if you will.

As to those who move out, a recent study (we sure are studied) by Cal Tech's Dr. Bruce Cain showed that half those moving out of East L.A.'s barrio to middle-class (read white, Anglo) San Fernando Valley neighborhoods registered—Republican. ###

AUTHOR'S NOTE—JULY, 2003—Segregated housing patterns are nothing new to America. In the 90s Blacks made some progress in moving into integrated neighborhoods, but like much Black progress, one step forward is in the face of two steps backward. Blacks complain in Los Angeles that "illegals" are coming to America and stealing their jobs, stealing the homes they have rented for years, stealing their neighborhoods and stealing their place in American.

It is true that Hispanics of all sorts, Mexicans, Salvadorans and Guatemalans have taken over South Central Los Angeles and Koreatown, areas that used to be Black and Korean, and turned them into Hispanic neighborhoods.

What is also true is that many Blacks who have been displaced in South Central have moved out to the suburbs in Riverside and San Bernardino counties.

And, though, many Blacks have done well in the 90s and will continue to do well, a huge percentage of Blacks are in a black hole where they were forced into by their "plantation" owners, the American white liberals who need to have millions of hapless subjects to take care of with our tax dollars.

Hispanics can shed their plantation masters by simply peeling off a few more votes for people who agree with them on many issues.

Four times as many Hispanics voted for President Bush in 2000 than Blacks. He returned the favor in the first 30 months of his administration by naming more Hispanics to office, to boards and commissions, than all previous Presidents together.

In the meanwhile, Blacks maintaining a status quo when they should be progressing is not good enough. All the Spike Lees, Al Sharptons and Jesse Jacksons in North America will not make it better for their community. Their anti-Bush and anti-white venom will scuttle the community in the long run because others, like Hispanics and Anglos, simply dismiss emotional clap-trap like reparations for descendents of slaves and blackmail payments to Jesse Jackson's Operation Whatever.

Thus, while untalented people like Jesse Jackson and Spike Lee get rich, more than one in three Blacks lives in abject poverty and their men suffer the highest unemployment rates no matter who is President. Under their favorite President, William Jefferson Clinton, Blacks, men and women, suffered through unemployment that was always twice as high as Whites and 50% higher than Hispanics.

◆   ◆   ◆

"THE BUSINESS OF HISPANIC AMERICA, IS BUSINESS"

We see them everywhere on television; we see them whining, cry-babying, acting like the victims they claim to be. They are the Hispanic activists who believe they are advancing the interests of the Hispanic community, empowerment, if you will. They are not.

Though they are the ones television normally turns to for comments when news needs Hispanic comments, they reflect the total failure of their methods and influence and should, in fact, be ignored by the media.

Proof is the huge success of the racist-inspired and supported Proposition 187 in the 1994 California election. Less than ten percent of registered Hispanic voters voted and twenty percent of them actually voted for the virulently anti-Mexican police state of 187.

For all the media attention their voter registration drives attract, they register precious few people. For all the money they get from foundations, fewer are turned out to vote.

Is there a solution for this Black Hole of Hispanic empowerment? Not as long as these activist failures continue to allegedly lead and keep drawing the attention of the media and the do-gooder foundations.

More importantly, the Hispanic community must wake up and drop its imitation of the Black activist movement that brought into being good civil rights laws and parallel economic disaster better described as subservience to new white masters-social workers and bureaucrats.

In a recent Yankelovich-New Yorker survey, 58% of African Americans "feel that conditions are worsening for them…and, half believe that race relations in America will never be better than they are." This is the legacy of Black activists who, in keeping their eye on the prize, forgot the real road to freedom which is composed of money, economics and business.

The Hispanic community has reached the cross-roads faced by Blacks in the 1960's. Will they go the same way, or will they take the road to true political and economic freedom?

Ladies and gentlemen, the decision has been made and it is for freedom.

According to HISPANIC BUSINESS MAGAZINE, there are now an estimated 613,000 Hispanic-owned businesses in the country, about three times the number in 1980 and, more importantly, six times the number of African American-owned companies. The combined revenue generation exceeds $27-billion and the purchasing power of the latest Hispanic census numbers (26.8 million people) exceeds $190-billion. Hispanic-owned firms employ 319,000 people.

Projections are being made that the number of Hispanic-owned businesses will triple again in the next four years as a result of the momentum and velocity built up during the Golden Years of Hispanic business formation—the Reagan-Bush years.

Finally, then, we have the beginnings of real power, the power to write checks that are real and don't bounce, checks that influence campaigns and the candidates that run them.

What's more important, a social activist telling an inner-city politician that he can deliver 200 Democrat votes for a politician that couldn't lose if he died during the campaign, or a Hispanic business man that can raise $10,000–$20,000 with a half-a-dozen phone calls for a candidate in a tight suburban race that will be won with a handful of votes? The answer is, the man or woman with the check, of course.

These people with the checks are usually, according to the HISPANIC BUSINESS MAGAZINE, 5% with some college, college graduates (31%) and an astounding 58% have post-graduate work. They (98%) have incomes in excess of $50,000 and only 44% are English-only speakers.

Almost half of them are for improving education and economics, while only two percent believe in defending affirmative action. As one of them, television's Geraldo Rivera, states emphatically, "Why support a dead issue?"

Interestingly, 36% believe small business is the vehicle to empower the Hispanic community, while 21% believe that empowerment will come from corporate America. In other words, 57% believe that business, particularly small business, is the way to real power. Conversely, only 14% think social activists are the path to power.

Business, then, is the path to power, real power and it appears that our educated business leaders have decided to step into the fray for power. Social activists get the attention, but produce little.

They must be moved aside and they must be moved aside now, for if not, the majority Hispanic population of the future California will look and act like America's inner-city people of today—powerless, poor, prison-bound, of illegitimate birth and decidedly not average, middle-class Americans.

What a waste of talent and human resources that would be just as it is today in New York, Newark, Chicago, Detroit, Los Angeles, etc., etc...###

AUTHOR'S NOTE—JULY, 2003—What can I add to this piece? Nothing. Except for updating the numbers, the entire piece stands on its own with complete clarity.

◆   ◆   ◆

AGREE TO DISAGREE

A favorite dicho (saying) of my octogenarian grandfather before he died a couple of years ago was: "Put ten Mexicans into a room and you'll have 11 opinions."

Never has this been clearer to me than in an interview with a small print shop owner I do business with.

Since he founded the Chicano Rights Committee in 1970, Herman Baca has become a familiar face on Southern California television with his numerous complaints against police and federal agencies.

It is not unusual to see Herman Baca quoted on the front pages of Mexico City's influential newspaper Excelsior.

"What problems do we face as Mexican Americans?" I asked.

"We don't know who we are," Herman replied.

"Who are we?"

"Before the Chicano Movement, where I grew up in New Mexico, there were people who called themselves Hispanos, Hispanics, Mexican Americans, Mexicans or Latinos. No one knew exactly what they were.

"The birth of the Chicano Movement in the 1960's, the Chicano Consciousness, gave us identity. It gave us a philosophy."

"A philosophy?"

"Yes. A philosophy based on the premise: This land (the Southwest) is our land, it was stolen from us by the Americans. All of our problems started with the piece of paper that set the theft in concrete, the Treaty of Guadalupe (1848)."

"Herman, do you really believe that today's 40% school drop-out rate of our people is caused by the Treaty of Guadalupe Hidalgo?"

"All our problems stem from the Treaty."

"Do you really believe that 25% of our people, those below the poverty line, can blame their status on the treaty?"

"Yes. The treaty disenfranchised and emasculated our people."

"How?"

"Our people have no economic power because they're not allowed to participate in this so called 'Free Market'.

"We don't have political power because we're gerrymandered and pushed around so white Democrat incumbents can get re-elected every two years at our expense.

"20% of the country's employers admit to discriminating against our people on job interviews and hiring, and no one does anything about it.

"The Migra, Immigration, kicks in doors and busts everyone with Brown skin in sight, even if their American, and deports them faster than you can say Enchilada.

"Sometimes, I'm ashamed to be an American. That's why I call myself a Chicano."

"How, Herman, do you account for 75% of our people living above the poverty line? How do you account for more than half of us owning our own homes? How do you account for the 50% increase in those of us making over $50,000 in the last few years? How do you account for a doubling and tripling of Hispanic business owners, like yourself, in the Eighties?

"How, Herman, how?'

"Bones. They throw bones to us."

"How do you explain that we have more officeholders than ever before and, in fact, increased another 5% in 1990?"

"Bones. They make it very difficult for us to register to vote, so they can keep us down."

"Difficult? Herman, to register, all you need to do is fill out a postcard, sign it and mail it in to the Registrar's office. You don't even need a stamp! Herman, you don't even have to prove you're a citizen!"

"That's too difficult. We should have registration at the polls on election day."

"Herman, as easy as it is to register today, less than 30% of our people bother to register. Isn't apathy the real problem?"

"Our people don't register because it doesn't do any good. What votes we cast are diluted by the establishment with at-large elections and with gerrymandering.

"They want us powerless and poor, the Reagans and Bushs."

"Herman, you're as wrong as you can be. I disagree with almost everything you've said.

"I don't even call myself a Chicano, I'm a Mexican American, or an American of Mexican descent. I don't think the Migra or Border Patrolmen are all jackbooted fascists. And, Herman, if 20% of businessmen admit to discriminating against us, doesn't that mean 80% don't?

"Herman, about the only thing we agree on is that the Americans stole this land from us. It was President Polk who secretly ordered American troops onto disputed Mexican territory with instructions to draw a Mexican attack.

"Congress was tricked into declaring war on Mexico by President Polk, so he could annex territory for his slave-owning friends."

"See, we agree on something", Herman triumphantly stated.

As my grandfather said, put 10 Mexicans into a room and you'll have 11 opinions. But, he also used to say, first, you have to get 10 Mexicans to agree to enter the same room." ###

OF SILVER EAGLES AND COVEYS OF QUAIL

There are 50th anniversaries being observed throughout the United States, the South Pacific, Asia and Europe this year. I saw hotel signs the other day with: "12th Defense Battalion, 50th Anniversary"; "5th Amphibious Tractor Battalion, 50th Anniversary". Hundreds of such reunions are taking place.

These are old men meeting to remember 50 years ago. Their memories are our history. 50 years ago evil challenged Western Civilization in World War Two. Evil lost. It lost to those old men meeting today; it lost to them when they were, as President Bush puts it, "just kids".

50 years ago, Marines landed on the beaches of Guadalcanal and engaged the previously unbeaten Japanese Imperial Army. Despite being abandoned on the beach without food, supplies and ammunition by the U.S. Navy, the Marines used Japanese equipment, ate Japanese food and turned Japanese guns against the conquerors of "The Greater Asia Co-Prosperity Sphere". The Marines lost three thousand men while killing 30,000 Japanese.

Commanding the U.S. Marine artillery during the fierce battle for Guadalcanal—Colonel Pedro Del Valle.

One wonders if a very young Pedro Del Valle is one of the men mentioned in "Semper Fidelis: The History of the United States Marine Corps" by Ohio State University Professor Allan Millett.

Describing the multi-year military intervention by the Marines in the Dominican Republic, Prof. Millett writes that during 1919, "Operating in the eastern area was a patrol of Mexican and Puerto Rican (U.S.) Marines…; this group, disguised as bandits, was the terror of Seibo province."

50 years ago a San Antonio teenager named Cleto Rodriguez joined the U.S. Army. A couple of years later, he was sent with a buddy to check out a railroad junction on the outskirts of the Philippines capital, Manila. Cleto and his friend held off a fierce Japanese attack and killed dozens of the enemy. His friend was killed. Cleto Rodriguez lived to return to San Antonio the second most decorated American soldier of World War Two. He died a couple of years ago of natural causes.

50 years ago, in addition to Cleto Rodriguez, Mexican boys from throughout the Southwest walked to recruiting offices and joined the fight against evil. Many, knowing that some of their fathers and uncles were the "terror" of the Dominican Republic "disguised as bandits", joined the Marines.

50 years ago, a Marine Staff Sergeant named Leon Uris took notes about his fellow Marines which he later shaped into one of the all time best sellers, "Battle Cry". One of the principal characters? "Spanish Joe", a tough and endearing Mexican boy from El Paso.

Mexican American boys would make history fighting all over the world, 50 years ago. They would fight as privates and colonels. They would win 30 medals of honor, thousands of silver and bronze stars and Navy Crosses for bravery. They would earn the respect not only of their enemies, the Germans and the Japanese, but of the Army, Navy and Marines. They, I repeat, won 30 medals of honor and thousands of silver and bronze stars, and Navy Crosses.

Spanish surnames are engraved on thousands of crosses in national cemeteries from Arlington to Manila, from Normandy to San Diego's Ft. Rosecrans. And, when a city in Texas refused to bury a Mexican boy who died fighting Germans, the true battle was joined, here in America. Even President Harry Truman, who called Blacks, Niggers, and Jews Kikes, who wouldn't have known a Mexican if he tripped on one, joined thousands of Mexican fathers, mothers and brothers and sisters in fighting for the right to bury our own warriors in our American cemeteries.

All this happened or started to happen 50 years ago. And though my sensibilities towards these events are particularly acute, a feature on National Public Radio (NPR) on Saturday, September 19th, jolted my sense of and appreciation of history and how men of brown skin have affected it and this country.

50 years ago, NPR told me, 400 of my cousins, Navajo Indian braves, some as young as fifteen years of age, joined the U.S. Marines and were organized into a top secret force of "Code Talkers". These men were specially trained to talk military jargon in Navajo. Why? Because no matter how many PhDs Japanese offic-

ers had from UCLA and no matter how good their English was from years in the U.S. as spies, they couldn't break the "code" that was the Navajo language.

Thousands of lives were saved by young bronze-skinned braves who talked of Silver Eagles (colonels) and coveys of quail (infantry). There's only a few of these men left and they are old. After 50 years these men are being honored with a special display unveiled last week at the Pentagon.

50 years ago the Navajos went to war against the Japanese. At their 50th reunion, each session starts with a young Navajo girl slowly and deliberately singing, acappela, a haunting rendition of the Marine Corps hymn in Navajo. It makes me proud of my Navajo cousins. ###

AUTHOR'S NOTE—JULY, 2003—The United States is fortunate to have had these men step forward to fight for the country in World War II. While no movie was ever made about Pfc. Cleto Rodriguez, or the other heroic Spanish-surnamed soldiers, Marines and Navy fighter ace Gene Valencia, one was made recently about our Navajo cousins.

That movie featured real Indians portraying the Navajo Marines. It was named "Wind Talkers." It is a fitting tribute to these fine men and people.

◆   ◆   ◆

I'M NOT ONLY A HISPANIC

Recently, a struggle for power in Spanish-speaking television surfaced publicly and was criticized by Mexican American commentators. Protesting the "Cubanization" of LA's Mexican American television station, an editorial writer from the LA TIMES suggested placing Cubans in charge was ill-advised.

The Eastern "Hispanic" media charged him with being divisive and disruptive. If they thought he was divisive and disruptive, watch this!

What is a Hispanic? This Hispanic thing troubles me because it's an artificial homogeneity promoted by Spanish-speaking splinter elements; the lazy media they've convinced to use the catch-all term and pointy-headed sociologists. This is all contrary to the cultural/ethnic interests of my people—the numerically and politically dominant Mexican Americans.

HISPANICS, according to THEM, are anyone in the Western Hemisphere who speaks Spanish, or comes from families who speak, or formerly spoke Spanish. This includes Pedro Guerrero of the St. Louis Cardinals, whose ancestors were from Black Africa; includes Zambas, part Black, part Indian people of Southern Mexico with nary a drop of Spanish blood; includes tiny Salvadoran Indians who sneak into Los Angeles in search of work; and, includes Puerto Ricans, many of whom trace their bloodlines to Spain and/or Africa.

A monolithic use of HISPANIC simply doesn't hold up. It's no more valid than the word SLAVIC to encompass those who came from Poland, Bohemia, Moravia, Serbia, Croatia or Russia. Just as there's no monolithic SLAVIC community in the U.S., with singular views or spokesmen, there's no monolithic Spanish-speaking community or spokesmen as the Anglo media would have us believe. No Cuban or Puerto Rican speaks for me.

19 million Spanish-speakers live in the U.S. Of these, there are four distinct components. 13 million are born in Mexico, or from families who came from Mexico sometime during the last FOUR HUNDRED YEARS(!). The next largest groups are 2 million from Puerto Rico, a million from Cuba and another million-and-a-half from Spain, Central and South America.

While all make contributions to the social and cultural environment, numbers dictate that Mexican-born or origin people have the largest impact on the U.S. The dog which wags the tail, so to speak. Not the Hispanic tail wagging the Mexican.

MEXICAN AMERICANS are those specifically born in the United States of families who came originally from Mexico; or those born in Mexico who choose to live here. CHICANOS: A 1960's term of hazy origin applied by some Mexicans to themselves and used by the media, a stylebook term, if you will.

Of these terms, which should one use in referring to the 13 million of us whose origin, directly or indirectly, is Mexico—try MEXICAN AMERICAN. Chicano is considered by most of us demeaning and insulting, the equivalent of CRACKER, when one speaks of blonde, blue-eyed folks from Jimmy Carterland. Also, consider: All Chicanos are Mexican American, but not all Mexican Americans are Chicanos.

Cuban-Americans are just that; Puerto Ricans, just that; Central Americans, just that. Fine, let them call themselves Hispanics.

Spanish, the Church and baseball are about the only common experiences we "Hispanics" share. We come in all sizes, skin, eye and hair colors, names, occupations, neighborhoods, cities and states.

But, Mexican Americans live, work and vote in every single American state, unlike Cubans, Puerto Ricans and Central Americans who concentrate in Eastern cities and Los Angeles. If, then, the only national presence of Spanish-speaking is Mexican American, why refer to us as Hispanics? Call them Hispanics, if they wish, but don't lump me in with them.

The Census Bureau projects Mexican Americans, not Cubans, not Puerto Ricans, not Central Americans, will outnumber the Black population in a couple of decades. Mexican Americans, not Hispanics.

If you're still confused, try this litmus test. Hispanics are like Peter Nunez, former United States Attorney in San Diego. Pennsylvania born of Spanish immigrant parents, he wrote in the WASHINGTON TIMES on a proposed ditch between the United States and Mexico. The proposed ditch annoys Mexico. Nunez comments "if Mexico doesn't like it (the ditch), too bad".

Nunez, of course, hasn't heard that the Drug Enforcement Administration states: "The ditch won't work!" Or, that, we need Mexico more than it needs us in the war against drugs. Or, that more than 400 Mexican cops have died at the hands of drug smugglers, while less than 100 U.S. cops have so died.

Remember, Mexicans don't grow cocaine; they don't sell it on U.S. streets; they don't fly airplanes full of the stuff up from South America, where Hispanics grow it. And, any expert will tell you only 30% of U.S. drugs come across the Mexican border. Where does the rest cross?

Like Nunez, "Hispanics" have little sensitivity towards Mexico, usually feel culturally superior to Mexicans and try to sound like their little countries (Guatemala, El Salvador, Cuba and Puerto Rico) are important.

They think they're more important than 90 million people in Mexico, America's fifth largest trading partner; than Mexicans, when Americans and they have fought side by side against foreign invaders a hundred years ago and as recently as World War Two, when Mexico sent combat pilots to the Pacific. No other "Hispanic" country did so.

No, to Mr. Nunez and all other "Hispanics", to all who lack sensitivity towards Mexico, I don't want to be called a Hispanic. I don't eat Hispanic food, I eat Mexican food; I wasn't born in Hispanicland, I was born in Mexico; I don't listen to Hispanic music, nor dance Hispanic dances, I listen to Mexican mariachi music and dance Mexican dances.

No. And, if that's divisive, then make the most of it. ###

AUTHOR'S NOTE—JULY, 2003—The argument continues to this day and will for some time to come. But, with the election of George W, Bush, more attention has been paid to Cubans (Florida) and Mexican Americans (California, Arizona, New Mexico, Texas, Iowa, Wisconsin and Oregon) than the other "Hispanics" for the simple reason that their votes truly count in states that are critical to success at the polls.

As the decade of the 90s wore on, two words rose in prominence in describing these people of the Spanish-speaking community: Hispanic and Latino. Latino is used by more blue-collar types and some newspapers, but Hispanic has become larger in prominence than all other terms. It is one completely understood by all, except the Chicano types who don't count, or by white racists who prefer the term, "mud people."

PART III

Chapter introduction—The thrust of this book and its component essays is that of the fast-growing Hispanic/Latino population, the country must know that Cubans, Puerto Ricans, Dominicans and South and Central Americans among that population are, in total, a distinct minority within the group.

The vast majority, almost two of three Hispanic/Latinos in the United States are of Mexican-origin, either actually born in Mexico, or descended from people born in Mexico. Thus, there are two groups within the Mexican-origin community: Those born in Mexico, and, those born in the United States. Those born in Mexico are Mexicans until they become American citizens; those born in the United States are Americans of Mexican descent, or better yet, Mexican (as an adjective) American (as the noun).

There are some among us who object to the words Mexican American because they don't like labels such as "hyphenated" Americans. These, of course, are the same people who call our society a "color blind" when Blacks are still the last hired and first fired, when only 3% of Fortune 500 Executives are Black and while the District of Columbia schools—full of Black children, of course, are churning out little kids that can't read or write who can only look to futures in prison and poverty, thanks to those who maintain we have a "color blind" society.

In the simple and final analysis, perhaps too simple for the feeble-minded "hyphenated American" critics, We need to be called Mexican Americans so that the feeble minded can tell us from Mexicans, of whom there are over 100-million just minutes south of where this is being written.

7

Chapter introduction—Education, intelligence and accomplishment are three areas in which the American media has badly covered the Hispanic population. There seems to be nothing but negative stories Here are both negative and positive essays about an issue that is as important to Hispanics as any issue there is.

WHO GRADUATES?

For every 10 Mexican Americans who enter the 9th grade, four will not graduate from high school, we are told. Exactly who these people are, or why they drop-out is not related to us because truth does not always fit the scheme of ethnic politics portrayed to us by special interests.

Mexican Americans mostly (60%) live in California, where, surprise, we graduate in more or less the same percentage as everyone else. In other states, however, drop-out rates among Mexican Americans have reached epidemic proportions. This California vs. Everywhere situation is not new.

Three decades ago, California's Mexican Americans earned twice what Mexican Americans did in Texas, and, in fact, annually made within a $100 of white, Anglo Texans. In San Diego, for example, we made 84% of what Anglos made in California, while making 100% more than our cousins in Texas. The reason then was, of course, education. It is today. We still make more.

There are as many theories why Mexican Americans drop-out as there are drop-outs. The most popular and self-pitying is that Mexican Americans are poor, thus they can't afford to go to school; that they need jobs at sixteen to help out their poor families. Thus, it is whined, they're unable to graduate.

This is valid in some cases, but doesn't explain such huge drop-out numbers, as the number of us in poverty is less than 25%. Besides, most immigrant groups have come to America in the past, poor and uneducated. The Irish, the Italians, the Japanese, the Polish, the Russians, the Chinese, they've all come poor and they've done well. In fact, Polish, Japanese, and Chinese Americans rank one, two and three in per capita income, ahead of Americans of English or German descent.

Not unlike other immigrant groups, children of Mexicans born in the U.S. do stay in school, and do graduate, in contrast to those whose parents were born in Mexico.

Some believe that Mexican American children are discriminated against by a conspiratorial Anglo education establishment to keep them uneducated and available for menial jobs. Our racist cousins believe Mexicans are too stupid, so why spend the time and money to try and educate people who can't learn.

To racists, I recommend they read (if they can read) Octavio Paz or Carlos Fuentes. Or, letters between President Benito Juarez and 25 year-old Matias Romero, his personal representative to President Abraham Lincoln during the 1860's. If there's any doubt, let them speak to United States Secretary of Education Lauro Cavazos or Interior Secretary Manuel Lujan, or me.

Here's one theory, my own. Some of today's Mexican American children have a mindset, a mindset which, along with our skin color, has been passed down from our Indian forefathers for thousands of years. Anyone can see that most of the drop-outs have brown skin, a color that is a badge of honor and dignity to most, as well as a life sentence for some of us to perpetual ignorance and poverty. Regardless of skin color, no education means peonage, period.

Years ago, I led my dehydrated Marine company to shelter before they were rendered dysfunctional by 120-degree heat and the desert's searing sun. Unlike my fellow Marines, I reveled in the heat, in the desert. I was home.

Asked how I managed so well in the desert, "Colonel", I laughingly responded, "Brown skin...I'm the perfect desert machine. Only a camel or an Apache is better equipped for the desert than we Mexicans with Indian blood."

I still feel that way. As in all equations, however, there is a minus for every plus, a negative for every positive. The drop-out problem is not caused by brown skin itself, but rather by attitudes, beliefs and conditioning of the Indian side of our brains; baggage we've carried since the dawn of time.

Our other side, the Spanish, destroyed Indian civilization, religion and culture during and after Mexico's conquest, but they did not destroy a special Indian mindset developed through several thousands of years. In fact, they nurtured it to enslave Mexico's Indians, who always outnumbered the white Spaniards.

The special mind-set began, appropriately enough in the beginning. From the dawn of time, Mexican Indians were all warlike and trembled in fear, subservience and humility before successful warriors. Nomadic, the tribes followed water sources and herd animals. Because of constant movement, a sense of material property never developed among rank and file Indians. They were just part of the earth, as was everything.

Living, hunting, ever-present war, everything was communal and collective; everyone had a function within the tribe. It was more than teamwork, however. There was no such thing as an individual. I repeat, there was no such thing as an individual. An individual's existence was measured by his contribution to the whole. In a word, total conformity. In fact, the words I and me barely existed in the languages of Indian Mexico, and were not used by common Indians.

Total conformity. No deviation was allowed by the clan/tribe. Peer pressure was so intense, deviates were cast out of the clan/tribe to die. If you didn't produce for the group, if you didn't do as the group commanded, you ceased to socially exist. Without the group's protection, you were dead.

Nature provided the Indian with everything needed to survive, including a natural curiosity about the world. As with all humans, there was an instinctive desire to know about their environment. This led to observation of the sun, moon and seasons, which led to development of the Aztec Calendar.

This feat, coupled with the development of corn (maize) and organized agriculture, led the Mexican Indian out of nomadic rudimentary food gathering and hunting to a more complex society, as complex as any in the world.

Indian Mexico, a two-tiered totally conformist society, the led and the leaders. A mass of conformist followers, dictated to and led by a tiny few.###

AUTHOR'S NOTE—JULY, 2003—No one can truly explain why Hispanics have the drop-out rate they do. It doesn't seem to be improving, either.

Two possible explanations come to mind: One, most such children are urban, many of them less than privileged and many from families that are recent immigrants; secondly, urban school teachers are lousy, so lousy they should be prosecuted for endangering children.

These two explanations lead to a collective wish by California Hispanics, if not all Hispanics in the country, to cast aside the public school system as we know it and to substitute some form of vouchers to enable urban, inner-city children to be taught to read and write by real teachers, not union shop stewards and rank and file union members more concerned about pay for no results than for competency.

◆   ◆   ◆

MEXICAN AMERICAN SCHOOL DROP-OUTS: THE WHY

Mexican American youths have high drop-out rates from school in many areas of the country, ranging from 11% in parts of California to 50% in some rural areas. Those who drop-out tend to be from families in which the parents are from Mexico who have only a few years of formal schooling themselves.

As noted in Part One of this essay, once the Mexican Indian settled into agriculture, his society changed. Corn is the American historical equal of the cultivation of wheat in the Middle East and rice in Asia. These three crops are civilization's bedrocks, joining with the use of weapons and the development of religion as civilization's fundamental precepts.

With agriculture came total dependence on rainfall and the seasons. Tribes could no longer simply migrate from waterhole to waterhole. Now sedentary, and much more populous, they looked to the sky and the elements for the elixir that produced bountiful corn crops, rainfall. Unfortunately, they had no control over the elements.

A lack of rain, too much wind, a hurricane, lightening-caused fires, too much rain and floods were some of the natural disasters these people faced. Unable to explain, or predict disasters, a religion based on disaster developed, which, in turn, led to priests and shamans who specialized in defining and trying to tame disasters.

As many disasters are seasonal, they refined a calendar allowing them to "scientifically" advise when corn should be planted. The entire civilization depended on bountiful corn crops. No corn meant starvation.

In thousands of years of subservience to more aggressive people; in the complete absence of individualism; in not having a concept of material property; in an elite group with knowledge and power unknown to the average person, i.e., the priests defining of disasters and their ability to tell people when to plant; and, in the ultimate fatalism expressed with the shrug, lie the seeds of our Mexican American school drop-out problem today.

We've seen how up to 40%, hundreds of thousands, of our children are dropping out of school, how lack of education means perpetual poverty and how better educated Mexican Americans make more money (California vs. Everywhere else), thus live better, and we've seen how children from families where the parents were born in the United States stay in school, while those from parents born in Mexico drop-out. We are pursuing a theory that many of these children are dropping out because of an Indian mindset developed thousands of years ago.

First, any casual observation of Mexican American school drop-outs shows that most have darker skin than those who stay in school.

For many of the dark-skinned, as it has been for thousands of years, there still are no individuals. Extended families, neighborhoods mean more than individuals. When the Mexican Indian civilization reached its peak, it consisted of many independent city-states, each with its own set of rulers or a single dictator. Loyalty was demanded and expected of each city-state resident over and above that to his family.

Most Indians were not only of the same racial stock, they were of the same tribes in most cases, speaking the same Nahua language, yet they constantly warred on each other over territory, tribute, people to sacrifice to the Gods and as important as anything, women. New women were constantly captured and brought into the tribe, to, believe it or not, replenish the gene pool.

Race and tribe aside, the city-state (Neighborhood) was all important. Its boundaries were clearly marked (Graffiti) and pity the poor straggler who wandered into your city-state without permission.

Lack of, and rejection of individualism is manifested today by many among the Mexican American community. How? Generally the drop-out boys dress, walk and talk identically; i.e., heavy woolen shirts, baggy pants, baseball hats pulled tightly down around the ears and white t-shirts and/or tank tops. Many wear their hair in the same style. Many belong to territorial, clannish "gangs", what the ancients would call, clans. Most have home-applied tattoos to their hands and arms. They are interchangeable clones, regardless of city.

Not to be outdone, Mexican American girl drop-outs dress alike, wear their hair the same and wear the same excessive make-up. Like the boys, they're interchangeable clones, also, regardless of city.

Almost without fail, a practiced observer can point out future drop-outs the first day of 9th grade with almost 100% accuracy. It's like picking out illegal Mexican aliens, if you know what to look for, its easy. We even have a name for these drop-out types, its "CHOLOS" or "CHOLAS", meaning half-civilized boys or girls.

Many make themselves subservient to those perceived as being stronger, just as the less warlike ancients did to warrior tribes. As a rule, they look at a car as the epitomy of property ownership, while the concept of owning land is foreign to most drop-outs, as it was to Indian Mexico. Paying rent is a way of life, a form of tribute not unlike that paid by the ancients to their elite.

And, lastly, the main ingredient of drop-out mindset, Fatalism, Indian fatalism. This trait comes from fear of natural disasters. Very simply, the Indian couldn't define, much less control the elements, so he shrugged and accepted them and their disastrous consequences as his fate.

As priests developed, the Indian relinquished to them the worry and fear of disasters. In time, priests developed a hereditary power elite which directed every aspect of Indian life. Everyone obeyed them; the priests were the only ones capable of, or had the time for, thought, scholarship, architecture, and leadership in the Indian community. Ancient Mexico was a theocracy, not unlike today's Islamic Republic, Iran. ###

MEXICAN AMERICAN SCHOOL DROP-OUTS: THE WHY II

Ancient Mexico was a theocracy, not unlike today's Islamic Republic, Iran. Led by a religious fanatics, Indian Mexico's society resembled a pyramid with millions on the bottom serving, feeding and paying tribute to an elite.

People planted crops when the priests told them; built great buildings, structures and cities when and where the priests told them; went to war when the priests told them; and sacrificed other people to Gods the priests told them existed (the Dung God, for example). When the priests failed in war, the Indian quietly paid tribute and fealty to whomever demanded it.

There were only two classes of Indians: A small elite with knowledge and its power; and, the masses who forfeited the power of knowledge to carry on ordinary lives, to endure, to get by. This system failed the Indians in a far less complex 1519 when the Spanish arrived. It is failing now.

Today's Mexican American school drop-outs belong to the latter group; a group developed thousands of years ago by our Indian forefathers, a group just trying to get by.

The drop-outs today convince themselves they need to work, thus have no time for study. They convince themselves there are others to do the thinking necessary to survive in our technological world. They don't participate, nor want to, in the community for the community good. They only want to impress their friends with flashy cars, low-ride up and down city streets built and paid for by others. Others will worry about the Russians, or where the next freeway construction dollar will come from, or who will build a new sewer system or school. Others always have.

They forfeit the power of knowledge because, they say, school is for others. Or, they say, they can't afford free schooling. Or, they say, teachers pick on them because they're Mexican.

To be part of the "gang", they forfeit their individualism to others, to those who finish school, the new "priests", the new "elite", the college graduates; the others.

Is there an answer to this disaster? Yes. The answer lies in the adversity of the desert, I think. Victor Alba wrote in The Mexicans, The Making of a Nation, "...in the deserts of Chihuahua, where hamlets lie far apart and only two small towns break the 200-mile expanse between Chihuahua (City) and the American Border...History tells us that during the Revolution (1910), the ragged, barefoot followers of Pancho Villa ranged those featureless plains under the broiling sun, mounted on worn-out horses loaded with weapons and booty, slept through the freezing nights—yet they had the stamina left to...fight." And, I might add, to win.

Compare, if you will, today's brown-skinned drop-outs and these brown-skinned men. These men were individuals. They were not communal peer-pressured people; they believed in owning land; they did not forfeit direction of their lives to an elite, to others. These men controlled their own destiny.

They took care of their families, then contributed to the nation, not their neighborhood. In many cases they made the ultimate sacrifice for nationhood. Only an idiot would die for his neighborhood. Most of these men couldn't read or write. But, they knew something our drop-outs don't know. They knew the ultimate freedom was to control one's destiny.

In his Nobel Prize acceptance speech, author William Faulkner stated, "Man shall not only endure, he shall prevail." I believe that. So did the desert soldiers of Villa.

School drop-outs don't, they just get by.

As certain as the sun rising tomorrow, critics screaming like banshees will call, write and otherwise convey among themselves, to me and to any media who will listen, that I have blasphemed my own people, that I have accused the victims, the drop-outs, of being guilty of victimizing themselves.

It will be said that I'm too hard on people. Over and over, we hear that drop-outs occur because Ronald Reagan "gutted" the Department of Education, because the "problem" needs more Federal funds. It will be said, ad naseum, that the problem is everyone's fault except the drop-out's. It will be said our children are too poor to go to school, that they need to work.

Baloney.

More money is spent today per child in America for education than Mexican Americans earned in Texas working a whole year in 1960. Teachers are earning more than ever. Granted, education, as reflected by standardized college entrance examinations, isn't as effective as it was thirty years ago. And, granted teachers seem more occupied with "working conditions' and union membership than with teaching children.

Despite the inherent defects of our educational system, not one expert maintains our children are not educatable. There are some problems in children from all-Spanish speaking households, true, especially in elementary grades. By the seventh grade, however, these problems pretty much disappear and are not noticeable at the high school level by researchers.

At the college level, a figure of 4% jumps out of almost every study conducted of various disciplines. 4% of American engineering students, for example, are "Hispanic"; 4% of Master's candidates in Business are "Hispanic"; 4% of U. of California, Berkeley, students are Mexican American.

I can also report a striking figure of 45 two and four year colleges and universities in Arizona, California, Colorado, Illinois, New Mexico and Texas with Mexican American enrollments of 25%, upwards to 87%. With these figures, questions arise about only 4% of UC Berkeley's enrollment being Mexican American.

This is a valid question, a very valid question, which we'll examine next time in Part Four. ###

MEXICAN AMERICAN SCHOOL DROP-OUTS: THE WHY III

Let's examine some numbers. At prestigious universities like UC Berkeley, only the cream of high school graduates are chosen for their limited freshman space. In fact, by a 30-year-old state law, passed by the White, Anglo Establishment, UC takes only the top 12.5% freshman applicants, which in 1960 were safely white. UC Berkeley is 400 miles from the large Mexican American community in Southern California.

There's also, I might add, racism in admission policies at UC Berkeley and the entire University of California system. The Berkeley Chancellor recently apologized publicly for flagrant anti-Asian racism.

You see, Anglo admissions officers, frightened that Berkeley is fast becoming an all-Asian student body, simply rejected applicants because they were Asian, despite many having perfect 4.0 (all A's) records in high schools.

There are many lawsuits pending against the University of California for this admitted practice. As far as Mexican Americans are concerned, however, the law suit outcomes won't have much affect inasmuch as most who do attend college do so closer to home, in Southern California.

They tend to be commuter students; they tend to work and attend college simultaneously; they tend to be Federal Pell Grant recipients (low income) or student loan borrowers. Attending college close to home, thus, helps spread dollars better than going to school hundreds of miles away.

Every public college in Southern California has decently high Mexican American enrollments, higher probably than can be expected, considering the bad rap of not being educatable that is accepted by many in the Anglo community.

It should be noted that private schools in the area have far fewer Mexican Americans than public institutions. With tuition in excess of $7,000-a-year at San Diego's Catholic university, for example, few of us can afford applying, no matter how great the university may be, when a few miles away, one can attend a fine San Diego State University for a thousand dollars a year.

What does this all mean? The rate of college graduates in Southern California among Mexican Americans is double the national average. It means that we have a head start in solving the drop-out problem, as studies have repeatedly shown that children from bi-lingual or English speaking households who have parents who graduated from high school and attended college—will finish school and probably go on to college—just like everyone else.

So, why such a high drop out rate? There are two blames to lay. Parents of and the drop-outs themselves.

What kind of a parent allows their child, or children to drop-out of school? The kind typified in the movie STAND AND DELIVER, the story of LA teacher Jaime Escalante and his Garfield High students. Two parents come to mind in the movie, one a father, one a mother. The father owns a restaurant and pulls his daughter out of school to help at the family restaurant, then becomes incensed when her teacher comes to ask him to allow his daughter to return to school.

The mother involved needs a full court press by her pretty daughter to sign a "contract". The "contract" stipulates homework and cooperation at home for the students, allowing them to study. After much pestering, the mother signs the "contract", saying, "Boys don't like girls smarter than them."

A real life example comes to mind of my great-grandmother taking me to visit her friends when I was little. While the women sat around drinking coffee, chatting in Spanish, I played in a corner. I remember them smirkingly remarking on an eighteen year-old girl who entered college that week.

"Huh!", one lady snorted, "A lot of help she's going to be to her family". "She's going to think she's better than the rest of us!", another remarked. "Boys don't like girls smarter than them", another sneered.

All nodded assent to the criticism of the eighteen year-old girl, including the girl's mother. Imagine the pressure this girl faced at home during her college career which, I might add, she completed successfully. She became a teacher.

All Children particularly Mexican American children, must be taught they are worthwhile, very special individuals. Individuals with a capital I. They should know they are not just tiny little cogs of society. We've seen how our Indian past has perpetuated a communal mentality, a tribal peer pressure system on these children and how there's no individualism in this mentality.

Yet, millions of us manage to not join gangs, to not drop-out of school and hundreds of thousands of us go on to college despite our own doomsayers.

These people know they are worthwhile individuals and they know they need education to progress, to step out of circumstances which might not be altogether pleasant. They know they can do it, they make no excuses, even if college takes ten years to complete, part-time.

In addition to teaching individualism to our children, we must teach them respect, desire and a hunger for private property. Private property is the difference between being peasants with no future and a people with one.

Peer pressure in dress, speech patterns and grooming must be overcome, or our children will allow their lives to be ruled by others, just as the Indians did. We must make sure they learn English and use it properly. Each must be taught they are capable of doing anything, regardless of skin color. Light brown, dark brown, medium brown skin, matters not.

For an individual, an educated accomplished individual, skin color doesn't matter as long as you produce and exert control of your environment and destiny. In other words, there's no reason one of our little boys or girls can't grow up to be President. To do so, they need to adapt to modern America, be smart, tough and educated, truly educated. Is that that hard to do? ###

EDUCATION: A VINTAGE PROBLEM

Months ago, I challenged Hispanics in general, Mexican Americans, specifically, to face the disastrous reality of as many as 50% of our children dropping out of school before graduation. I suggested an operative statement from comic strip Pogo, "We have seen the enemy and it is us.", as it applies to those among us who point fingers in all directions, at schools, at teachers, at administrators, at poverty, et. al., but not at those with whom the fault specifically lies—the parents, the fathers and mothers of the drop-outs.

The article resulted in attacks on my "insensitivity" towards poverty conditions which, according to my critics, cause the massive drop-outs. BALONEY!

Little, if any, linkage exists between poverty and schooling. Moreover, only 25% of us live in poverty, thus, how do we account for a 50% drop-out rate? Current poverty, notwithstanding, the rate of poverty among Mexican Americans has declined by 28.5% since 1960, yet the drop-out rate stubbornly clings to 50%. Poverty is a handy excuse for shortsighted handout artists, but is not provable, nor quantifiable in its affect on drop-outs and academic achievement, or lack of it.

For example, Polish Americans are number one in per capita family income; Japanese and Chinese Americans, numbers two and three. Certainly, no one claims these people (most of whom arrived in the past 100 years) arrived with dollar-stuffed pockets, waving master's, legal, medical and doctorate degrees. And, how does one explain a statement by the late Chairman of the United States Civil Rights Commission, Clarence Pendleton, regarding the fact that every single Black judge in New York City, every single one, at every level, local, state and Federal, was of poor West Indian background.

Poverty, therefore, is no rationalization for sub-standard academic achievement. It hasn't stopped any other group from succeeding in the U.S.A., particularly the Japanese who lost most of their property while locked up in internment camps during World War II, just 45 years ago. So why us? Why are we Mexican Americans different, or are we?

Twenty years ago, a group of UCLA professors studied Mexican American students in Los Angeles and reached some conclusions which are more valid today than then.

Professors Gordon, Schwartz, Wenkart and Nasatir concluded:

1. The most consistent and important influence on school attainment is family educational level and family aspirations for their children's education.

2. Ethnic composition of elementary and middle schools substantially affects performance of Mexican American students, but has no effect at the senior high level.

3. The exclusive use of English as home language contributes consistently and positively for Mexican American students at all levels.

4. Family economic level contributes less to school performance of Mexican Americans than does family educational level.

Other interesting facets of Mex-Americana: Dr. Leo Estrada (UCLA) says of 21 Mexican American PhD's who met recently, 20 were Protestant. Concurrently, 65 Spanish-speaking medical doctors, mostly Mexican American, organized an association in San Diego. Of the 65, most are Roman Catholic. Conclusion: Religion has no bearing on academic achievement.

So why are we so deficient in academic achievement; why do so many of us drop-out of school? Poverty and religion can't be blamed. Teachers and administrators can't be blamed, either, as they want more kids in school because it means more jobs, more money. Segregated demographics have some bearing, true, but not at the high school level. Do we lack in basic intelligence; can we not learn?

Remember the new association of 65 Spanish-speaking doctors in San Diego? Forty years ago, there were none. Today, there are half-a-dozen Mexican American judges and scores of Mexican American attorneys in San Diego—forty years ago, there were none. Ipso facto, we can learn, we can learn like anyone else. Why, then, such a drop-out rate?

A teacher in East L.A., Jaime Escalante, has half the answer—GANAS (gah-nahs, desire), or lack, thereof. As portrayed in the movie, "Stand and Deliver", he proved that poverty-saddled East L.A. pachuco (pah-choo-koh, punk) students with giant doses of ganas (desire) can accomplish anything academically. Anything. All it takes is desire and hard work.

But, that's only half the answer, half the equation. The other: Tough, no-nonsense parents, or lack, thereof. Drop-outs are their responsibility, not society's, not mine, not yours. We only pick up the tab. Unfortunately, there's no punishment for the criminal act of allowing a child to drop out of school. Yes, a criminal act, an act of child abuse on par with sexual or physical abuse. Our legislatures should make it a criminal offense for a parent to allow a child to quit school. Period!

Unless we cut the Mexican American drop-out rate, millions of us will be doomed to social and economic poverty and, worse, to be a permanent underclass; an underclass existing on government hand-outs and welfare checks, with no hope of climbing higher, ever.

An underclass "living" a life without dignity, without pride, without hope, without future—a life of Whine, not champagne. ###

"EVERYONE TELLS US"

Mexican American kids are stupid, lazy, drug-abusing school and societal drop-outs. We know this because everyone tells us so. Anglo newspapers and Anglo television newscasters tell us every day.

Mexican American kids can't learn anything especially when they attend poor, under-equipped, crowded inner city schools. Mexican American kids can't succeed in school because they are poor and the Anglo community hates them so much that they deprive the kids of good, well equipped schools. So Mexican American radical activists tell us.

Everyone tells us these things, except the Massachusetts Institute of Technology, or, as it's better known, MIT. For, you see, MIT, the premier American university in science and physics, has just admitted Alicia Ayala, 18; David Villareal, 18; Enrique Arzaga, 17; Liliana Ramirez, 17; and, Jesus Martinez, 16.

Count them. Five, yes, five Mexican Americans all from one of the poorest high schools in the USA. Count them, five, yes, five Mexican Americans from Ysleta High School in El Paso, Texas. Most of Ysleta's students are Mexican American and most are poor, to boot.

Ysleta High hasn't enough computers and scientific equipment for its students to use, according to Principal Roger Parks. Yet, these five students have accomplished what no other group from any other school in US history has ever done. Never, ac cording to MIT's Joe Jasso, assistant director of admissions, have five students from a general attendance (public) high school ever been admitted at one time.

Before critics scream affirmative action, let us lay that red herring to rest. Affirmative action had nothing to do with this mass admission of five poor El Paso kids to MIT. According to Jasso, 7,000 prospective freshman apply each year, of which 1,000 are admitted, with only 600 accepting.

In other words, kids who apply to MIT are special to begin with. These five kids are even more special than the extraordinary kids who normally apply for admission.

"We are part of a community that has drugs, violence and gangs", says Ysleta High's Principal Parks.

"We have our share of students who scorn intellectual achievement," he continues, "Our drop-out rate is as high as any in this area."

Nevertheless, Ysleta High has, what he calls, "personality, (and) a soul. The school is more than this ratty building." To that, we can say amen.

Who are these kids? Ayala is valedictorian of the class of '92 and Villareal is salutatorian. Liliana Ramirez could not speak English two years ago, and her parents still don't, though they attend all school functions accompanied by a translator.

The 16-year-old baby of the class, Jesus Martinez, skipped two grades early on and works part-time as a janitor. His father died eight years ago, so he works to help his mother. When Ysleta High held a reception honoring these kids, he had to work until 2:00 a.m. to make up the time he spent being honored.

Will these kids succeed in life? Do they make their school and community proud? Do they make their people proud? Do they?

They make me proud. And, I know they will succeed. I only wish we could bottle their success formula for the millions of other poor kids attending "ratty" high schools.

What is their success formula? Caring, though poor and sometimes immigrant, non-English speaking parents, who, according to Ysleta High teacher Paul Cain, "push them to become achievers". Caring teachers like Cain and principals like Parks and a school with "soul" round out the formula.

But, some will say, these five kids are a flash in the pan. Not so, says Principal Parks. "Our valedictorian last year, an immigrant, went to Harvard, and the salutatorian went to MIT."

Let the record show, that each of these kids, as well as other Ysleta High grads who've attended Harvard, Amherst, Vassar and Yale is a Mexican American.

Remember this when you hear about the next drive-by shooting in East LA, or Southeast San Diego, or Any Pueblo, USA, where Mexican Americans live. Remember this when some Mexican American activist pleads poverty as an excuse or reason for school drop-outs. Remember this when the declare there are no jobs in the community for those who wish to better themselves.

Remember Jesus Martinez, 16-years-old, who attends school full-time and works into the night as a janitor so he can attend MIT and help his mother at the same time.

Remember these kids. Or, as teacher Cain states, "You can't help but fall in love with them…They are winners. When they wake up in the morning, they are winners." ###

THE BELL CURVE BALL HITS THE GROUND

Uh, huh! Oh, oh! Colored people (Negroes, African Americans, Blacks) aren't as smart as white people. Everybody knows that. At least most white persons secretly know that. There's proof, you know. You can look it up.

Yes, Charles Murray and the late Harvard professor of psychobabble, the recently deceased Richard Herrnstein, just published a book, THE BELL CURVE, ,which flatly concludes that Blacks are intellectually inferior to whites who are intellectually inferior to Asians. Luckily for me and my fellow "Hispanics"-"Latinos"-"Mexican Americans"-"Mexicans," Murray and Herrnstein haven't discovered us. I mean they obviously would find us inferior because some of us don't speak English well enough to successfully handle intelligence tests in turn ,of the century English designed by white pyschobabblists to measure what is obvious to anyone with eyes, ears, and a brain—intelligence.

Thank God Murray and Herrnstein weren't around when 5,000 students in San Diego and Miami were tested for intelligence by two professors who were interested in how monolingual and bi-lingual students do against each other.

They found that bi-lingual students did better than students who speak one language and that English speakers did better than students who speak mostly Spanish at home. Surprise.

At the same time the San Diego schools (one of the largest systems in the country) had a difficult time explaining why the proportion of Spanish-speaking and Limited English Proficiency (LEP) students in the Honors-gifted program was far below their percentage of the student body.

The question was how could there be less than 10% of the Gifted program minority when the Minority percentage of the student body is over 50%. The answer lay with the qualification tests for the program.

The traditional tests were heavily weighted towards English-language verbal skills, thus precluding those who spoke much Spanish or Black English. Monolingual middle-class white kids simply ran off with the test scores, thus claiming the vast majority of gifted slots in the special programs.

Murray and Herrnstein would have been proud of the "superior" white students because they would have validated their theories of whites being superior to Blacks and Hispanics. They would have been wrong. Very, very, wrong.

What happened is that the tests were changed to non-verbal tests, the kind one takes in the military to select potential pilots. Using squares, triangles, rectangles, circles and myriad patterns and, of course, numbers, tests were devised to measure logical thinking, ability to reason and other brain chores that are stimulated by sight. Guess what?

The proportion of minority students in the gifted program exploded and now more or less equates to the over-all enrollment in the city schools. What a surprise.

Now, back to Murray and Herrnstein. Are Blacks less intelligent that whites in America? They say yes and its important; I say maybe, but so what? IQ scores are just that, IQ scores. Intelligence, however, is far more important. I am not alone.

"Murray and Herrnstein," Newsweek Magazine writes, "say the evidence of black-white IQ gap is overwhelming. They think the difference helps explain why many blacks seem destined to remain mired in poverty, and they insist that whites and blacks alike must face up to the reality of black intellectual disadvantage."

Newsweek concludes that, "A close reading of the THE BELL CURVE, however, suggests they may be contradicting themselves."

The New York Times calls the book a "flame-throwing treatise on race, class and intelligence…", and calls the Murray-Herrnstein theory "a grisly thesis." It further notes that "The notion that one group could be genetically superior to another has a long and sordid history in this country and abroad."

"Similar arguments led to the rise of the "eugenics movement" in the United States and Europe during the 1920's and '30s. Eugenicists favored policies to encourage selective breeding by desirable population groups: Nazi Germany, with its explicitly racist ideology was the highpoint of the movement," Newsweek writes.

How can anyone expect an entire race to be equal in test scores on tests written by white for whites when the American black was held in slavery and forbidden to read, write and acculturate for three hundred and fifty years?

Let me put it into terms even Murray and the late Professor Herrnstein can understand. How can we expect an entire race to have equal IQ's as those who kept them down, and repressed them educationally until just 25 years ago?

How? ###

AUTHOR'S NOTE—JULY, 2003—The Bell Curve was financed by those who still believe in "eugenics," that is, the purification of the white race, the superior race. Specifically, it was financed by people associated with the Pioneer Fund. That Fund was, according to IRS filings organized by Harry Laughlin, who also founded the American Nazi party in the 1930s.

Recent Pioneer Fund research is what the relationship between Black male penis size and Black crime rates.

No responsible universities or colleges accept research grants from the Pioneer Fund.

The Fund also contributed the majority of the founding funds for the Federation of Americans for Immigration Reform (FAIR) the anti-immigrant organization founded by Dr. John Tanton. He was called a bigot by conservative Linda Chavez when she resigned as the President of U.S. English, another bigoted group founded by Tanton.

The Bell Curve was and is silly. Its authors dumb and dumber. Its financiers bigoted and racist.

◆　　◆　　◆

HISPANICS CAN'T FINISH SCHOOL

Hispanics don't finish school. Many don't attend college and those who do, don't finish. We are told this every day by "experts" who conduct surveys and studies.

Most studies are done by education professionals in Washington D.C., by people such as Rafael Valdivieso of the Hispanic Policy Development Project and Deborah Carter and Reginald Wilson, authors of "The Ninth Annual Status

Report on Minorities in Higher Education", which was commissioned by the American Council of Education of Washington.

According to the report high school graduation rates for Hispanics in general and specifically Mexican Americans have declined since 1985. Valdivieso states, "It's the ones who are poor and have language problems who drop out."

With all this depressing news, one is tempted to muse on why Hispanics, Mexican Americans particularly, don't finish school. Or do they? Can we believe the PhDs and their studies?

We can believe their studies only if they conduct them properly and honestly. Unfortunately, proper and honest studies are hard to come by. It seems our vaunted PhDs can't tell the difference between native-born Americans of Mexican descent and people born in Mexico.

Specifically, we find the experts include in their studies the million-and-a-half Mexican farm workers legalized by the 1986 Immigration Reform, as well as the million-and-a-half amnesty candidates who snuck into the country prior to 1982, who between them also have precious few years of elementary school. And, they include hundreds of thousands of Salvadoran and Guatemalan refugees who've managed to sneak into the country.

In other words, the studies are faulty because the numbers they study are skewed with millions of uneducated people from Mexico and Central America.

Given this built-in bias, its no wonder that over-all Hispanic high school completion has fallen from 62.9 percent in 1985 to 56 percent in 1989. Moreover, their statistics indicate that Mexican Americans over 25 drop out at such a rate that they have the highest proportion of drop-outs among Hispanics.

Again, they err in their statistical sample. How? By studying bodies over 25 and not being able to spot any of the 10,000 illegal Mexicans who find their way across the Border, El Bordo, every night heading for jobs in Los Angeles, New York, and Chicago. Few, if any, of these illegals have but a few years of schooling, and few, if any, speak English.

Despite biased survey samples, there is hope for Hispanics in education, specifically for Mexican Americans. When the 1990 census data is released the PhDs will find, to their surprise, that native-born Americans of Mexican descent attend and finish school in percentages comparable to anyone.

They will express surprise that Mexican American drop-out rates in some areas, such as San Bernardino, California, are half that of white students—yes, half. They will, of course, label this an aberrations. Hispanics, they will tell us are too poor in treasure and English to do well in school.

Yes, too poor and too unable to speak English well. And, no mathematical ability, to boot. So speaketh the PhDs and so believeth America's body politic.

Keeping these "truths" in mind, I commended Emmy-winning Mexican American actor Edward James Olmos at the National Association of Hispanic Publishers Convention for, in my view, doing more for Mexican Americans than anyone in the country. He did so, I told him, by portraying Bolivian-born Los Angeles teacher Jaime Escalante in the movie "Stand and Deliver".

Escalante, one of President George Bush's heroes, took Mexican American students from a barrio high school in East Los Angeles and taught them calculus with fervor, insight and thoroughness. They all passed the nationally administered Advanced Placement Test—for college credit—an achievement which caused a national scandal when the Eastern educational big-wigs who run the national tests accused Escalante's students of cheating and forced them to retake the test while under heavy scrutiny.

They did and they all passed. Escalante doubled and tripled his output of college level achievers and proved that Mexican American students, regardless of economic status, can compete with anyone in the country, anyone.

By dramatizing Escalante's achievements for Public Television and for the local movie house, Edward James Olmos did more for Mexican American self-esteem than all the PhD studies ever done. Olmos received an Academy Award nomination for best actor and Escalante received the attention he deserved as America's finest teacher.

As for Mexican Americans, in the Escalante story, they can see for themselves, without middlemen, that they can succeed at calculus, at college, at anything they choose, as long as they're willing to study and work hard.

For example, Brian Naranjo, a 17-year-old senior in Garden Grove, California, sick with influenza, recently took the Scholastic Aptitude Test (SAT, used for college admissions) and scored a perfect 1600 points. Only ten of the 1.8 American million students who took the SAT last year had perfect scores, with the average score being 900 points. Not bad for a Mexican kid.

Naranjo takes honors classes in physics, calculus and English. He plans to study physics at UCLA.

Naranjo's achievements won't show up in the PhD's studies because they'll be classified as aberrations. Everyone knows that Mexican kids don't finish school because they are too poor and can't speak English well. Everyone knows this. Everyone but Edward James Olmos, Jaime Escalante, Brian Naranjo and me. ###

DROPPING OUT, WHY?

This year, more Hispanics, particularly Mexican Americans, will graduate from high school and college than ever before. Of all who started the ninth grade in America's towns and cities, the majority will graduate.

These graduates have much in common besides diplomas and degrees. Almost all were born in the United States and speak good English from homes where it is spoken by their parents. Most come from homes where at least one parent is a high school graduate. Most come from the statistical majority of Hispanics, and Mexican Americans, who are middle to upper income. And, lastly, most will have lighter skin color than is expected of Hispanics.

On the other hand, the almost 40% of Hispanic students, again mostly Mexican American, who drop-out—those nationally infamous Hispanic drop-outs—have many things in common, also.

Usually, they are born outside the United States or are born of parents from outside the United States. Their English is not good, nor is that of their parents. Spanish is the dominant language at home, regardless of length of U.S. residence. As a rule, neither parent has much schooling. If they do, it's usually grammar school. Because they are usually recent immigrants and have little schooling and English capability, these people are usually lower income types. And, lastly, most will have skin color that is darker than most Hispanics.

Skin color doesn't cause the drop-out problem and it doesn't necessarily bring on discrimination from our dominant White society, though it can, sometimes. No, skin color reflects the amount of Indian blood one has, and usually denotes the cultural balance one grows up with.

One notes that Mexican Indian culture and it's fifty-thousand man army failed miserably in staving off a couple of hundred Spanish free-booting soldiers of fortune in 1519. The Spanish succeeded like no other empire in history in absorbing its conquest of the Mexican Indian and his culture. This was no accident.

For example, though the Romans spent hundreds of years in empire, few of their conquered ever spoke Latin. In India, the mighty British pulled out in 1946 after a century of colonial rule and the average Indian still spoke his native tongue.

In Mexico, within one generation the Indian gave up his native language and switched to Spanish. Most gave up their human sacrifice based religion to become Catholics. Even today, the most pious and energetically religious Catholics of Mexico are Indian.

Indians are great followers. They have been since the dawn of time when they were wandering bands of food gatherers moving from water hole to water hole. These were extended families, clans and tribes. They demanded total conformity of each tribe member, with deviations punished by death or expulsion. This was the ultimate in peer pressure.

Around 5,000 years ago one of them discovered that a grass with edible seed kernels could be planted and harvested in the temperate Valley of Mexico. Maize it was called—corn.

No longer a wanderer but a farmer, the Mexican Indian became sedentary and discovered he was dependent on weather, on rain, on the sun, and, on the seasons. But the average Indian couldn't calculate when to plant or when to expect rain. Some exceptional Indians, however, could. These became the most important men in Indian civilization—priests.

Education was limited by priests to themselves and their own. The average Indian revered the educated priest class, paid tribute to support the class and, because the priests could predict rain and clear skies, allowed priests, the "smart" ones, to tell them where and what to build; what to believe and think, and how to live their lives. All this on faith in and respect for the "smart" ones.

For hundreds of years and dozens of generations, the Mexican Indian subjected himself completely to the "smart" ones in matters educational, religious and political. He followed. He didn't deviate. He belonged to the tribe. An individual, he was not.

Nothing has changed. The Indian still bows to peer pressure, to "smart" ones.

Almost without exception, the boy or girl who will drop-out can be pointed out the day they enter the 9th grade. They dress identically; they wear their hair the same; they speak the same broken border "Pocho" (poh-choh) talk, a combination of Spanish and English.

They generally come from large families, live in cramped housing and are not pillars of the great American Middle Class. And, they don't aspire to be. They leave that to "smart" ones.

They have cars to buy and girls to impress. Thus, they have to work, to make the money needed for their cars and girls. Some will even help their families, though pregnancies and teenage marriage statistics belie this poverty argument. There's no time for school in this vicious cycle.

Will this vicious cycle ever end? Or, will it doom our fastest growing minority group, the Mexican Americans, and their potential contribution to a great America?

It will end because every day more of them are native born Americans of Mexican descent raised differently from their Indian cousins, raised as individuals by "smart" ones to become, of all things, "smarter" ones. ###

AUTHOR'S NOTE—JULY, 2003—No matter how hard I try, I cannot be diplomatic about this subject of school drop-outs.

But, then again, why should I be diplomatic? Why shouldn't I attack the parents who allow their children to quit school? They truly deserve to be called to account.

If a child drops out of school, the parents ought to be charged with child neglect or child abuse. Such parents need to be sent to jail, even if only on weekends. The drop-out problem must end.

Laws should be changed raising the drop-out age to 17 or 18. Parents should be charged for allowing their children to drop-out.

◆   ◆   ◆

WHERE'S MEXICO? WHERE'S CANADA?

What are we getting for the billions of dollars we're spending on education? Very little, it seems. A third of our children can't find Latin America on a map. Across the country, an estimated 23 million adults are illiterate (9.5%), that is, they can't read or write. We are told 15% of our work force is functionally illiterate.

America, land of liberty and opportunity. The problem is, too many of our people can't spell opportunity, can't read a blueprint, or instructions and can't even read street signs, stop, go, live.

Proof. One in ten Navy recruits, usually 20-years old, can't read well enough to graduate from boot camp. It costs the Navy $75.00-a-day extra to help these recruits raise their reading level. This $75.00 is, however, a drop in the bucket.

In 1989, American private business spent $25 billion on its own initiative for employee reading and writing programs.

And, its not just in the Navy or in the private work force that we have literacy problems. How many precious educational resource dollars are wasted on teaching remedial English—BONEHEAD ENGLISH—to college freshmen in our largest public universities and colleges? Millions of precious dollars is the answer, millions.

Let's go a little farther. Over half our high school seniors don't know in which half of the 19th Century the American Civil War was fought in. And, for Pete's sake, don't even bother to ask these seniors where Gettysburg is or why it's important, or who commanded the Confederate rebel forces, or who the Union Commander was.

Sadly, we speak of high school seniors, those left after 40–50% of "Hispanics", 30–40% of Blacks and 20% of Anglos have already dropped out.

The creme de la creme of American high schoolers, and many can't read, can't write, don't know our history and can't find Southeast Asia/Vietnam (37%), Canada (13%), or Latin America (29%) on a map.

Worse, in states where teachers are required to take competency examinations, huge percentages fail. These are teachers, working teachers, not students, not children, failing these tests.

And what does the national teacher's union, the National Educational Association (NEA) say about teacher competency examinations? They refuse to approve such tests and have successfully blocked their use in many states.

Let's take another example, one in Texas. At a high school in North Dallas, a predominantly Black and Mexican American school, only 5% of its students could pass statewide mathematics tests a few years ago. Today, 95% of these Black and Brown kids pass these tests. A miracle, you ask? Yes.

A miracle named John Saxon. A retired Air Force officer, Saxon developed a technique of teaching math which uses repetition for problem solving. In a word, the student works on the same problem every day until he learns how to solve it. Period.

Now, considering critics and commentators are busy littering our landscape with prognostications of mathematical illiteracy toppling the USA from its decades-old position as the world's technical aristocracy, one would think American education would trample a path to Saxon's door. Have they?

No. In fact, his institutional critics, the educational monopoly of teachers and administrators, have forced Dallas schools to drop his methods and textbooks by next year. And, wherever his methods and textbooks are used, the monopoly fights their use in every school, in every district, in every state.

Teachers want to teach, they insist. They collect their pay and want more and more pay. But apparently, they don't want their students to learn. How do we know? We know because our children don't know where Latin America or Canada is; because they don't know where Vietnam is; because they can't write a simple declarative sentence, even after they're admitted to college; and, because they can't add two plus two.

And, again, I stress that I'm not talking about kindergarteners, I speak of high school seniors and college freshmen. Regrettably, I also speak of credentialed teachers, teachers working in our schools today, protected by tenure and union contracts.

One teacher in my community was suspended from teaching FIVE years ago, then fired, and she is still collecting her pay. She keeps appealing and she's not even in the courts yet. Five years!

Educational Armageddon is fast approaching and drop-outs aren't our only problem, educators are as much of a problem, as well. Education is too important to be left to educators.

There are many factors contributing to America's illiteracy, including television, working mothers, divorce and teachers. Teachers, however, are paid for their contribution, and so are their administrators.

America's parents must retake our schools from the monopoly. How? By abolishing tenure, by merit pay for teacher excellence, by universal teacher competency tests, and class-action damage law suits against bad teachers, schools and administrators for openers.

An educational Line of Death must be drawn, now! Before it's too late. ###

AUTHOR'S NOTE—JULY, 2003—VOUCHERS, VOUCHERS, VOUCHERS. With a move this year to change the Washington D.C. schools into voucher schools, perhaps someday, the vast majority of Hispanics will get their wish and get vouchers for their children to attend better schools than they have now.

◆   ◆   ◆

"THE TESTS, STUPID!"

If you took a thousand white kids, a thousand Mexican American kids and a thousand Black kids, which group would have the highest rate of gifted kids?

Using the standard IQ tests, white kids have dominated the gifted programs of city after city, school after school.

In San Diego, for example, with only 50% of the student population in 1982, white kids made up 82% of the city's Gifted and Talented Education (GATE) classes.

Theoretically, 50% white kids should only produce 50% gifted kids. Conversely, if minorities make up 50% of the student population, they should make up 50% of the gifted.

Theory, however, doesn't cut it when huge cultural differences exist between the test takers and the test makers. Given that most intelligence tests currently in use were devised by white professors decades ago when most schools in the country were segregated by race and given that the "Hispanic" population was miniscule at the time, intelligence tests were designed for white kids, only.

The result, of course, was that Mexican and Black kids were thrashed in test scores and relegated to the educational dustbins of vocational schools to prepare for working lives as laborers and semi-skilled workers.

This situation was encouraged by business and industry and implemented by priggish old maid school teachers and counselors who fondly declared, "People like you need to learn a trade"; or, "College? Silly boy! People like you don't go to college…"

That's how it was. Really. The system was preserved as such until only recently. The tool to keep it so? IQ tests. Intelligence tests. Tests used to prop up the system. Tests used to keep kids in the eternal slavery of unskilled and semi-skilled work, of minimum and poverty wages.

No more. No Mas. After a ten year struggle, the San Diego schools have destroyed the old maxim of white kids are brighter than Mexicans and Blacks. In fact, last year's numbers show a majority of minority kids in the GATE program for the first time in its history.

"Statewide (California) we look at San Diego City Schools as the model," says Judy Witt of the California Association for the Gifted.

Keeping this in mind, it should be pointed out that San Diego County schools—those outside the city—still use the old methods, the old tests, which result in 69% of gifted children being white. White students make up only 51% of County students.

Mexican American students make up 29% of the County's students, yet account for only 11% of gifted students, while Black kids are 8% of the County student population and make up only 4% of gifted kids.

What's the difference between the city and county schools? Why is the majority of gifted kids in the city now Mexican and Black, while they still lag in the county?

To paraphrase Bill Clinton's campaign motto—The Tests, Stupid!

The old tests, you see, test language-verbal skills and prior knowledge. If you know things like, "It was the best of times. It was the worst of times.", you score well. If you don't, you don't.

I submit and San Diego proves that Mexican kids with limited English proficiency and Black kids without benefit of books in the home can be just as bright as white kids. Why? The Tests, Stupid!

Change the tests and we have a miracle on our hands. San Diego is now using Ravens Progressive Matrices instead of the old Wisconsin tests. The new test does not rely on vocabulary or language to determine intelligence. It's a visual test that allows non-English speakers to use their brains in the same way any kid does. It also allows quiet and deliberative students to do well.

Almost everyone is happy about the new situation except some grumblers who complain that Spanish-speakers should be required to take tests in English. Others complain because they believe that intelligence should be measured by what you know, not what you can reason with, nor problem-solve with.

Once again, "If you took a thousand white kids, a thousand Mexican American kids and a thousand Black kids, which group would have the highest rate of gifted kids?

Actually, skin color doesn't matter anymore, finally. ###

AUTHOR'S NOTE—JULY, 2003—Bell Curve, anyone?

◆   ◆   ◆

DAVID DUKE'S ANTI-CHRIST, THE ILLEGAL ALIEN...

The long predicted, anticipated and feared Anti-Christ has arrived. He lives and works In Los Angeles, Chicago, Houston, San Diego, El Paso, or the Great American South. His power among us is growing by the day. He directs a complete razing of America and its treasure. He has been in charge of redistributing wealth from those who have and giving it to those who don't have. According to the David Dukes of the country, the anti-immigrants, and the anti-Catholics, he is the Hispanic.

David Duke, longtime Ku Klux Klan, White Supremacist, ersatz Republican, former Louisiana legislator and founder of a European White group, goes to Siler, North Carolina, where Hispanics have converged to take hundreds of jobs and holds a demonstration. A couple of hundred protesters show up to hear Duke protest "illegal aliens" and the destruction of North Carolina and its schools by Hispanics.

Hispanics are lowering school test scores, critics cry. They are breaking every town's treasury. They are destroying the hundreds year old South, town by town, factory by factory, school by school.

Yes, some test scores are dropping in Siler. Are they because Hispanic kids are stupid, or just don't yet understand English well? Are those Hispanic kids tested in Spanish as they are in California? In California it is not unusual to find that Spanish-speaking kids, otherwise known as English-learners, score better on language and reading Spanish tests than English-only children on comparable English only tests.

For example, Vista, California, schools, with 28% Spanish-speaking English learners and a 49% minority student body (95% plus Mexican American), test well on Stanford Achievement Tests (SAT-9), though, as Dr. Bill Loftus, assistant Superintendent for Instruction, says, "We could do better." Considering, however, that national SAT-9 scores only have 1% non-English speakers built into the averages, Vista test scores show well. In fact, Spanish-speaking students score well in comparison to English-only students.

Vista's English learning Spanish-speakers actually score better on their Spanish version language tests than English-only scores on the SAT-9 test in grades 3, 10 and are even in grade 9. In grades 2, 4, 5, 6, 7 and 8, English only SAT-9 scores are higher than the Spanish version. Vista English learning Spanish-speakers score better than national averages in all grades but the 6th. That includes North Carolina and its 98% plus White/Black student body.

Another example and more proof that Duke and anti-Hispanic hysterics are wrong, is in the college-bound Scholastic Assessment Test (SAT) scores, The Hispanics in Vista (and in North Carolina) are almost 100% Mexican American, so let's examine the Mexican American SAT taker.

According to the College Board, the organization that administers the SAT, 37% of Mexican American SAT test takers have parents without high school diplomas, 38% have parents who do. 7% have parents with Associate Degrees from community colleges; 10% have parents with Bachelor's degrees and 8% with graduate degrees. Only 1% of Whites have parents without high school diplomas. 32% of White parents of White SAT takers have Bachelor's degrees, as do those with graduate degrees (32%). Only 3% of Black parents of SAT takers do not have high school diplomas. Black parent Bachelor's degree and graduate degree holders are double that of Mexican Americans.

The average GPA of Mexican American SAT takers was 3.06 (on a 4.0 scale) in contrast to a 3.31 GPA for Whites and 2.84 for Blacks.

Income categories of test takers tells us more about Hispanics who are "dragging down" test scores in Siler, North Carolina, and elsewhere. 35% of Mexican American student SAT test takers come from families with a total income of under $20,000, 34% from families with incomes between $20,000 to $40,000, 15% from families with $40,000–60,000, 9% with $60,000–80,000 and only 7% with incomes over $80,000.

Back to Vista, California. Vista SAT test takers (25% Hispanic, an all-time record) scored 523 in verbal in 1999 (18 points higher than national) compared to 500 in 1998 (5 points less than national). So, who dragged whom upward?

David Duke probably doesn't know this, but North Carolina's SAT verbal scores are laughable and always have been, always. In fact, though the North Carolina (490) and South Carolina (480) verbal SAT scores are lower than the rest of the USA (505), their scores are rising slightly. Can it be that as more Hispanics come to the Carolinas, SAT scores will rise as they are in Vista, California?

So, the anti-Christ's children are presenting themselves at the schoolhouse door. Given a warm welcome and a concentration of good, professional teaching and help, the Hispanic child can do quite well, thank you. Look at Vista, California.

If, however, they are met with the hostility and cry-babying of Southern White supremacists like David Duke, they do have options. They can go back to Mexico or, they can buckle down, work and study hard. In doing so, they can raise the level of culture and education in what has been a social and intellectual wasteland for too long, thanks to people like David Duke. ###

AUTHOR'S NOTE—JULY, 2003—Bell Curve, anyone? Official English, anyone?

David Duke is serving time in Federal prison for fraud and tax cheating.

Who would the reader rather have as someone to look up to, federal prisoner David Duke, or Jose, the hard working Mexican illegal who send 80% of what he earns home to feed his family?

◆   ◆   ◆

"ANOTHER JUDGE, ANOTHER STUPID DECISION"

A California Superior Court Judge has ruled that illegal immigrants must pay non-resident tuition when attending the largest public university in the world, the California State University. Whoopee!

Judge Robert O'Brien bought the argument that a kid who has lived in California for 5, 10 or 20 years has to pay out-of-state tuition of $7,000 if not in the U.S. legally. The plaintiffs argued that there are up to 10,000 illegals among the University's 360,000 students.

The University estimates there might be 500 illegals somewhere in the 20-campus system, exactly 9,500 less than the plaintiff's claim.

Speaking of the plaintiffs, who are they? Are they upstanding, legitimate, concerned California citizens? They have names such as, the American Association of American Women; the American Federation of Police; the California Coalition for Immigration Reform; Citizens for Law and Order; the Coalition for Immigration Law Enforcement, and the Valley Citizens for Fair Immigration.

Am I the only person who sees the similarities in the names of the suing groups and the Federation of Americans for Immigration Reform (FAIR)? Am I the only person who knows that FAIR's principals have a history of organizing front groups to create the illusion of many people and groups striving for the same goal? Am I the only person that sees that FAIR follows the organizational, propaganda and legal methods created by Communist Party USA?

The judge doesn't concern himself with the backgrounds and affiliations of plaintiffs, nor where their money comes from—but I do. The judge has probably never heard of FAIR's founder, Dr. John Tanton, nor where he secured founding funds for FAIR—but I have.

Dr. Tanton is best known for founding U.S. English, a group dedicated to erasing all traces of the Spanish language from the United States, and for founding FAIR. He is also known for raising millions of dollars for these efforts and for lobbying to keep Spanish-speaking and Roman Catholic immigrants, even if legal, from entering the U.S.

This lawsuit against the University bears every sign of being a Tanton operation. The names of the groups and the wildly exaggerated claims of tuition-sucking illegals all point to Tanton.

Oddly enough, the pin that punctures the wild exaggerations of the anti-immigrant forces is a recent study by two San Diego State professors for the Auditor General of California. Professors Louis M. Rea and Richard A. Parker overestimated the number of illegal aliens in San Diego and California, then purposely underestimated the amount of revenues these people pay the State of California.

The study specifically mentions illegals in the two State University campuses in San Diego. At San Diego State University (30,000 students), the study estimates 70–80 possible illegal resident students. At Cal-State San Marcos, a campus surrounded by up to 50,000 illegal immigrants, the study estimates one possible illegal.

So, is there a problem? There might be. When three million illegals applied for amnesty under the 1986 Immigration Reform Act, we found that they came from 150 countries. Illegal Irish, or Canadians, or British might be enrolled at the University. We simply don't know.

One thing we know for sure, however, is that there aren't many illegal students from Mexico or Central America. Why? Because most of these illegals have less than 7 years of schooling. How, then, can they enroll in the University? To enroll, one must first apply, provide transcripts and test scores, then pay $1300 in fees.

How does an illegal with 7 years of school, pass the SATs', produce high school transcripts and fill out the application? Chances are, then, that most illegals in the University are white and not Indians from Oaxaca.

Too bad Judge O'Brien made his dumb ruling, as, if it is upheld on appeal, the University will have to check out the legal residency of each and every one of the system's 360,000 students.

Because, to assume that all illegals in the University are Mexican and to, as a result, check only those with brown skin or Spanish surnames, is against Federal law. It'll be awfully expensive to check 360,000 students.

Another dumb judge makes a stupid decision and we, the people, have to pay for it. Isn't that always the case? ###

AUTHOR'S NOTE—JULY, 2003—Despite the judge's ruling, the State Legislature passed a bill in both the Assembly and Senate that permits any child who attends California high schools for three years, graduates and enrolls in the State University or the University of California to pay in-state tuition no matter his or her residency status.

Strangely, until the anti-immigrant activists listed in the law suit stuck their little noses into college tuition charges, the law clearly stated that anyone who lived in California for a year prior to enrollment in the community colleges, State University or University of California were deemed to be residents, period. There was no question about legal residency.

California Democratic Governor Gray Davis signed the bill into law. Texas did the same. Other states are debating the issue now. Only Virginia has passed a law denying in-state tuition to illegal alien students, even those who attended Virginia high schools and have perfect grade averages and high test scores.

Federal law allows individual states to determine in-state tuition issues.

◆   ◆   ◆

LEARNING THE WRITE WAY

Western civilization survived the fall of Rome to the German barbarians, attacks by the Mongol Hordes of Genghis Kahn, invasion by Moslems into

France and Southeastern Europe, the Imperial German Kaiser, Adolf Hitler and, finally, Communism. Despite this millennium and half of triumphs by Western Civilization, today, American Civilization is in danger of being brought down and destroyed by American children.

Standing behind the children are teachers, the true perpetrators of the crimes abounding in the nation's educational system.

What is the crime? American children can't write, according to a giant national study released by the U.S. Department of Education. Only one in four can put together a paragraph or two proficiently enough to succeed in school or future jobs.

The report was issued by the Education Department's National Assessment of Educational Progress and contained the results of testing 60,000 students in public and private schools at the 4th, 8th and 12th grade levels. Supplementing this sample, 100,000 8th graders in 35 states, the Virgin Islands and schools operated around the world by the Defense Department were separately tested.

Girls did better than boys. Asian-Pacific Islanders did better than Whites, Blacks and Hispanics. Whites did better than Blacks and Hispanics. The poorer the student's family and the less education parents had accrued, the lower the test results. California did less than average and scored lower than Texas and New York, states that are comparable in population diversity.

"The Average or typical American student is not a proficient writer," summed up Gary W. Phillips, acting chief of the National Center for Educational Statistics, an office in the U.S. Department of Education.

Even below the average incompetent writing American student is the California student. 56% of California students wrote at basic level and 24%, 25% worse than the national average. Among children who eat free federally paid for lunches, and/or whose parents never graduated from high school, the scores were the worst in the country. Children with limited English skills were also lower than average. They numbered 13% of students who took the California tests in contrast to only 2% of the national test takers.

Hispanic kids, thus, appear to have done worse than others. Or did they? Something is wrong here. I say that because we are observing a huge new marketing campaign by one of the country's largest and best-known computer companies, Gateway Computers. It is launching a multi-million dollar campaign to sell computers to Hispanics, particularly Mexican Americans.

R. Todd Bradley of Gateway says, "It's (Hispanic population) huge; it grows very, very aggressively. More important, it's under-served." Brad

Shaw, Gateway Vice-President says, "We see a great opportunity" in marketing to Hispanics.

There are 8-million Hispanic households in the country and we now know more about them than ever, thanks to a study commissioned by Gateway. A Forrester Research survey of 100,000 American households produced some of the most astounding results vis a vis Hispanics this writer has ever seen. No wonder Gateway is spending millions to pursue the Hispanic market.

Hispanics, according to the survey, are SECOND ONLY to Asian Americans in being connected to the Internet. 64% Asian Americans are likely to be Internet-connected, 36% of Hispanics and third-non-Hispanic whites with 34% Internet connections. Forrester Research analyst, Ekaterina Walsh, projects that Internet access by Hispanics will increase by another 30%, to an over-all 43% in the next few months.

On one hand, we find Hispanic children who are worse than many at writing an English paragraph and on the other, experiencing more access to the newest font of knowledge, the Internet, than even the dominant non-Hispanic whites, the Anglos, among us.

This, ladies and gentlemen, is what we call a conundrum.

Obviously there are many Hispanics interested in their children, interested enough to be buying computers to help their children succeed. There will be more after Gateway spends millions to advertise to Hispanics and creates even more demand. Let me repeat that statement. Gateway will spend millions in television and other advertising in a campaign directed at Hispanics and they will buy more because they are asked to do so. That is market creation. Gateway will have success with its Hispanic campaign. Observing that success, other computer companies will weigh in with millions more in Hispanic marketing and, coincidentally, computer prices will probably come down and more Hispanic children will have Internet access. Everyone benefits.

Everyone except many of the limited English speaking children and children whose parents never finished school. They can't compose a decent English paragraph today and may never without some form of intervention. They obviously aren't getting the help they need in school, or at home. The community, you and I and private enterprise, must intervene on a one-to-one basis to help these children and we must do so today. Tomorrow may be too late. ###

AUTHOR'S NOTE—JULY, 2003—Newspapers screamed with headlines that Hispanics had more Internet use growth than any group in the Country in the year 2003. Blacks were second, Asians close by and White last in Internet use growth. Looks like Gateway was right, despite that company's market share shrinking.

◆   ◆   ◆

SCHOOL VOUCHERS AND PUBLIC MIS-EDUCATION

In a recent poll conducted for the Public Policy Institute of California of over 2000 Californians, only a tiny number thought illegal immigration is a serious issue. So, out goes the theory of fanatical alarmists and not-so-subtle racists that illegal immigration is a burning issue with most people. It is not, nor should it be.

The Public Policy Institute of California conducted a 2000 person state-wide poll and concluded that:

"Education continues to rank overwhelmingly as the single most important issue to Californians, with nearly one-third statewide naming schools as their priority. Crime (8 percent), immigration and illegal immigration (7 percent), guns and gun control (5 percent) and economy/jobs (3 percent) complete the top five issues." So, there.

We are constantly bombarded with phony charges that everyone is up in arms about illegal immigration or immigration in general, yet California the ultimate destination of most immigrants, seems to think other issues are more important. In USA Today (Sept 2), a University of California, Los Angeles, researcher comments that in 1950, the California White population had a high school drop out segment of 2/3rds and a 25% child poverty rate. Education, he said, was the key to reversing those statistics and that as we did it before, we can do it again.

The mobilization of education and financial resources to bring California into the forefront of education worked in the Fifties. It must be done again, for again we find a major portion of the population, Hispanics this time, in a situation where four in ten haven't finished high school and about 25% of their children live in poverty. But will the same techniques that worked to upgrade the White population in the Fifties work in the new Millennium?

Test scores are down everywhere, including non-inner city schools. Inner city schools are a disaster. 4th graders that were tested this year showed only minimal improvement over last year. Of course, at former Governor Pete Wilson's insistence, children with limited English skills were forced to take tests for full English speakers, thus guaranteeing lower scores. He was trying to make a point, something about limited English children being stupid, or that bilingual education doesn't work. Whatever his motive, it was political.

Unluckily for Wilson and his rabid anti-Mexican followers, the private testing company botched the statewide test results. In a word, they are worthless. Another Pete Wilson fiasco was not passing some form of school voucher program during his 8-years as Governor.

When publicly funded school vouchers were on the ballot, the teacher's union spent millions to defeat the issue. Vouchers may not be the total answer, but they most certainly are more help than harm. Sure some of those monies might be spent on private and parochial schooling. But, is that bad? No. Is that unconstitutional? One lonely federal judge thinks so in Cleveland, but other judges have said no. Moreover, the issue of public monies being expended on religious educational institutions was settled almost sixty years ago when the first government check was cashed by Notre Dame University, wasn't it?

Politically, vouchers have had a tough climb up the hill of public opinion, but a poll announced last week startled everyone with the news that all major segments of the population now endorse vouchers. That is a giant leap forward for reform in education. Blacks, for example, who last year were 52% against vouchers have reversed themselves and now favor vouchers by 57%. Hispanics have always favored vouchers and dwarf the Black and White pro-voucher percentages. In fact, two thirds of Hispanics favor vouchers. Do they know something the rest of the country doesn't? Yes, they do.

Hispanics know that unions will strangle schools so that teachers only benefit from the educational process and benefit only in shorter workdays, more money and no accountability. Teachers unions don't care about test results; they don't care about SAT scores, they don't care whether or not children can or cannot read. If they did, they would make certain each and every child could read and write. It doesn't take perfect two parent families to teach children to read or write, it only takes committed teachers.

They must not be allowed to succeed. The will of the people must prevail. The public schools have been discounted by most of the populace as effective institutions. A half dozen states are creating innovative voucher programs aimed at disadvantaged children. Last week, in front of Latino business people and a national television audience, the leading candidate for President, George W. Bush, presented a comprehensive federal voucher program. It will allow children in schools that fail at their task to receive federal vouchers redeemable anywhere.

Vouchers, then, will be a key difference between Republican Bush and his Democratic rival next year. Education, therefore, will be the most important issue of the 2000 campaign, as it should be, and voters will have a clear education choice available when they vote. That, is more than parents currently have while teacher's unions have a stranglehold on public schools.

AUTHOR'S NOTE—JULY, 2003—Vouchers used for parochial school education are legal and constitutional, so ruled the United States Supreme Court.

As this is written, there is a move in Congress to use Washington, D. C. as a test for federal vouchers. The D.C. schools spend over $10,000 per student annually and have totally failed to meet even minimal standards for the predominately Black student body.

Naturally, the teacher's union is opposing such a move, but the Democratic mayor of Washington, D.C. is supportive of the proposed experiment.

◆   ◆   ◆

TEXAS SCHOOLING

There are many among us who decry the growing presence of children of Mexican immigrants, legal and illegal, in schools throughout the Southwest and other job magnet cities of Chicago, New York City, Atlanta and scattered cities and towns throughout the Midwest and Northeast.

We are told that most Mexicans don't finish school. There is a claim that they will be a drain on future social services. There is a claim that these uneducated people will not be equipped to work in 21st century America. These people point to the deteriorating Los Angeles schools as an example of what we can expect in the educational systems that must deal with Mexican-origin children. They used to point to Texas as an example of rotten schools and more rotten students, especially the Mexican ones. They cannot point to Texas schools any longer.

New teaching methods have been created by the El Paso Collaborative for Academic Excellence, a seven-year old program conceived and implemented at the old Texas Western campus, now known as the University of Texas-El Paso. Sports historians will note that Texas Western forever broke the Whites-only strangle-hold on college basketball when an all-Black Texas Western team won the NCAA tournament.

It may be that these educational innovators may have broken the choke-hold of bad teachers in Texas and, perhaps, elsewhere. Everyone should remember that teacher competency examinations have only existed in a few states for a few years. In California, only new teachers can even be tested. The teacher's unions have strangled any attempt to test existing teachers for competency. Moreover, "minority" teacher candidates have extraordinary high failure rates in competency examinations. This, of course, is another issue for another day.

School reform started in 1984 with a Ross Perot chaired commission that demanded radical changes in less-than-acceptable Texas schooling. Unhindered by strong schoolteacher unions, radical reform measures were passed by the Texas electorate and successive legislatures. The result is that today, under Governor George W. Bush, 75-per cent of high school sophomores are passing the graduation test they are required to pass in the 12th grade to graduate from high school. In 1994, only half passed, according to Texas education officials.

For a concrete example of what a horrendously bad state school system can do to create a "poverty" state of affairs for its own people, we can take a peek at the per capita income of "White" Texans in 1960. In that year, the Census Bureau reported that the per capita (per person) income of Whites in Texas ($5100) was actually less than that of Mexican Americans in California ($5400). Only 8-per cent of Mexican Americans had high school diplomas in 1950, yet by the end of that decade made more money in California that the "better educated" Whites of Texas.

Texas has cast off the inferior school mentality that pervaded the state for a hundred years and there is proof. According to national test results released by the U.S. Department of Education last September; Texas eighth graders ranked over-all fourth in writing, with Black and Mexican American children ranked first and second, nationally.

To truly measure Texas schools we must focus on El Paso, one of the poorest cities in the country, which also has the highest percentage of Mexican-origin people. El Paso congressman, Democrat Silvestre Reyes, represents the fifth-poorest district in the USA. Two/thirds of the city's 135-thousand students live in poverty ($16,400 for a family of four) and half enter school with limited or no English.

Five years ago, according to school officials, two-thirds of white students and only a third of Mexican American and Black students passed the state-wide mandatory mathematics tests. Last year, 91 per cent of whites, 80 per cent of Mexican Americans and 75 per cent of Blacks passed the tests. All this progress in just five years.

We have here, a total rout of teacher's unions and their friends in the Democratic Party. The rout comes by innovation and a rah-rah attitude of real teachers who believe in their students. Texas is living proof that Mexican-origin children can succeed in school, graduate and go on to college. All they need is attention by well-prepared, motivated teachers who ignore unions. Their alleged impediments of English deficiency, lack of parental input and poverty are excuses used by incompetent, ill-prepared and unmotivated teachers to cover up their own professional failures.

How else can we explain the quantum leap of these El Paso and Texas Mexican American students from cellar test score levels to high nationally ranked scores? Won't it be a pleasure to point to our own students and their rising test scores once we derail the powerful teacher unions?

This pleasure will come when we impose radical educational change and innovation that unleashes the promise of the hundreds of thousands of Mexican-origin children in schools where ever they are in the country, as has happened in Texas.

AUTHOR'S NOTE—JULY, 2003—Reformed education is but a wisp of a dream among Mexican Americans in the United States. In every state and local school district, teachers and their unions oppose reform. They oppose merit pay for good teachers; they oppose competency examinations for all teachers; they oppose vouchers; they oppose charter schools; they oppose any change in the current system.

The current system is dooming hundreds of thousands of Hispanic and Black children to a doomsday scenario of under-educated school drop-outs thronging our streets and competing against each other for scarce jobs.

We must reform the entire K-12 system everywhere in the country, and do it now.

◆   ◆   ◆

THERE GOES THE NEIGHBORHOOD

A generation ago America's conscience was battered by the way it treated African Americans. Decades of lynchings, bigotry and total discrimination and segregation in housing, jobs and politics caused widespread revulsion and the beginning of legal redress for the millions of long suffering Blacks.

While this was occurring, no one paid attention to Latinos, as they weren't very numerous and their complaints weren't as egregious as those of Blacks.

According to a recent the Los Angeles Times Poll, a third of "Blacks say they live in a mostly Black neighborhood, about the same as those who live in evenly mixed ones. Notably, about one in six Blacks now say they live in mostly Latino neighborhoods."

One-fourth of Latinos, the Poll states, live in mainly Latino or mostly Anglo neighborhoods, with "42% (saying) they live in evenly mixed areas and only 3% live in principally Black areas."

While no one was looking, Latinos have overflowed from their traditional neighborhoods and snapped up housing and jobs which, under the best of conditions, are in short supply for low income people to begin with.

In ethnic demographics, Latinos have increased by leaps and bounds during the last two decades to now number 22 million. And without exception, most Census observers and employees are now predicting that Latinos will pass America's Blacks in numbers within the next 20 years.

If true, what will happen when Blacks look around and see millions of Latino living in formerly all-Black neighborhoods, in former ghettos with names changed to barrios?

And what will they think when most entry level and low-pay jobs are snapped up by willing Latino workers able to and desirous of working more than one job a day?

And what will they do when Latino Congressman, currently outnumbered two to one (22–11) by Black Congressmen, find those numbers reversed?

In a word, can the Black population live with the fact they will no longer be America's largest minority group, nor the beneficiary of the country's gigantic guilt trip and its manifestations of affirmative action, race-norming, political correctness and reverse discrimination.

We see, for example, that many Blacks are demanding reparations for their ancestors being brought to these shores in chains.

Quotas in hiring are deemed desirous and necessary as a means of making up for years of discriminatory hiring by White males.

Undercover government agents are used, with Black encouragement, to ferret out landlords and property managers who discriminate in housing.

Colleges and Universities race each other to pass restrictions and sanctions on free speech "fighting words" that cannot be tolerated in the academia now run by children of 60's flower children who believe they are helping the cause of Blacks by murdering First Amendment free speech.

The country has begun to unravel at the seams because of racial intolerance and antagonism between whites and blacks. Or is it the end, in reality?

While many of America's Latinos complain about discrimination and bigotry aimed against them by white America, sometimes with reason, are they as bad off as Blacks claim to be?

An examination of the facts clearly answer that question.

While 34% of America's Blacks live under the poverty line, 75% or more of Mexican Americans and Cubans live above the poverty line. University of Chicago studies reveal that a Latino making $2500 a year has a better chance of living in a "mixed" or integrated neighborhood that a Black with a PhD.

Unemployment among young Black males runs as high as 40% in some cities, while Latinos, particularly Mexican American males, have a labor market penetration rate of 82%. School drop-out rates of native-born Latinos in California are substantially less than that of Blacks.

The only category in which Blacks have outperformed Latinos is in college degrees. This stands to reason as over 40 colleges and universities were specifically founded over a century ago to educate Blacks. The United Negro College Fund raises millions to support these schools.

Latinos have never had colleges and universities founded to educate them. Only 4% of Mexican Americans, for example, have college educations. There are glimmers of hope, however, as the number of college-educated Mexican Americans in San Diego doubled during the Eighties to 12%.

The question is, therefore, are America's Latinos as bad off as some of them claim to be? The answer is no. And anyone that thinks so can't support their position with facts.

Truth or fiction, amigos, which will it be? ###

AUTHOR'S NOTE—JULY, 2003—With the announcement that Hispanics now outnumber Blacks in the country, the old paradigm of issues being of Black and White connotations, is dead and a new paradigm has come on line.

Despite what the media would have everyone believe, Hispanics, generally, don't care much for Blacks. Sure the less-educated poorer Hispanics identify with all poor people, of which there are plenty in the Black community. It is also certain that a small splinter of the Hispanic community, the ultra-liberal, radical Chicano types, identify with the Black cause because they want to be victims.

Most Hispanics do not consider themselves to be victims. They want the best of America for their children and believe they will have better lives.

A CBS/New York Times poll released the same day as this note is being written concludes that 75% of Hispanic immigrants to this country, legal and illegal, consider their lives to be better than their parents and 75% project that the lives of their children will be better than theirs. That's twice the percentage of non-Hispanics (Whites and Blacks) who believe their children will have better lives.

◆　　◆　　◆

"THE MISSION OF TEACHERS: POWER OR RESULTS?"

There was a time when teachers, though grossly underpaid, worked hard and long hours and attached themselves to their students like remoras do to sharks in order to push students upwards through the system so they might succeed and leave, in many instances, lives of poverty and ignorance. Not today.

Years ago, practically every teacher I knew came from economically modest circumstances and attended teachers colleges or state colleges and universities that charged precious little in tuition and were designed to cater to such students; students who worked their way through college.

When they hit the classroom, they did so with glee and enthusiasm, despite little pay. They had a mission. The mission was to take little kids and teach them to read, write and to add and subtract.

In 1940, less than one in 40 American adults had a college education. Today, one in 5 have college educations. In my San Diego, it's almost one in three (29%) adults with college educations, the highest such percentage of any major city in the world.

What we have, therefore, is a confluence of rising educational expectations among all Americans, better schools and better educated teachers. Or do we?

Any survey of urban California schools indicate that these schools are of lesser quality, in physical terms, than suburban schools—even though the United States Supreme Court ruled years ago that school financing must be equal regardless of location.

And, all statewide test scores indicate that urban schools are deteriorating or remaining stagnant. The same is true throughout the United States.

One evident deterioration nationally is the Scholastic Achievement Test (SAT) that is taken every year by millions of students with college in mind. The SAT is the national test that most college use as the basis of college admissions.

Compared to my graduating class (1958), the SAT scores have taken a dive. They have plunged so far that the grand poo-bahs that run the SAT have reconfigured the test so that they can raise the averages by artificial means.

There is plenty of blame to go around. Television, for example, occupies more time than ever of a child's life. The deterioration of the American family, be it by divorce, illegitimacy or two-parent working households plays a significant part, as well.

And, I believe, as important as any other factor, the decay of the teaching profession has destroyed the public schools as I knew them.

Ever since teachers organized into unions, their pay has increased, while test scores have gone done. While class size has gone down, test scores have dived. More people are graduating, yet more have to take remedial classes in college. With more money in their jeans and much smaller class sizes, teachers have demanded and received more power in the administration of schools.

In California, the teachers contribute over $600,000 a year in political contributions to legislators and have moved into local school elections with thousands of union high-jacked dollars. For example, a teacher ran for my school board in the last election and raised less than $2,000 on his own. The Teacher's Union raised, by individual teacher payroll check-off, $35,000 and spent it as an "independent expenditure" on behalf of the teacher, who went on to win by a tiny vote margin.

Despite putting one of their own on the Board of Education, the union has gone out on strike. 133,000 students and their parents are left out of the loop while teachers strike for 16% more pay and more power to run individual school sites by demanding 50% of the Governance Boards of each school site.

What happened to the dedicated teacher of my day and to their enthusiasm to teach? What happened to teachers who sacrificed money for tenure, lifetime job security, pensions and satisfaction of a job well done?

What happened to public schools run by elected citizens? Almost 50% of America's adults are categorized as "functionally illiterate", why? Many of today's students cant' read or write, why?

The dumbing down of America is on course and it is directed by teachers, not parents, in my opinion. It pains me to say so, considering the many fine teachers that grasped me by the neck and pushed and shoved me into college.

In fact, it was one of them that told me that during World War I, then French Prime Minister Clemenceu stated that "War was too serious to leave to Generals."

In view of today's schools and the teachers who collect their paychecks there, particularly those that service people who look like me, let me rephrase that: Education is too serious to leave to teachers. ###

AUTHOR'S NOTE—JULY, 2003—In recent days, news from Lawrence, Massachusetts, broke that the Superintendent of Schools in Lawrence, a Puerto Rican earning $155,000 annually, failed the English competency test required to be passed by all teachers and administrators in the state.

This is not news to observers of the education scene. Most teachers are competent, having, of course, college degrees. However, a substantial number simply can't pass competency examinations in the fields they teach in.

All one has to do is to catalog statements and positions of teachers who opposed the War in Iraq (March, 2003)and compare them to the facts.

Most teachers, and their students, couldn't find Kuwait on an unmarked map when the first Gulf War broke out even though it was the entire mission of the United States and its allies to eject Iraqi armies from the small oil-rich country they had invaded and occupied.

Education must be taken away from educators, period. If not, they will condemn the Hispanic population to peonage, the same peonage they left behind in their petty little dictatorships. That statement also includes Mexico, the country of my birth, the Mexico that was strangled and ripped off so badly by the one-party dictatorship of the old ruling party, the PRI.

8

Chapter introduction—Much of the intra-Hispanic struggle can be noted visually. For some reason, clothes seem to separate many Hispanics from other Hispanics. Social and educational position seems to follow various fashion fads.

Watching CBS's 60-MINUTES Show, I saw a New York Puerto Rican activist complaining that his son was always being stopped and hassled by New York's men in Blue. When asked why, he responded because my son "wears baggy clothes." I yelled at the television, "Stop wearing baggy clothes, moron!"

Like Blacks wearing "colors" and "do-rags" these mostly young Hispanic boys and girls self-identify as the worst of America's fears, of thugs, simpleton criminals complete with tattoos, mustaches, scraggly little chin whiskers, of promiscuous bearers of babies they can't support and of school drop-outs growing America's underclass even larger.

This view may be considered to be mean, cruel and disrespectful of young Hispanics. It is, for I have no benevolent or benign views of punks, criminals and drug addicts, no matter their color, ethnicity or gender.

Punks are punks.

CLOTHES MAKE THE MAN

A true homeboy, he was. We used to call them pachucos (paw-choo-kohs). Hair slicked back, red bandana wrapped tightly around his head, plaid woolen shirt unbuttoned except for the top button, overlarge white tee shirt, baggy khaki pants, wispy immature mustache and an earring in his ear. This, splendid representative of American Hispanics is a homeboy.

He stood there, as if fixated, staring at the attractive young Yuppie woman as she walked by.

"What are you gawking at, you stupid jerk?", she snapped.

Clothes and how they're worn, today, set each of us apart and tell the world what we think of ourselves and everyone else. To homeboys clothes are their badge.

In Chicago, for example, young Black boys proudly wearing satin athletic jackets with the names of their favorite teams and wearing $100 hi-top athletic shoes named after their athletic hero, are gunned down when they won't give up their expensive jackets or shoes to less fortunate boys.

In Los Angeles, young Black boys are shot because their baseball hats aren't cocked at a certain angle; or because they're wearing red, or blue, in the wrong neighborhood. Wearing colors, gang colors, is what we're talking about.

In San Diego, an elementary school prohibits the wearing of red or blue clothing by its little boys, who by the sixth grade begin wearing gang colors in the hope of not being shot while walking to or from school.

In New York, bullet proof coats are being sold for young children, to protect them from stray bullets.

And now, the banning of clothes has reached a new plateau. Mini-skirts that hide nothing and tight tube tops that hide little are permitted for our daughters, while black Los Angeles Raider jackets, shirts and caps have been banned for boys in several San Diego area middle schools.

One principal emphatically states that the black Raider jackets are worn to intimidate other students. He says, "You can't allow kids to intimidate or be intimidated because I'm here to educate, not play any games."

Some of the kids complain the ban affects how they make fashion statements, or how they present themselves to their peers. In fact, they claim, the ban interferes with how they portray their manliness, their machismo.

A few complain the ban is racial. Why? Because of statements such as that of a San Diego Unified School District police officer, Larry Miller, who says, "It's also a tradition in the Hispanic community to wear black, as a fashion statement." It is? I thought only Sicilian mobsters, La Cosa Nostra, the Mafia wore black.

One Hispanic eighth-grader says that some gang members wear Raider jackets because the gangs want "to look cool". Another principal says, "Sure, the Raider jackets can symbolize a macho attitude—the kids know the team's reputation—and they like to associate with that bravado; it's a status symbol."

Looking cool, status symbol, macho attitude—Baloney!

We used to call people like this Pachucos. The word, Nobel Laureate Octavio Paz states is "a word of uncertain derivation, saying nothing and saying everything…"

"Since," Paz continues, "the pachuco cannot adapt himself to a civilization which, for its part, rejects him, he finds no answer to the hostility surrounding him except this angry affirmation of his personality…instead of attempting a problematical adjustment to society, the pachuco actually flaunts his differences."

At the heart of the matter, Paz writes, is, "The pachuco has lost his whole inheritance: language, religion, customs, beliefs…His disguise is a protection, but it also differentiates and isolates him: it both hides him and points him out."

Pachucos are called homeboys now; homeboys can only be Mexican. They don't shoot each other because hats aren't worn right, or because blue is worn rather than red. They don't kill each other for shoes or jackets.

But, they do kill each other and any innocents that happen in the way to protect "territory",; to avenge insults; and, to scream to the world that they are macho. They wear black Raider jackets and shirts to declare, "Hey man, I'm cool; I'm tough."

But, they're not cool and they're not tough. They're just drawing attention to themselves, for they have no other means. Almost without exception they do not finish school; nor do they speak English or Spanish well. They can't read or write well. They can't reason well, nor are they good a simple arithmetic.

They're not even good at being rebels against American society in that their manner of dress, Paz writes, "is only an empty gesture, because it is an exaggeration of the models against which he is trying to rebel, rather than a return to the dress of his forebears or the creation of a new style of his own…"

"…his clothing spotlights and isolates him, but at the same time it pays homage to the society he is attempting to deny."

The homeboy-pachuco stood there, stunned, wondering why the young lady was so vehement in calling him a "stupid jerk." He'll never know, nor will he be able to figure out why—he'll be too busy picking up garbage, digging ditches or, serving time. ###

AUTHOR'S NOTE—JULY, 2003—Punks who dress like punks will always be punks. Punks who cover their bodies with tattoos will always be punks.

Seldom do Hispanics like me step forward and criticize these punks and call them what they are.

We must discard these people and their victim hood now and forever.

◆   ◆   ◆

LA LUCHA (LAH-LOOCHAA), THE STRUGGLE

In this corner, Hispanics who live in a fantasy where every other American picks on them, holds them back, tries to crush their cultural heritage and their right to speak Spanish.

In that corner, Hispanics who seek facts, analyze them and conclude that many Hispanics succeed and manage to hold on to their cultural heritage, Spanish, and excel at being unique, successful Americans.

In another corner, are Hispanics who are tired of whining and whimpering, and advocate that they assert themselves, become self-sufficient, as well as political and that they take control of their destiny.

These are the protagonists in the struggle for the souls of the 22-million plus Hispanics of America. Moreover, the winners will set the agenda for the decades to come when Hispanic numbers will grow to such totals that in a hundred years it's conceivable that one in three Americans will be Hispanic.

Of the three corners of the struggle, two are emotional and one is analytical.

Facts and intelligent analysis are the property of those who seek truth. We find both in "Out of the Barrio" (Basic Books) by Linda Chavez, former Executive Director of the U.S. Civil Rights Commission—a good job—and former President of U.S. English—a bad career move.

She startles us with, "We cannot assimilate—and we won't...", a statement made by Mexican American Arnold Torres at the politically so-correct Stanford University.

Torres, former Executive Director of the League of United Latin American Citizens, the oldest Hispanic civil rights group in the U.S., fervently believes this baloney and, unfortunately, is joined by many so-called Hispanic leaders.

For example, Antonio Stevens-Arroyo, an instructor of Puerto Rican studies in New York, attacks Linda Chavez, personally, for her book, its facts and her conclusions.

Like Torres, Stevens-Arroyo's emotions leave him vulnerable to objective examination. Rather than counter Chavez with facts, the Puerto Rican Studies instructor uses words such as "fat cat", "right-wing", "very dangerous propaganda" and "defeated political candidate", referring to Chavez' unsuccessful Maryland campaign for the U.S. Senate.

Stevens-Arroyo invents facts when he writes "that most Latinos in this country are...third, fourth, fifth or even sixth generation Americans." Some of us are, of course, but Stevens-Arroyo and "most" Latinos are not. Most Latinos, particularly non-Mexican origin Latinos (e.g., Puerto Ricans) have been in this country less time than the Irish, Italians or Russian Jews.

Score one for Chavez.

He writes that "some Latinos used (the Liberal War-On-Poverty) opportunity created in the '60s and '70s to get ahead in the '80s", a position Chavez challenges. Some, of course, did. They became instructors in Puerto Rican and Chicano Studies; they became social workers; and, some became "poverty warriors".

They did not, however, become businessmen and women; they did not become the economic backbone, the producers, of the Hispanic community.

While the instructors, social workers and poverty warriors collected tax-supported paychecks, hundreds of thousands of Latinos started businesses in the Eighties and built an economic base which produced a whopping 67% increase in after-tax Latino income while non-Latino after-tax income increased by only 33% during the same period (1982–1990).

Stevens-Arroyo writes that Chavez claims that Hispanic culture and the Spanish language are impediments to upward mobility. Actually, she writes, "Winning court battles to have His panic children taught in Spanish in a society in which the best jobs go to people who speak, read and write English well hardly empowers Hispanic youngsters."

She's right, isn't she?

There's another emotional position, one that KO's Antonio Stevens-Arroyos—one from Daniel Munoz, Sr., Publisher of La Prensa-San Diego.

Munoz, a political maverick who equally shafts the Right and Left, Republicans and Democrats, writes, "The thing is, gente (heh-nteh), get off the welfare and the hand out trip you have been on and suck it up...Time we take things into our own hands and turn this thing around...there is dinero (dee-ne-roh, money) to be made...otherwise ten zillion Mexicanos would not be coming over daily to work...They find work!

"We (Mexican Americans) went to war and built airplanes. We went to war again and we built missiles. Then we went to war again—flew the planes and commanded ships...and our numbers grew. Porque (pour-keh, why), we can't take control of our lives?

He continues, "It's 1992 very soon gente…shall we pass it crying in our beer or are we going to take el toro (bull) by the horns? I for one accept the challenges of life…how about you?

In this corner, Chavez and Munoz and millions of successful Hispanic Americans. In that corner, the crybabies, Puerto Rican and Chicano Studies instructors, poverty warriors and their supplicant clients.

The struggle continues. ###

AUTHOR'S NOTE—JULY, 2003—Linda Chavez so far outclasses her critics that it isn't funny. Between her arguments and those statements from Daniel Munoz, Sr. the arguments of the victims are pathetic.

◆   ◆   ◆

CACIQUES, CHIEFS

Among my fellow Mexican Americans, most go to bed at night planning no more than how to survive another day; how to get a better job, any job, for that matter; or how to better their lives. There are those, however, who dream of political power, glory, and how to lead us. These are would-be CACIQUES (kah-cee-kehs), an old Mexican Indian word for tribal chief, appropriate here because we are a tribe, albeit millions strong.

Power seekers find three distinct groups within the Mexican Americans population. First, social activists, who are mostly from the 25% of us below the poverty line. These people relate to Mexico's left-leaning political system.

Then, those from the 75% of us who are above the poverty line; educated, with decent jobs, or entrepreneurs, small business people. These people are Americanized, to say the least.

The third group is more or less indifferent to, and ignorant of, their socio-economic and political environment, a condition which is quintessentially American.

In the first group, the prevailing philosophy is activist politics first, which is how they fill the media with activities and mischief. The second group first seeks a solid economic foundation, then enters politics, usually Republican, surfacing in the media as successful newsmakers, not rioters, picketers, or boycotters. The third group seems to pay some lip service to the first, acts like the second, but has no commitment to either, or to themselves.

Let's apply labels for identification. The first group generally call themselves Chicanos. However, based on observing activities of this group, I call them "Statists." Why? They demand an activist and larger government, financed, of course, by taxing the rich, to solve all problems of those below the poverty line. Concurrently, they blame those problems on previous American governments. Most see Mexican Americans as subjugated and discriminated against because of ethnicity. They argue this land (California, Texas, Arizona, New Mexico, Colorado, Utah and Nevada) was forcefully stolen from Mexico through an unjust war(1847–1849); by the war-ending treaty, the Treaty of Guadalupe Hidalgo, imposed on a prostrate Mexico by an unjust and deceitful United States of America.

Moreover, they reason, there's been and continues to be, systematic discrimination against us aimed at keeping Mexicans in peonage. This is why there's poverty among us, they claim. Examples: Cesar Chavez of the Farm-workers and Toney Anaya, former New Mexico Governor, currently a Jesse Jackson lieutenant.

Those from the second group take a less-jaundiced view of the Mexican American experience in the U.S.A. They proudly call themselves Mexican Americans; i.e., Americans of Mexican descent. While they recognize there's discrimination, past and present, they shrug it off and charge ahead. As to this land being formerly Mexican and how it became American, they say, so what? Examples: educated, hard-driving Mayors Pena (Denver) and Cisneros (San Antonio); Secretary of Education Lauro Cavazos; and, zillionaire aerospacer, Manuel Caldera, who parlayed $16,000 into $55-million.

One of these, a newspaper publisher, calls the first group, POVERTY PIMPS, as he perceives them to be non-productive whiners, with their hands out for government-welfare dollars and grants. The "Statist-Poverty Pimps" would call his group, "COCONUTS", BROWN on the OUTSIDE, WHITE on the INSIDE, and/or "TIO TACOS", Uncle Taco as in Uncle Tom.

This group I call ENTERPRISERS, who's view of government is: "Get out of our way!" They find welfare-poverty-oriented government distasteful and as providing a haven for effete Anglo bureaucrats, a public sector petit bourgeois, if you will, useless in a rough and tumble private sector.

For example, 15 years ago I started a business with $500 borrowed dollars. Full filling Anglo-imposed stringent permit and licensing codes, I found myself regulated by an Anglo 20-year veteran cop who never reached sergeant's rank. This was a very picky man. So much so, he actually lifted my license when I promulgated group discounts, because, he ruled, the law required me to charge only what the city (he) permitted.

Where were "Statist-Poverty Pimps" when I was fighting cops and City Hall for the right of all businessmen to charge whatever the market would pay for services? They weren't around, they were too busy yelling "Coconut". This, while I created jobs with an annual six-figure payroll.

The third group? "Statist-Poverty Pimps" call them "Limps", for, what is to them, obvious reasons. "Enterpriser-Coconut-Tio tacos" call them invisible, because they're nowhere to be found when battles need fighting. I would call them-"LEGS", short for Legumbres, Spanish for Vegetables.

They're best exemplified by Cheech Marin's characterization in his hit movie, BORN IN EAST L.A. Like them, he couldn't speak Spanish; he knew so little of his Mexican heritage, he didn't know why East Los Angeles, with millions of Mexican Americans, has a Cinco De Mayo Parade every year; he didn't even know what Cinco De Mayo commemorates. When asked to name the President of the United States, the character Marin portrayed couldn't remember.

Like it or not, we Mexican Americans find ourselves in one or another of these groups and not by accident, but by choice. Who, then, are our CACIQUES? In the "Statist-Poverty Pimp" group, they appoint themselves, then look for followers. In the "Enterpriser-Coconut-Tio Taco" group, they rise naturally, as Thomas Jefferson wrote, "By talent and virtue," talent and virtue recognized by others. In the numerous third group, the "Limp-invisible-vegetables," Caciques are invisible, like the group. Numbers, you ask. How many in each group? Who knows? Groups one and three don't want counts, and group two, is too busy making money. ###

AUTHOR'S NOTE—JULY, 2003—One of the examples I used for the money-making group, Manuel Caldera, turned out to be a crook who bribed government contract awarders with hug sums of cash to give him contracts. He was convicted of bribery and sent to federal prison.

Despite his prison time, he managed to keep a large sum of money. After prison, he resided in the lap of luxury Palm Springs, California, until his concubine girlfriend shot and killed him for fooling around with another woman.

◆   ◆   ◆

OF COATS, TIES AND HUARACHES

Screaming epithets and obscenities, a small group of Radichics (Radical Chicanos) heckled at and disrupted a recent California university speech by our Mexican American playwright/movie director Luis Valdez (ZOOT SUIT, CORRIDOS, LA BAMBA, and I DON'T NEED NO STINKING BADGES).

Upset with the symbolism of his wearing a coat and tie rather than huaraches (wahr-ah-chees, sandals), the Radichics accuse Valdez of "selling out" a peasant heritage, for commercial success.

I was reminded of this incident while watching the first elected Mexican American councilman of a 98% Anglo (white, non-Spanish speaking) city, drive by in a new Volvo, talking into a car phone, wearing a crisp blue button-down shirt and striped tie. Has the Councilman sold out? Has Valdez?

The first determination is: Sold out what? From 1848, when this land was forcibly taken by the United States, until recently, we Mexican Americans have lived culturally isolated lives, segregated into colonias (neighborhoods) almost exclusively Mexican.

What few who could read and write turned to Mexico for books, plays and movies. Slowly, however, a few of us made it through American schools/colleges and began to tell our story to the world. This is a recent phenomenon. Most noteworthy has been Luis Valdez' efforts, first with his Teatro Campesino (Peasant Theater), and adjunct of Cesar Chavez' United Farmworkers struggle, then with plays and movies.

"ZOOT SUIT", a play relating Anglo bigotry and injustice in Los Angeles, played before packed Los Angeles audiences, moved east to New York and flopped. "...STINKING BADGES", examines our collective identity crisis and played before enthusiastic audiences in Los Angeles and San Diego, but has yet to move east.

His "CORRIDOS", which appeared on Public Broadcasting, was heavily criticized by one Tex-Mex critic for what he saw as stereotyping of our people. "LA BAMBA", his $6 million movie, grossed and made mega-millions. This huge commercial success brought Valdez to the forefront of American entertainment and solidified his position as a Mexican American intellectual, at least a commercially viable one.

Valdez describes, chronicles and dissects our struggles against Anglo bigotry, prejudice and injustice. With the success of "LA BAMBA", success measured in millions of dollars, we now have Hollywood access for our stories and can expect more such movies in the future. For this we can thank Valdez. In accusing him of "selling out", the huarache-wearing Radichics display a campesino (peasant) mindset based on little more than a wish for a mythical cultural background.

Facts: Of the over 100 million American workers, only 3% work in agriculture; only 15% of Mexican Americans do. So who wears huaraches? The Mexican farm workers in my area don't. Certainly, I wear 15-year-old rubber tire-soled huaraches during leisure time, but are they a cultural bridge to my Mexican heritage?

What heritage are we talking about? As I see it, there are two. The first I discovered after an arduous climb to the top of the Pyramid of the Sun at San Juan Teotihuacan, outside Mexico City. There, I realized I was a direct descendent of fierce Aztec warriors, who forged an Empire, and the courageous band of 200 Spaniards, led by Hernando Cortez, who conquered the Aztecs. Later that day, I observed memorabilia of Pancho Villa and his Division Del Norte (Army of the North), which won the Mexican Revolution.

On this Mexico City visit, I traced the steps of Aztec warrior-kings, Spanish Conquistadors and touched the oaken doors of my birthplace, doors smashed in by Pancho Villa's troops, twenty five years before I was born.

With great delight, my great-grandmother told me many times how Emiliano Zapata's peasant, huarache-wearing soldiers came to our back door, politely knocked and humbly begged for food. In contrast, she told me, Villa's troops, wearing cowboy boots and Stetson hats, kicked in our front doors and took what they wanted including my great-grandmother.

Villa's men, individualistic, tough, lean, frontier cavalrymen swept through Mexico like a furious hurricane. They were rebels. Zapata's men were tiny, humble huarache-wearing Indians, more at home on burros than horses. They were revolutionaries. These two disparate armies and their leaders, Villa the rebel and Zapata the revolutionary, were living examples of our dual heritage.

We can choose lineage from Aztec Emperors, Spanish Conquistadors and Villa's tough, victorious horse soldiers; or, from Ejideros (communal Indians), beggars of food and government hand-outs, wearers of huaraches. The parents of our children can freely choose either heritage to pass on to the young. Choosing is simple. The results, however, are not, as such choices directly affect our collective future.

The Radichic hecklers have chosen their path, a path trod on huaraches, a peasantry in perpetuity, if you will. That is not what my America is about. Others have chosen a path of symbolic coats and ties, a path preceded by fierce warriors and Conquistadors.

As for me, my Aztec-Conquistador-cavalryman heritage is summed up for all the world to see in the words of our famous folksong, "La Bamba", "Yo no soy marinero (I'm not just a sailor), Soy Capitan, Soy Capitan (I'm the Captain)", and in the title of Luis Valdez' play: "I Don't Need No Stinking Badges." ###

AUTHOR'S NOTE—JULY, 2003—So there!

◆　◆　◆

"A DEAL THEY COULDN'T REFUSE"

Magnificent, that's what US Senator Carol Moseley Braun was when she stood in front of the United States Senate attacking the idea that United States sanction of the Confederate flag as personally offensive to her as a Black person, a descendant of slaves.

Not so magnificent was her performance at the Judiciary Committee hearings on the appointment of Judge Ruth Bader Ginsberg. Specifically, her remonstration of Senator Orrin Hatch for using the infamous Dred Scott case (slaves are property in all states) and Roe vs. Wade (making abortion legal in all states) in the same sentence caused her to blow all the good will she earned fighting the Confederate flag.

In the persona of the first Black female United States Senator in history we find an example of how contradictory a person or group can be and how deficient they can be on one hand and brilliant on the other.

For example, many of my Mexican American colleagues brilliantly espouse causes such as fair and humane treatment of illegal immigrants. Some propound the cause of the poor and of the working poor so eloquently that congressmen scurry about passing laws to help the underprivileged. Others argue for better education for Spanish-speaking kids by teaching kids in Spanish to read and write, then to convert them to English. Laws and funds quickly follow their entreaties.

Some argue for political empowerment, even for non-citizens, by organizing and voting for leaders and politicians who will move the entire Spanish-speaking community into modern America. Non-citizen voting, of course, is not a new idea. Most states allowed white male European immigrants to vote before they became citizens prior to 1922. All these ideas and causes are worthy of consideration and implementation.

My Mexican American colleagues cover themselves with glory when they fight for the community like they do. Some, however, emulate Senator Carol Moseley Braun and blow it.

Specifically, there are those who preach that what is now California, Arizona, New Mexico, Texas, Colorado, Utah and parts of Oklahoma (the Southwest) was stolen from Mexico after the imperialistic "Manifest Destiny" of the United States was implemented in the Mexican and American war of 1846. There is, of course, some truth in this position.

If these people let it go as simply a foreign policy peccadillo by the United States, they would perform a public service. Where they and their position fall apart is in insisting that this land is still Mexican because it was "stolen property".

They neglect to point out that the Mexicans accepted $15 million for these lands. Granted it was a "Don Corleone" Mafia-type deal in that the Americans made the Mexicans a "deal they couldn't refuse." But a deal is a deal and like scrambled eggs, we can't go back 143 years to unscramble the Treaty of Guadalupe eggs. They never mention this.

Moreover, they insist that this land must be returned to its "rightful" owners, the Mexicans. And, that any Mexicans who come here "illegally" are not really "illegal" as this is Mexican territory. They encourage Mexicans to come here and they do so in an effort to somehow grab the land back.

They call this the "Reconquista", the reconquest. Their historical precedent is that of the Spanish battling the Moslems for 700 years to drive them out of Spain, a feat they accomplished finally in 1492.

There are some critical differences in the Spanish and Southwest experiences, however.

In Spain, the Spanish were the native peoples and they had their own culture, religion, language and nationality. In California the Hispanos had only been on the land for 75 years, in New Mexico for three hundred years. They were not politically independent they were Spaniards, then Mexicans.

There were, in fact, only about 75,000 Hispanos in all the conquered lands of the War. Most of my Mexican American colleagues (and me) are not descended from any of these few people who became, by the Treaty, American Citizens in 1851.

We must grant that those 75,000 people, their descendants and their immigrant cousins from Mexico have been badly treated by the United States on many occasions and in many ways. But in no way can our experience be erased by hyperbole and political rhetoric based on emotion and fantasy.

Mexican Americans who cover themselves with glory one minute must make sure that they don't stumble, intellectually, the next minute for they look like fools when they do and, unfortunately, they make all Mexican Americans look like fools, also. ###

AUTHOR'S NOTE—JULY, 2003—The constant whining of the tiny number of people who continue to cry about the Mexican and American War of 1846–48 is tiresome and boring. Yes, the Americans provoked a war to steal territory. Yes, that move did not pass today's international law observed by most countries. Yes, the war was provoked to annex territory as slave territory for the benefit of the Southerners. Yes, many in congress, led by Whig-Republicans-to-be like Congressman Abraham Lincoln objected to the war.

Nonetheless, it happened and it happened a long time ago. California entered the United States as a no-slave state and produced great success for the United States when the country was plunged into Civil War by the rebel South.

◆　　◆　　◆

OCTOBER 11TH, 1492

With Christopher Columbus and political correctness in mind, the Swedish Nobel Peace Prize Committee awarded this year's Peace Prize to a Guatemalan Indian Woman, Rigoberta Menchu, for her work against the tyranny of whites over Indians. Her government labels her a Communist.

She will be the idol of this country's white liberals, who have turned historical revisionism into an art, in their crusade against D.E.W.M. (Dead European White Men).

The politically correct will pressure white wimps into changing Columbus Day to Indigenous People Day in places like Berkeley, California. They will threaten violence to stop Columbus Day parades. They and their white sycophants who run America's schools will propagandize school children into believing that Columbus was a bad man.

Despite these politically correct efforts at changing history, the most important contribution of the clash of cultures in 1492, the Mestizo (part Spanish-part Indian), becomes more important to our world each and every minute of every day.

A true mestizo revels on the 12th of October, El Dia de La Raza, the Day of the Race. Without Columbus there would be no Mestizos, no modern Mexico, no Mexican Americans. Without Columbus, the English might have "discovered" America. And they might have implemented a policy of "the only good Injun is a dead Injun". Mestizos, you see, can only come from live Injuns and live white folks.

Mestizos live because of Columbus and a true Mestizos honors the man and his voyage despite his failings as a governor and as a 1992 liberal.

The politically correct among us would keep us in our place, we mestizos, and have us join our Indian cousins in wishing for yesteryear and phony-baloney nobility and some connection to, or communion with nature. We must demur. We mestizos are people of the modern world.

We gained independence by shedding blood, not by United Nations resolution, nor economic sanctions. We run countries while more civilized Europeans "ethnically cleanse" their cities, towns and country sides. We wheel and deal in international commerce while Kurds and Bosnians, pure white-blooded peoples, look forward to freezing and starving to death this winter.

There are those, like the Indians of Guatemala and Peru, who claim their white establishment governments mistreat them and, in some cases, kill them, and they are correct. But, on the other hand, I do not know very many educated people in Latin America, nor very many educated Mexican Americans who would trade places with those noble and spiritual Indians—indigenous people—who lived in the Americas on October 11th, 1492.

Mexico, with the 13th largest economy in the world, is the mestizo nation to which all lesser developed nations can look up to. On the African continent, only white-run South Africa can equal Mexico's economic might. In the Middle East, only Israel can compare with Mexico in per capita non-oil income. In the East and Far East, only India and China can match Mexico in economic output and international purchasing power. Only better-developed Japan, Taiwan, Hong Kong, Singapore and South Korea can be compared to Mexico economically.

Nevertheless, Mestizo Mexico will, by dint of population, natural resources and economic alliance with the United States, outstrip all but Japan and mainland China in a few years.

Without Columbus, this could not be. Without Columbus there would be no mestizo Mexico, or white Costa Rica, or mixed Panama, or Venezuela, et al. Without Columbus, there would be nothing but Indians, indigenous people.

They would be burning jungle to plant small patches of corn. They would be sneaking up on buffalo with bows and arrows. They would be throwing maidens into wells to appease the gods of "Dung". They would be cutting the hearts out of prisoners of war. They would be eating their enemies in victory banquets, giving new meaning to the term "medium rare". What male enemies they didn't kill and/or eat, they would force into slavery; the women would become sex slaves to their conquerors and, coincidentally, broaden the gene pool.

Without Columbus, we would not be here, we mestizos.

We mestizos do not need politically correct white folks to fight non-existent battles for us. Maybe the Indians, I mean, indigenous people, need the white folks to fight their battle for them, but we don't.

After all, this is 1992 and we run countries and we've done so for a long time, thanks to Columbus.###

AUTHOR'S NOTE—JULY, 2003—Many of the bigoted in America refer to Blacks, Indians and Mexicans as "mud people."

It is my theory that most Mexican haters hate Mexico because it is a country of Mestizos. Even in Spanish, the word Mestizo is defined as mixed blood, half-breed. Such mixed blood people have never met with approval of the Northern European.

I may be wrong, but I don't think so. Never underestimate the bigotry of the Northern Europeans, or of the Southern Europeans like the Spanish and Italians.

The Spanish had 32 different racial classifications in the Spanish America they ruled for 300-years. It was the Spanish and Portuguese who ran most of the slave trade to the Americas (Remember the Supreme Court case about the AMISTAD, which was memorialized in Stephen Spielberg's great movie, AMISTAD, even if it didn't strike the fancy of most White movie goers).

The Italians who have come to America have spawned some of the worst bigots in the country on the subjects of Blacks. They will deny it, but it is true.

◆   ◆   ◆

A TRUE WINNER

The 499th anniversary of Christopher Columbus' discovery of America is here and now begins the countdown for the 500th anniversary. Most of us will celebrate but a few disgruntled losers will drag their "politically correct" allies out of their intellectual black holes to attack and denigrate Columbus.

Columbus was a man of his times. He was a capitalist/adventurer. He was a merchant seaman who sailed throughout most of the known world. He was a devout Catholic. He traded in slaves. He was a man of his world. He was a man of his times.

He was also a man of tremendous vision and courage. Every one knows that he convinced the Catholic Monarchs of Spain, Ferdinand and Isabella, to finance his three-ship fleet on its westward voyage to find the spices and gold of India and Asia, as well as a good dose of glory.

Those who denigrate Columbus the man and his accomplishments are quick to suggest, with precious little evidence, that many people from Asia, Europe and Africa came upon the Americas before Columbus. They say dumb things like, "The Vikings, the Africans, the Phoenicians, the Polynesians, they all came...They all left on good relations."

That comes from Bob Castillo, a Chiracahua Apache and "spokesman" for the International Indian Treaty Council. This group consists of Indians from North America and Mexico who object to any celebration for Columbus because he caused a genocide, a mass murder of the indigenous people of the Western hemisphere.

They blame Columbus for the high rates of diabetes, alcoholism, unemployment and suicide among Native Americans.

In Castillo's words, "Columbus was no hero. He brought genocide. He brought murder, disease and land theft. Since he came, Indians have gotten a raw deal."

Ramon Gutierrez, chairman of the Ethnic Studies Department at the University of California, San Diego, states, "Since Columbus we've had five centuries of indigenous genocide."

The National Council of Churches proclaimed in May of 1990 that, "For the descendants of the survivors of the subsequent invasion, genocide, slavery, 'ecocide' and exploitation of the wealth of the land, a celebration is not an appropriate observance of this anniversary."

Are these people right?

Were Columbus and those who followed from Europe murderers and plunderers of a simple, peaceful Indian, native society? Are those of us with Spanish and European heritage—albeit with substantial Indian blood—guilty, also, of murder and plunder?

Are we? No! I repeat, No!

James Axtell, who teaches history at the College of William and Mary, remarks that the Council of Churches "got suckered by the left." The resolution, he says, is, "a very intemperate, ahistorical view of things. It's so skewed that it's doing a disservice to modern parishioners who believe they've got to feel guilty about what happened 500 years ago." Amen.

What the Spaniards found 500 years ago depends on where we're talking about. The Indians Columbus found on the Caribbean islands were peaceful and, in 1991 terms, laid back. He noted in his log that they would make good servants. He was wrong, of course. They weren't tough enough.

The Indians Hernando Cortez found in Mexico twenty years later were the total opposite of the island Indians. They were hard working, industrious, artistic farmers and builders. They were highly organized by a priest class and were the lords of great Mexican city states.

They were also sadistic, murderous, plundering despotic kidnapers of women and children, killers of men on religious altars, that is, they believed in human sacrifice. Some sacrificed young virgin girls to appease their wicked and mean-spirited gods. They even had a "dung" god.

These were not nice people. Their society was not particularly nice either. A hereditary nobility and a tightly knit priest class controlled every single aspect of Indian life. In a word, they live in a fascist state. There's no thing noble about Fascism, whether it's under Hitler or Mussolini, or Moctezuma.

Moreover, without Columbus and those who followed him to America, there would be no United States of America, no Mexico, no democracy, no "unalienable rights" and no system on earth where everyone is guaranteed, "life, liberty and the pursuit of happiness."

Some will say that this all would have happened eventually, but it didn't. It started with Columbus.

Columbus was a great man. What he accomplished was great. We are his offspring and we are what we are today because he, Christopher Columbus, was a winner, a true winner. ###

ILLITERACY IN AMERICA

Over half of 696 American seniors at 67 colleges surveyed by the Gallup Poll couldn't identify the Magna Carta, or the author of "The Tempest". Less than two-thirds of these rah-rah college seniors knew that the American Civil War was fought sometime between 1850 and 1900. 60% couldn't name the U.S. President serving when the Korean War broke out in 1950.

Some good news came from the survey. For example, only 25% didn't know that Christopher Columbus discovered the Western Hemisphere before 1500. And only 23% thought Karl Marx's words, "From each according to his ability, to each according to his need." are in the United States Constitution.

These are college seniors. Applying national percentages to the sample, only four percent of the surveyed 696 seniors would be Latinos, leaving the remaining 96%, heavily white, with a sprinkling of Blacks.

A study of high school seniors concluded that 37% can't locate Southeast Asia on a world map, the same Southeast Asia where America fought its longest war just twenty years ago. Almost a quarter of those surveyed think the Mississippi River empties into the Atlantic or into the Great Lakes. 16% think that ships traveling from New York to London pass through the Panama Canal. A third of these high schoolers think Finland's climate is either tropical or arid desert.

Remember, these studies were conducted with college and high school seniors. Remember, also, that Education's propaganda machine makes a big deal of Latino school drop-outs and goes out of its way to twist drop-out statistics and studies into a massive emotional barrage against Latinos.

The propaganda machine jams into overdrive when it says there's a 40% drop-out rate among Latinos. It waves educational establishment drop-out studies like red capes in front of a bull prompting cries of outrage from politicians, professors, principals and teachers.

One professor writes that Latino parents don't give their children "tough love," the "tough love" white parents give their educationally gifted children, the ones who don't drop out, the ones who go on to college. The same ones, I presume, that Gallup polled.

Every time the Educational Establishment conducts one of its studies it draws from within for surveyors and draws on itself for methodology. Unfortunately for Latinos, for everyone actually, scientific objectivity is sorely lacking in these self-aggrandizing studies.

The first defect in their methodology is in selecting their study samples. A Puerto Rican in New York, a Nuyorican, is different than a Cuban, a Nicaraguan or a Colombian in Miami, or a Salvadoran in Washington D.C. or Los Angeles. They are all different from Mexicans. Another basic truth is that even among Mexicans, there's a difference.

There are native-born Mexican Americans of parents from Mexico and native-born Mexican Americans of native-born Mexican American parents. There are legal resident aliens from Mexico, as well as amnesty candidate Mexicans legalized by the Immigration Reform Act of 1986. There are also hundreds of thousands of illegal Mexican immigrants.

Guess what? To the Educational Establishment all these Mexicans look alike. Rarely does one see a study that breaks down educational attainment of the native-born vs. illegal immigrants, that is, Americans of Mexican descent, mostly urban and immigrant Mexican Indians from rural Southern Mexico.

Nor does one see studies that pick-up former drop-outs who return to adult school years after dropping out as kids. Nor does one generally see in study methodology student tracking from the ninth grade through graduation. They usually count the number of Latinos who enter a ninth grade, then count again four years later. This does not account for inter-district, inter-city or inter-state moves or, moves back to Mexico.

Remember, Mexicans look alike.

America's Educational Establishment needs Latinos and their drop-out rate; it needs Latinos to deflect attention from its own failures and deficiencies.

If America is concerned and disgusted by an alleged 40% Latino drop-out rate, it won't concern itself with a 20% Anglo drop-out rate. If Latinos are derided for dropping out, maybe no one will notice functional illiteracy among many of its White/Black high school graduates.

If Latinos have documented educational shortcomings, maybe no one will notice that more than half of white college seniors can't identify the Magna Carta, the Medieval English charter from which our Constitution draws directly. Or, maybe no one will notice that half of white college students can't identify

William Shakespeare as author of "The Tempest". God only knows how few can name the author of "Don Quixote".

Perhaps the best summary of America's Educational Establishment's achievements are noted in a current test of cultural geography students at the archetypical bastion of White, Anglo Middle Class society, Ohio's Bowling Green University. One must note that the number of Latino students at Bowling Green University can't be counted on one hand.

With over half-a-million American soldiers, sailors and Marines making war on Iraq at this very moment, of 112 Bowling Green University cultural geography students, only two could identify 13 Middle Eastern nations on a map. Less than half could identify six nations. Six of the 112 students couldn't name one, not one.

Maybe we should give these students a couple of bucks to rent the movie "Lawrence of Arabia". Maybe they'll learn some geography, more than they have in America's public schools and universities.

It would certainly be cheaper. ###

AUTHOR'S NOTE—JULY, 2003—What a disgrace that so many seniors can't find the very place their fathers, uncles and cousins fought in for so many years just a generation ago, Southeast Asia. Also disgraceful is the fact that these Middle-America seniors can't identify the countries where Americans would bleed and die, first in the first Gulf War, then, again, in 2003 when we returned to finish off the butcher of Baghdad, Saddam Hussein.

PART IV

9

ONE STEP FORWARD, TWO STEPS BACKWARD

Chapter introduction—I have discussed the warring intra-Hispanic communities many times. Nonetheless, we are confronted by criminal and uneducated Hispanics everywhere we turn. No matter how many try to crawl out of the proverbial bucket of crabs that keep dragging back those climbing out of their dead-end life, there seem to be many more Hispanics unwilling to try for success, for an education, for a better life.

These kind of people are the weak ones who belong to gangs, who rape and pillage the Hispanic community, who deal in drugs, who drop out of school, who cry and whine that America doesn't want them, that America doesn't care about them. But, one must ask, why would America care for these punks if these people themselves don't want to work to succeed, to study, to learn to read and write.

"LOOKING OVER YOUR SHOULDER"

Latinos are fiercely rushing away from a "romantic" peasant-like status and, in so doing, are, regrettably, leaving many behind, including some of their own.

As recently noted in studies of the Black community, affluent Blacks have doubled in the past decade. Blacks left behind, even poorer than they were ten years ago, are bitter and blame successful Blacks for some of their plight. Latinos, I believe, are experiencing the same phenomenon.

Perhaps the best example of Latino political and social progress is this: In a survey by the Spanish-language television network Telemundo, over 50% of Spanish-speakers identified themselves as Democrats. When asked who they voted for in 1988, over 60% said George Bush (41). In California's 1990 gubernatorial race, 47% of the State's Latinos voted for winning Republican Pete Wilson.

Voting Republican is as good a measure as any in tracking economic and social progress.

In contrast, the best example of bitterness by those being left behind are words by George C. Balderas in the Los Angeles Times: "Republican principles is an oxymoron. As an American of Mexican descent, of several generations, a Latino and a registered Democrat, I can reasonably conclude that the Republican Party is the party of special-interest groups and that we Chicanos are not one of those sought-after, Republican-courted special interest groups. So excuse me if I want nothing to do with fascist Republican politics."

The struggle, then, for the political soul of the Latino community is waged between polarities, and is being waged by people and institutions as diverse as American politics can be. Diverse as the pressures are, however, Latino political progress is affected by the same old sociological, ethnic and racial bromides faced for generations by Spanish-speakers.

"Each race has its own special characteristics. I meant to show that Hispanics and blacks aren't well suited to a high level, electronic, industrialized society, but that they are suited for something like an agricultural society."

We find these words in Newsweek Magazine by Yuji Aida, professor emeritus of Japan's Kyoto University, in an essay discussing how America's work force will soon be dominated by minorities. This view is, unfortunately, held by many in this country, as well. And, it affects how Latinos are viewed by other Americans.

Cesar Chavez and his followers, for example, concentrate all their efforts on agriculture, ignoring the 92% of Mexican Americans and 95% of Cubans and Puerto Ricans who don't live on farms, but rather, live in cities. The rural poverty these people decry exemplifies what many suffer but that, in the over-all context of Latino life, doesn't truly reflect it or what progress has been made by most of the other 20-million Latinos.

Only in the cities can we measure the status of Latino life in America. Here we must be careful in who we deal with, when studying the Spanish-speaking population.

In Los Angeles, for example, we find that 42% of welfare recipients are immigrant Latinos, many of whom are Central Americans who've only arrived within the past few years, as penniless refugees from civil war, political turmoil and the economic disasters known as Guatemala and El Salvador.

Only 10% of LA's welfare recipients are native-born Mexican Americans. 25%, two and a half times that percentage of welfare recipient, are white.

Poverty, then, and its liberal cure, welfare, belongs to someone other than native-born American Latinos in Los Angeles.

Latino success must be measured by high labor market penetration (82% for Mexican American males), 80% and higher high school graduation rates, higher home ownership rates every year, more and more college attendance and huge percentage increases in business formation and ownership.

These measurement can only be used by objective people and here is where we have problems. Can Mr. Balderas be objective when he calls the party of Abraham Lincoln "fascist"? Can Professor Aida be objective when he offhandedly relegates 20-million American Hispanics and 200-million Mexicans, Central and South Americans to the growing fields?

Unfortunately, objectivity is in short supply in 1991. For those left behind, there is only bitterness. For those sprinting ahead, they only need look over their shoulder to see that no one is catching up, and that, though shameful, is not their fault. ###

THE GANGS OF LOS ANGELES

The punk gangsters of Los Angeles have gone too far this time.

The other night a young woman and her fiancé, both unable to hear, were driving to dinner "talking" to each other in sign language. Seven or eight boys riding in a pick-up truck apparently mistook the sign language the woman and man were using for gang signals.

The boys caught up with the fiancée's car and several of them appeared to be carrying rifles. One jumped out of the truck with a rifle, according to the young man, and ran up to his car and started firing.

At least eight bullets were fired, with two hitting the 22-year-old woman in the face and shoulder.

The fiancé sped back to his parent's house, where he carried her into their house, screaming, "I saw the bullet holes and the blood…Oh my God, how could this happen?"

How could this happen?

"This is not a case of mistaken identity", declared anti-gang detail Deputy Margarito Robles, from the Pico Rivera Sheriff's station. Pico Rivera is an LA suburb. "I suspect," he says, "her hand signs were misinterpreted as gang signs."

"The woman was shot in the face, there is no doubt they were trying to kill them", said Lt. Juan Rodriguez, the station commander.

How stupid can young punks be that they would try to kill a young woman because they mistook her sign language for dumb gang signs—how stupid can they be?

How stupid can a community be that permits young punks like this to run wild carrying rifles, pistols and Uzis? How stupid can parents be to let their kids enter "La Vida Loca", the crazy life, the gang life? How stupid can parents be to allow their kids to even dress like gangsters?

Baggy pants, too-large shirts, LA Raider jackets and shirts, bare-midriffs on girls, tattoos on boys, stacked hair on girls and slicked back hair on boys topped off with baseball hats worn backwards—these are the gangsters.

Along with the clothes is an insufficient number of brain cells which mandates that these youngsters function on less than normal consciousness.

I speak here only of Latino gangsters and I speak here only of the Southern California gangsters, the Chicago-New York-Jersey City-Miami-Houston, et al, gangsters don't interest me today, nor do the Black "gangstas". These others will draw my attention in another space, at another time.

My concern is for those gangsters who look like me, who live in the neighborhoods I lived in when young, who attend the same churches and schools I did, who play ball on the same school yards I played on.

I wonder how they can be the way they are and so different from me, considering we come from the same neighborhoods, speak the same languages (Spanish and English), make the same sign of the cross and share the same culture, history, diet and streets.

The Mexican gangs of Los Angeles are almost sixty years old. They came to public consciousness with "Zoot Suits." They were viciously attacked by white World War Two sailors and soldiers, then charged by racist LA authorities for being the victims of a riot.

As illicit drug use increased, so did gangster numbers, in and out of jail. Eventually they organized into two competing groups, the Mexican Mafia (urban) and La Familia (rural). From California prisons, they spread like a contagious disease into the federal prison system and neighboring state prisons of Nevada, Arizona, new Mexico, Colorado and Texas.

As they grew in numbers, so did their power. In prison, white power gave way to Black power and now the power flows to the Mexican Mafia and La Familia. Nothing moves in or out of California prisons worth money that doesn't pass through their hands.

And so, the gangs run wild in Los Angeles. Almost 70,000 Mexicans, Salvadorans and Guatemalans wear the baggy pants, Raider jackets and too-large shirts. They carry shotguns, Uzi machine guns, AK-47 and M-16 assault rifles. They carry everything but books.

The result: A young woman who can't hear or speak with a bullet in the face; a young man who can't hear or speak nor, now, sleep anymore.

The boy's mother puts it best and reflects the times with, "These were just two innocent kids going out to dinner". ###

AUTHOR'S NOTE—JULY, 2003—When Los Angeles was declared the "murder Capital" of the country when its murder count inched over 600 in 2002, the Mexican-haters had a field day blaming Hispanic LA gangs as leading the city into murderous anarchy. That wasn't true. Half of the 600-plus murders were committed by Black gangs in Los Angeles.

Nonetheless, the gangs of Los Angeles are punks who must be dispersed and rendered ineffective. My suggestion would be to arm them all with AK-47s and too lock them up in the Pasadena Rose Bowl and offer a million dollars to the last man standing.

◆   ◆   ◆

AN EVIL OCCUPATION

A nocturnal walk around my old neighborhood is impossible, without fear of being mugged, or being shot at by punks in a drive-by. A new word in our vocabulary: DRIVE-BY, an Urban American description of a random shooting from slowly moving cars, usually on residential streets. Victims: innocent men, women and children; communities; and, ultimately, our country.

Undermanned and outgunned, the police have basically withdrawn from crime-ridden ghettos in a classic military re-grouping to protect flanks and rear. They've forged a ring of steel, a perimeter of firepower around the problem. Now they stand back and watch.

It's not that they don't care, they do. That's why they risk their lives every day to protect you and me, black, white, brown and yellow. But, most smile when another drug shooting goes down. One less bad guy to chase; to bust; to watch walk out of court because it's "society's fault" the bad guy is bad.

What is larger than the Canadian Army? The gangs of Los Angeles. What is many times larger than all the police and sheriffs of Los Angeles? The gangs of Los Angeles. What is larger than black LA gangs, (Crips, Bloods, the Grape)? The Mexican gangs of Los Angeles.

Of 70,000 plus Los Angeles gang members, Mexicans outnumber Blacks by 2–1. Black gangs get publicity because they so flagrantly and stupidly kill people, sometimes in politically powerful, white neighborhoods. When such occurs, thousands of police flood the streets and street-suspend civil rights, busting every young man of color they see. Drastic? Yes, and sure, few such arrests stick. However, for the police, it works—fewer people die.

An informal suspension of civil rights is what we have, as during the Civil War when President Lincoln suspended Habeas Corpus for the duration. He did so because there were so many traitors to America to deal with. The traitors are still with us. Only now they're not Southern spies, they're black/Mexican gangs, vicious, murderous drug-dealing punks.

They're easily identifiable. So identifiable, in fact, schools from kindergarten on up are implementing anti-gang dress codes. No bandanas will be worn; no black shirts; no red shirts; no blue shirts; no earrings.

Earrings? And—plastic shower caps. That's for Blacks.

For Mexicans it's more difficult because our punks wear baggy work pants, woolen work shirts buttoned at the top, clean white t-shirts and darling, very darling, hair nets. These are traditional Mexican gangs.

There's new Mexican gangs in L.A., called "Stoners". These punks deal in and heavily use methamphetimines, and wear hair down to their waists. They live/ breath heavy metal music. Unlike the traditional gangs of East L.A., Wilmington and San Pedro, who cling to their Mexican background, these guys don't. They can't speak Spanish, nor, for that matter, English. They have no code of honor like their traditional predecessors. Pleasure is their reason for killing. In this, they have much in common with Black gangs.

Yes, this battle is lost. The police can't help, they just watch. When they do mobilize, they ignore civil rights to pack our jails with punks, punks who walk in hours. Punks who return dealing in crack cocaine, methamphetimines, heroin and guns. And, it's no secret where. Every ten-year old knows where crack houses are; where to buy dope and guns. Surprise! The cops know, also.

So, how do we stop this evil occupation? Call a cop? Have a little protest march? Write Letters to the Editor? Write newspaper articles? Yes.

More important, we must mobilize to snatch our neighborhoods away from the punks. Surely, our neighborhood churches are full of good people sick of the evil occupation; surely they're sick of their children exposed to drugs before they watch Sesame Street; surely they're sick of not being able to sit on their porches on summer nights, nor take an evening walk.

Sound, then, a clarion call for a thousand good men to say enough is enough. These good men can arm themselves with baseball bats, surround the operating crack houses in every town, city and village and so NO MORE, NO MAS.

If good people do this, the police will gladly come back. Like Mao's Communist guerillas, who, according to Chairman Mao, lived safely among the people with the people's help, the bad guys own a neighbor-hood because the neighbor-hood allows them to. An Evil Social Contract, if you will.

Does neighborhood justice, vigilantism, work? Remember the "Night Stalker" multiple killer in Los Angeles? Remember how he was captured? Not by police. In fact, he tearfully thanked police when they finally showed up.

Who caught him? A bunch of guys, Mexican guys protecting their East L.A. neighborhood from thieves, punks and bad guys. An ad hoc Spanish-speaking Neighborhood Watch, if you will.

The "Night Stalker" tried to steal a car in this neighborhood. Discovered, he ran, chased by a gaggle of Mexican guys, armed only with tire irons and baseball bats. Catching him, they called police and "held" him until they arrived.

I wonder if these Mexican guys read him his rights. ###

AUTHOR'S NOTE—JULY, 2003—When I sent this article out to editors around the country, some ran it some didn't. Interestingly, one op-ed editor, a woman from back East, wrote me a note that she considered running it but was hesitant because it appeared to her that I was advocating vigilante violence. To that, I would plead guilty.

But look at what happened in New York City when Rudy Giuliani was elected Mayor. He turned the police loose to heavily enforce minor laws against minor offenses. He stationed many cops where they were needed. He applied force when needed. New York is a far better place than it was before he became Mayor.

My theory of having grown men patrol their neighborhoods to handle the local punks with diplomacy or baseball bats. May be a form of vigilantism, but if that is what it takes, why not?

◆   ◆   ◆

WORDS REALLY MEAN SOMETHING, EVEN FROM RADICALS

If we use words, can we determine who the bad guys are around us? Or must we use actions, only; or, perhaps words and actions? Do words really mean something?

Read these words published in a student publication in May at the University of California, San Diego, named VOZ FRONTERIZA and edited by Mexican American students; the words:

"Luis A. Santiago, DEATH OF A MIGRA PIG—By El Chingaso-On Tuesday March 28, Migra pig Luis A. Santiago fell to his death chasing his own Raza, along la frontera falsa. Hundreds of Migra pigs, including INS pig Doris Meissner and the biggest pig in the nation Janet Reno, attended his funeral. The local news media even made a big deal about the death of this traitor in numerous stories, especially the anti-Mexicano paper the San Diego Union/Tribune, which ran a front-page story.

We're glad this pig died, he deserved to die. All Migra pigs deserve death. This Migra chases our people, in our barrios, on our land, land that was stolen from the Mexican people, and he is treated like a hero in the white community. He is no hero in the Mexicano community, because the community knows the atrocities that are committed against us, in our neighborhoods and across la linea, across la frontera falsa.

We feel absolutely no remorse for this pig, for he is the worse kind of pig there is, this Luis A. Santiago, Migra pig, ex-military man, Puerto Rican born, chasing his own raza. Chasing his own people instead of fighting for independence of Puerto Rico. We know where this pig comes from, we have a name for him, its called neo-colonialism or in a different term, Vendido, sellout.

We have no remorse for the sellouts who prey on their own people and then die chasing them. Death is everywhere in the Mexican community, why shoul we care about one less neo-colonialist oppressor? As far as we care all of the Migra pigs should be killed, every single one. There are no good Migra agents, the only good one is a dead one. But there are many Raza who wear the colors of the Migra. In reality these "raza" are not really Raza, they are the enemy. They have chosen a way of life, and they revel in beating their own kind. Do not accept la Migra in your communities, defend yourselves Raza.

The Border Patrol is the most racist violent organization in all of the occupied territories. On an every day basis Raza are harassed, beaten, humiliated and even killed by racist Migra agents. The time for this to stop is s now. The Mexicano community will no longer tolerate the Luis A. Santiago's of the world. The time to fight back is now. It is time to organize an anti-Migra patrol. A patrol that will follow la Migra. And if la Migra harasses or beats one of u s, we will defend ourselves accordingly. For we seek justice for our people. We do not mourn the death of Santiago, instead we welcome it. We are glad he is dead, unfortunately there will always be another pig to step in his place. Yet it is to bad that more Migra pigs didn't die with him. Migra Fuera de Aztlan!"

Without a doubt, this article, a poorly written one at that, is a fine example of free speech even for people with defective minds and would not be tolerated in any other country that I know of, including some "civilized" European countries. But more importantly, it reflects an intense lack of communal self-esteem among it's authors and publishers, as well as hate.

These conditions happen to apply to others among us, as well.

Let's change a few words in this article and see who it applies to then.

"On Tuesday March 28, Bureau of Alcohol, Tobacco and Firearms (BATF) agent John Doe fell to his death chasing a fellow American, on American territory. Hundreds of BATF pigs, including leading BATF pig, BATF Director, and the biggest pig in the nation Janet Reno, attended his funeral…

We're glad this pig died, he deserved to die. All BATF pigs deserve death…This BATF chases our people, in our neighborhoods, on our land, land that the Federal government stole from Americans without compensation to protect Spotted Owls and he is treated like a hero by the elite…

We feel absolutely no remorse for this pig, for he is the worst kind of pig there is…As far as we care all of the BATF pigs should be killed, every single one. There are no good BATF agents, the only good one is a dead one…The time to fight back is now. It is time to organize an anti-BATF patrol. A patrol that will follow the BATF. And if the BATF harasses or beats one of us, we will defend ourselves accordingly. For we only seek justice for our people, the Randy Weavers and Branch Davidians among us."

While the pony-tailed, radical, pseudo-peasants who published the original article in VOZ FRONTERIZA sit around and try to promote class warfare and will never make it to the middle class, the people who would subscribe to the slightly changed version are middle-class, usually, and they stockpile assault rifles, uniforms, underground supplies and run around the hills pretending to be militia soldiers.

There are some of these "weekend warriors," however, who go further. The rubble of the destroyed Federal building in Oklahoma City is proof, as are the continuous rumbles among enemies of this country who cry, BATF! BATF! RANDY WEAVER! RUBY RIDGE! WACO!

AUTHOR'S NOTE—JULY, 2003—There are extremist people on all sides of all issues. Race hatred, however, is particularly heinous because it is based on superiority fantasies of White people and hatred and victim hood fantasies of these Hispanics. They are both ugly.

Never mind that Randy Weaver was awarded over two million dollars by the government because an FBI sharpshooter killed his wife. Her death was his fault, not the FBI's. he was the fugitive, not the FBI. He was the criminal, not the FBI.

As for Oklahoma City, the hatred manifested there is unmatched by anything ever done or said in this country by Americans and is only topped by the mass murder of Americans on September 11th in New York City. That hatred was by White Americans against all Americans, White, Black, Asian and Hispanic.

The bomber, Timothy McVeigh, was executed for his crimes, executed because he deserved it.

◆   ◆   ◆

HEALTHY LATINOS

Presidents Clinton, Hillary and Bill, are hell bent to force a national health plan down the throats of every American this year.

I know one group that doesn't need the Clinton health plan. At least the group doesn't need a plan if a recent report in the Journal of the American Medical Assn is accurate.

The group, Latinos.

Though facing tremendous odds in health care, Latinos are less likely to die of most chronic illnesses such as cancer, heart disease and pulmonary disorders. Some exceptions, including diabetes and liver disease, exist.

Health problems are compounded for the Latino community because, though they have the highest labor market penetration of any group in the country, 39% of them don't have health insurance, a rate three times that of Anglos and twice that of Blacks.

Research done on Latinos indicates that they delay doctor visits because of this lack of insurance, thus delaying the discovery of major illnesses. Moreover, recent immigrants look upon American doctors with suspicion and have a fatalistic attitude towards disease.

Nevertheless, studies conducted among Mexican Americans in California, New Mexico, Texas and other states show lower rates of breast cancer, colon and lung cancer among them than among Anglos.

Death records of 40,000 Latinos, 25 and older, were compared to similar age groups among 660,000 "non-Hispanic whites", as the study referred to them. The study period was 1979 to 1987.

Joyfully, I must report that Latino men are 74% as likely to die as Anglos during a given time period and Latinas 82% as likely. Latinos also are less inclined to kill themselves than Anglos, thus they need not Dr. Kervorkian's home visits. They are less likely, also, to die of accidents.

Unfortunately, Latino men are 3 1/2 times as likely to be murdered than Anglos and Latinas twice as likely as Anglo women to be murdered, as well. Can't win them all, can we?

Latinos are about two-thirds as likely as Anglos to die of heart disease and cancer, respectively. They are half as likely to die of colon cancer than Anglos. Latinas are half as likely as Anglo women to die of breast cancer.

On top of these statistics, Latino babies have a lower infant death mortality rate than Anglos or Blacks.

So, why are Latinos so healthy? Except for those that drink. Cirrhosis of the liver and diabetes are the two main exceptions to the study's principal conclusions that Latino disease rates are lower than Anglo rates.

Most of them work. Most have high protein diets and lots of fiber. Most drink less than their Anglo counterparts, especially among the women. Most that smoke, and that is more than among Anglos, smoke less than their Anglo cousins. Most don't even visit doctors unless it's a matter of life and death, thus delaying diagnosis when real sickness occurs.

Another factor is that Mexican Americans have a median age of 19 years. Puerto Ricans and Cubans, however, have a higher median age.

What do doctors say?

"It remains a paradox," says lead author of the study, Paul Sorlie, of the National Heart, Lung, and Blood Institute.

Other researchers theorize that strong family bonds in the Latino community provide an environment of nurturing that "magically" protects Latinos against devastating diseases.

These researchers think that Latino culture frowns on smoking and drinking, thus cutting down the prospects of cancer and other vice-related diseases. They may or may not be right, but we know that if a Mexican reaches the age of majority, he usually is already drinking or he will never drink. The same is true for smoking.

We are healthy; we are strong; we do not need a national health plan. We need to only tell the Anglo our secret of long life and he can live longer, too.

First, the report's conclusions, then the secret: "The lower rates of heart disease, cancer and pulmonary disease do not seem to be explained by the major known risk factors for these diseases", declares the report.

We are healthy and the Anglo doesn't know why. Why? Jalapeno chiles, of course. ###

AUTHOR'S NOTE—JULY, 2003—Jalapenos taste great, less filling, but delicious and a cultural icon for 100-million people.

◆   ◆   ◆

"FOOD OF THE GODS"

Enough is enough. My character, my intelligence, my skin color, my culture, my first/second language, my religion and my race have been insulted, attacked and demeaned by bigoted people of all ethnicities and nationalities. In sum, they do so by snarling the words Mexican, beaner, wetback and. most usually, "foreigner". Enough is enough.

One such person went too far the other day when she called in to my radio talk show and declared that Mexican food was "foreign". I asked, "Chocolate"? She said, "Ah, ha, I'm glad you brought that up, chocolate is from France!"

Enough is enough. In a country where the most consumed food on Super Bowl Sunday is Guacamole (Mexican avocado dip) and tortilla chips, and where the most consumed specialty bakery product is all manner of tortillas and salsa outsells ketchup, Mexican food is the food of choice of millions upon millions of Americans far in excess of the 17–18-million Mexican-origin people there are in the country.

But, first, what is Mexican food? It is food or food products developed within the geographical boundaries of Mexico, past and present, that are unique from that of the other country that contributes to the Mexican history and culture, Spain.

Corn, without doubt, is the most important, for it is consumed by hundreds of millions of people all over the world. Corn, most experts agree cannot grow wild and was heavily cultivated in the Mexico that Spaniard Hernando Cortez invaded in 1519. Thus, it must have been developed by primitive farmers in Mexico thousands of years ago. The oldest known fossilized corn is about 5,000 years old and was found in a cave in the Valley of Mexico, outside Mexico City.

In recent days we have seen reports that squash seeds have been discovered in Mexico that indicate that farming was in practice as long as 10,000 years ago by Mexican Indians who were leaving the hunting and gathering stage of human development and entering Alvin Toffler's "First Wave," organized agriculture.

There are beans and chiles, there are the famous Jalapeno hot peppers, but the most significant Mexican food, as far as most Europeans are concerned, besides corn, is the tomato; the most widely used vegetable in the world.

Yes, the tomato originated in Peru, but it migrated by trade to Mexico about three thousand years ago. From the original grape-size, it was developed by Mexican Indian farmers into large fruits that were entirely different than the tiny Peruvian version, say a kilo or so in weight (2.2 pounds). In Mexico it was enjoyed by Cortez and taken back to Spain with the Aztec name, tomatl.

The tomato reached Italy about 1550 where it became such an integral part of the diet that tomato is used in almost all food preparation. It's so important that one has to ask—What did the Italians eat before they had the tomato?

And, then, there is chocolate. The very foundation of a worldwide billion-dollar industry, chocolate is as purely Mexican as are the pyramids of Teotihuican. Montezuma served a chocolate drink to Cortez; Cortez took chocolate to Spain where sugar, vanilla and cinnamon were added and where it became a favorite of the Spanish aristocracy. Within a hundred years, chocolate became the favorite beverage of England and France. But, chocolate, which comes from the cocoa tree of Mexico, cannot be grown in Europe, thus it remains a purely Mexican product, a Mexican food, even if now cultivated in Africa.

Chocolate does not come from France, lady. Tortillas and tortilla chips come from Mexico. Beans, pinto and others, come from Mexico. Squashes and pumpkins come from Mexico. Jalapenos come from Mexico. Salsa, a combination of tomatoes, jalapenos, cilantro, onions and garlic, is from Mexico. The taco, enchilada and prepared avocado, guacamole, are from Mexico. And, what would pizza, spaghetti, lasagna and cannelloni be without the Mexican tomato?

Enough is enough. Let me give fair notice to all the bigots, racists and anti-immigrant and anti-Mexican people out there across the purple plain: I will tolerate your insults and attacks on me and my people, on my religion, on my precious United States Marines, my brothers and even my mother, but—I will not tolerate attacks and lies on and about my cuisine, for my food is sacred.

Simply stated, my view is that the world isn't fit to live in without the food known as Mexican. But, in reality, it can't function without corn, corn eaten by millions of people in most of the world, or tomatoes, without which there would be no Italian food and chocolate, the Aztec word for chocolate, the same chocolate that is worshiped and eaten by millions of people, people that don't even know it's Mexican.

Enough is enough. Leave my Mexican food alone! It feeds the world! It gives the world pleasure! It just plain tastes good! Better, for example, than borscht, sweet breads, okra or kidney pie. ###

AUTHOR'S NOTE—JULY, 2003—Ah, Mexican food...

◆　　◆　　◆

RUFINO TOMAYO, ARTIST, 1899–1991

This man knew how to paint. Strange and fantastic creatures, bright colors, stark and distinctive forms were his subjects and methods. He longed for the accumulated cultural expressions of all who lived before Columbus; these were his inspirations. We can see pre-Colombian artwork in stone, in pottery, in gold and, more importantly, we see their work in his work.

Rufino Tamayo died the other day at 91. He was the greatest living Mexican artist, and, perhaps, the greatest Mexican artist of all time. His art was true, though exaggerated.

His art was not political, so he was ostracized by his world-famous contemporaries, Diego Rivera, David Siqueros, and Jose Clemente Orozco. They painted with Marxist anger and hyperbole to please Lenin and Stalin. He painted Indian angels.

They were the artistic heart and soul of the Russian import, Communism. His inspiration was the dust of Mexico and the lives of and cultural heritage of Mexicans.

Their work was totally political. He painted watermelons and stark landscapes. He painted, according to art critic Robert L. Pincus, for the "eye and heart rather than the mind. Or, as the artist once put it, 'Painting is a matter of the senses more than of the intellect'."

"Tamayo," Mexican Nobel Prize winner Octavio Paz says, "radically changed Mexican painting, liberating it from academic superficiality and the revolutionary triviality of the (Communist) muralists."

He strived to anchor his art in Mexico, but his grasp and appeal are universal and international. His paintings are appreciated wherever people can see and wherever they can appreciate honesty, not propaganda.

Ostracized and bitterly attacked by his Communist propagandist contemporaries, Rivera, Siqueros and Orozco, he moved to New York where his work attracted attention, despite its foundation in Mexican Indian art. He single-handedly mainstreamed Mexican art.

It was in New York that he and his work were affected by the 1939 exhibition of Pablo Picasso's "Guernica".

Even Tamayo, the apolitical painter, had to admit that with the Spanish Civil War-inspired "Guernica" some, if not all, art is political. In this, of course, he was no different than any other intelligent person who has seen "Guernica". His work, nonetheless, remained non-political and it emerged as the quintessential art of a nation of art.

After years of international acclaim and the development of a generation of Tomayo-ist young artists, his work was exhibited in 1968 in Mexico City to the cheers and OLES! he deserved. Two museums now house his work in the City.

In Los Angeles, his work adorns a restaurant named for him in 1988, the same year Mexico declared "The Year Of Tomayo". Tomayo paintings are part of the fabulous "Mexico: Splendors of Thirty Centuries" art exhibit which opened in New York, is currently in San Antonio and will arrive in Los Angeles in October.

His work can be seen and touched; it can be devoured intellectually, despite his senses approach; and, it can be appreciated for its modern manifestation of ancient disciplines, of ancient beauty. It is, an intellectual and cultural feast.

Tomayo, in the final analysis, was a pure blood Indian, a Zapotec like President Benito Juarez a century ago. And, it was this blood from which he drew inspiration, not in white European static form. The spirits of those before us, those who carved the great stone Olmec heads, built the mighty pyramids of Mt. Alban, Chichen Itza and Tenochtitlan, carved the great Mayan stone monoliths and designed and built great cities guided his brush.

As Tomayo once remarked, "Always there is Mexico…There are spirits in my country…I strain to listen to their voices."

Now, he is one of the voices and future Mexican artists can strain to hear him. I need not strain and I need not hear, for I can see him in his work and see what he strains to tell me.

Gracias, Maestro…Thank you, Master, your work is the mirror to my people's soul, to my soul. Thank you. ###

AUTHOR'S NOTE—JULY, 2003—I have seen some of Tamayo's work. It is spiritual and not something I would fall apart about, but, his artistry is unchallenged; neither is his scope.

◆   ◆   ◆

THAT'S LIFE

His name was Fuji. He came from Samoa and he had birds tattooed on his chest. A full head shorter than me, we weighed the same. They told me he hadn't lost a fight. That didn't bother me, I, too, was undefeated. Fuji would not present a problem.

Two rounds later I croaked to my trainer, "Please, let me finish, I've got to finish—on my feet!", as I lurched out for the final round having been bludgeoned by the tiny Samoan, having been hit so many times people lost count. I finished the fight, on my feet, then retired from boxing with a record of 6 wins and one horrendous loss.

Years later, I watched a fellow Mexican, light-heavy weight boxer "Yaqui" Lopez from Stockton, California, totally outclass an eastern "contender" for eight rounds. Lopez was masterful, quick, and obviously the best fighter. His only career drawback was that he was a "bleeder", that is, when cut he bled like a pig. At the beginning of the ninth round, the Easterner landed his only punch of the night, just above Lopez' right eye splitting the skin. Blood spurted.

When the referee called a technical knockout (TKO) in favor of the Easterner, Lopez pleaded that he could continue, that he wasn't hurt, despite being blinded by flowing blood. When interviewed, he remarked, "I've never been knocked out; I've finished every fight on my feet!"

Boxing is an art, a sport, some say a brutal undertaking which should be outlawed. Such do-gooders are usually white, Anglo, liberals who fervently believe they know what's best for us little brown folks. I disagree with them on many things, boxing is one, for we Mexicans have a special affinity for this contest of individuals, of skill and, ultimately, dignity. As the famous New York Times sports writer Red Smith used to say, "Ah...Boxing."

Rarely do Mexicans play as vital a role in a worldwide event as they did in Tokyo's heavyweight championship fight won by Buster Douglas in a knockout of undefeated former champion Michael Tyson. The principal players, referee Octavio Meyran and World Boxing Council (WBC) President Jose Sulaiman from Mexico City and New Mexico Congressman Bill Richardson.

Referee Meyran picked up the official timekeeper's count late the Eighth round allowing Buster Douglas to spend more than ten seconds on the canvas while Champion Tyson watched. But, like professional football's video replay system, their is no protest when the next play is run. Neither Tyson nor his people protested before the ninth round and never mentioned it until Tyson picked himself up off the floor, champion no longer.

The next Mexican in this drama is Jose Sulaiman, WBC President who echoed Tyson's manager's complaint that his fighter was cheated. Sulaiman, whose reputation in boxing circles is suspect, proclaimed the sponsoring WBC would not recognize Douglas' victory. Sulaiman backed off, of course, when every newspaper in the world pointed out the stupidity of trying to cheat Douglas out of victory, a victory won in the ring.

Now, New Mexico Congressman Bill Richardson has introduced legislation to set up some type of Federal oversight of boxing. It's about time!

Every state has its separate athletic of boxing commission; each has its own licensing system; each has its own set of boxing rules. A boxer can be banned in one state and fight in another, sometimes under his own name, sometimes using an alias. Doctors in different states use different medical criteria for evaluating boxers.

And, then, there's the element of organized crime's alleged control of boxing. Though promoters Don King, Bob Arum and newcomer Donald Trump will deny gangland connections, any ten year old knows the stench from boxing is from something other than cigars.

To the rescue, then, comes Mexican American Congressman Bill Richardson of New Mexico, who states, "I'm a fan". He has introduced legislation to place boxing under federal control, with uniform rules, standards and licensing. This is good. Why?

Because Mexicans do very well in boxing, practically dominating the lower weight classifications, both in amateur and professional boxing. For many its a way out of the barrio, for others it teaches discipline, physical conditioning and breeds dignity in people who would not otherwise be exposed to anything but a miserable street life.

One of my early idols was LA's Art "Golden Boy" Aragon a fine middleweight contender who went on to a Hollywood acting career. Another was Mexican Pajarito (Little Bird) Moreno who knocked out over thirty victims in the first or second round of his fights. He was an untouched, invincible warrior, a champion.

The boxing world marveled at Pajarito Moreno. A championship fight was signed with an Algerian challenger, Alfonse Halimi, who experts predicted wouldn't last a round.

Finally, for Pajarito, money, glory, beautiful women, international fame and lots of money for the former street urchin. The night of the fight, the stadium was packed and was a sea of white, green and red Mexican flags. The capital of Mexico was in that stadium.

The bell rang. The fighters circled each other cautiously, Pajarito looking for an opening for his devastating overhand right, his killer punch. Halimi wished he were somewhere else. Pajarito threw a jab, Halimi ducked and brought a right upper cut squarely to Pajarito's chin. Pajarito crumpled to the floor, knocked out.

My hero, untouched for thirty fights, my champion, had a glass jaw. Oh, well, Asi es la vida, that's life, I learned. A glass jaw, or an Achilles heel, everyone has one, even invincible warriors, heroes, and champions. ###

AUTHOR'S NOTE—JULY, 2003—Mike Tyson just filed for bankruptcy. He is currently in trouble for attacking two young men in Brooklyn. He served time in prison for raping a young woman who came to his hotel room voluntarily. He bit a chunk or ear off one opponent. He is suing promoter Don King for fraud.

Congressman Bill Richardson was appointed Ambassador to the United nations by President Clinton, then Secretary of Energy. His boxing bill died.

Mexican American boxing champion Oscar de La Hoya reigns as the king of boxing today. Crime bosses still call the shots on much of boxing and no one seems to care. Without great White heavyweight fighters, our governing establishment doesn't care about boxing. That's a shame.

A SUMMARY AND THE FUTURE

Illuminating an entire community with 75,000 words.

There are as many opinions and views expressed on these pages as there are issues. Readers will choose sides on these issues. Some will agree, some will disagree. Nonetheless, the views are out there and I stand by them. I make no apologies if anyone is offended.

It has been ten or more years since some of these pieces were written. Some of my views have changed in that time and I have so noted in Author's Notes. Some of my views and observations have become even stronger than when I wrote the original article.

Some of the facts have changed and, when applicable, I so noted.

The best example is how the country and this writer were so surprised by the explosive growth of the Hispanic population during the Nineties. The almost exponential growth of the Spanish-speaking numbers. With that growth, many issues changed in the minds of many. Issues we thought wouldn't arise for another decade or two are with us today. The issue of immigration, for example, has worked its way a little higher than it was during the Nineties.

In 2003, we find a minority in Congress led by maverick Republican Tom Tancredo of Colorado wanting to limit immigration, especially of the Mexican variety. We see Tancredo lying through his teeth on C-Span making up facts about Mexicans and the Border that are truly despicable. He has an audience in 2003. Those who call us "mud people" have a congressional champion.

He objects to the President's more benign view of Mexicans, immigration and illegal aliens. For his trouble he is banned from the White House.

President George W. Bush has a long range vision for immigrants, Mexicans and Mexico. If not for the tragedy of September 11th, 2001, accords solving, or at least handling problems along the Border with Mexico, problems of immigration, legal and illegal, would have been arrived at between the Bush White House and Mexico. History intervened and changed the entire direction of Mexico and United States negotiations.

What the future brings to the U.S. and Mexican situation, and that of the Border and immigrants is something we cannot project. What the future brings for the Hispanic community in education is something we cannot predict. What we can predict is that the 600,000 Mexican American college students who enrolled in California colleges and universities in the Fall of 2002 will keep growing in number. They are the future of California.

That is, if the entire public college system in California doesn't collapse from budget deficits and yearly increases in tuition. The largest educator of Hispanics in the world is the California Community College system. Over 400,000 of them enrolled in the 100-campus system in the Fall of 2002. With a tuition increase forced by Governor Gray Davis and a Democratic legislature of almost a third, thousands of Hispanic students will be forced to leave the community colleges and fewer new ones will enroll in the Fall of 2003.

Like the respondents of the CBS poll release within days of this writing, I join Hispanics in claiming that my life is better than my parents was and that the lives of my children and grand-children will be better than mine.

After education, economics is the most important issue among Hispanics. Jobs, income and standard of living and quality of life are economics as far as Hispanics are concerned. Bad schools and high taxes, for example, are daggers into the Hispanic community heart. Logically, therefore, Hispanics should politically reject those parties and candidates that protect bad schools and high taxes. They don't; they don't because they think they are supposed to vote for people who claim to be for the poor and working poor no matter what.

That idea, of course, is what has politically cornered the American Black. They wasted their political efforts by handing Democrat losing candidate Al Gore 92% of their vote and the result is isolation, perhaps, for all time. That lesson must be learned by Hispanics if they are to truly become a part of society that governs for all. If they don't, they risk isolation.

Hispanics must develop and present people the community will listen to and co-opt as part of the over-all community. Hispanics must learn to speak and write

English well, to present the community clearly acceptable spokespeople and social participants.

The future can be bright for the Hispanic community if they see to it that schools improve, if parents guide their children into better reading and writing of the English language. Better educated Hispanics can then get better jobs and earn more money, bettering their families by providing a better standard of living.

Better education, better English skills and better jobs are only possible if Hispanics grab the social problems by the throat and demand better schools. It all starts in kindergarten. It continues through high school graduation. It becomes vital then to enlarge the Hispanic college population and college graduation. This is only possible with desire, political impact and English language skills.

The end, for now.

AUTHOR'S BACKGROUND

◆

RAOUL LOWERY CONTRERAS
BACKGROUND AND EXPERIENCE

Author:

1. THE NEW AMERICAN MAJORITY, HISPANICS, REPUBLICANS AND GEORGE W. BUSH, Writers Showcase Press, July, 2002, ISBN 0595232493

2. A HISPANIC VIEW: AMERICAN POLITICS AND THE POLITICS OF IMMIGRATION, Writers Showcase Press, November, 2002, ISBN 0595256910

3. Books being prepared for submission—A HISPANIC VIEW OF THE CLINTON PRESIDENCY, VOLUMES I & II…

Political Columnist:

1. www.CalNews.com, 1998 to present

2. www.JWR.com (Jewish World Review), December, 2002 to present

3. North County Times (San Diego daily), 1998 to December, 2002

4. New York Times Syndicate New America News Service, 1995 to 2001

5. Daily Californian, 1998 to 2001

6. La Prensa-San Diego, 1990 to present

7. Published from time to time in: USA TODAY, LOS ANGELES TIMES, SAN FRANCISCO CHRONICLE, BOSTON GLOBE, KANSAS CITY STAR, CHICAGO TRIBUNE, LOS ANGELES DAILY NEWS, ARI-

ZONA REPUBLIC, DALLAS MORNING NEWS, SACRAMENTO BEE, FRESNO BEE, PORTLAND OREGONIAN, SAN DIEGO UNION/TRIBUNE, ORANGE COUNTY REGISTER, PHILADEL-PHIA INQUIRER, ARIZONA TRIBUNE, WWW. HISPANICVISTA.COM

Radio/Television:

1. Radio talk show host, San Diego's KOGO-AM600, 1994–2000; San Diego's KCBQ-AM1170, 2000–2001; 2. Television News analyst and commentator, San Diego's Fox News Channel 6, September 11, 12, 13, 2001 to present; 3. Preparing to produce and appear on daily CONTRERAS COUNTRY, A NEWS AND VIEWS program on San Diego's Channels 61 and 9

Professional: Senior Loan Officer, Citigroup's Citimortgage, 2001 to present; With the Republican Lincoln Club of San Diego, organizing the LINCOLN/ JUAREZ INSTITUTE, a 501 (c) 3, non-profit with mission to elevate the educational, and social levels of American Hispanics

Personal, Military and Education: Born Mexico City, 1941, came to United States in 1943. Attended public and parochial schools in San Diego, and San Diego State University with major in Political Science and minors in Economics and History. United States Marine Corps, Active and Reserve, 1959–1967, 4th Tank Battalion, 4th Marine Division, Training and Operations (S-3), Honorably Discharged, June 1967

Political: Campaign Surrogate, Bush for President, 2000; former appointee to California State Republican Party Central Committee; Official Statewide Spokesman for No on Proposition 10, 1998.

0-595-29256-9